WORLD OF KNOWLEDGE

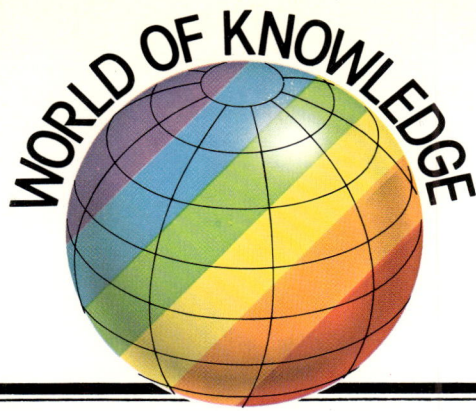

Peoples and Places:
Asia, Africa and Oceania

Peter Way

Ron Carter

Macdonald/Silver Burdett

Editorial Manager	Chester Fisher
Senior Editor	Judith Maxwell
Editors	Bridget Daly
	Brenda Clarke
Series Designers	QED (Alastair Campbell and Edward Kinsey)
Designer	Howard Dyke
Series Consultant	Keith Lye
Consultant	Dr Charles Gullick
Production	Penny Kitchenham
Picture Research	Jenny De Gex
	Janice Croot
	Georgina Booker

© Macdonald Educational Ltd. 1980
First Published 1980
Macdonald Educational Ltd.
Holywell House,
Worship Street,
London EC2A 2EN

Published in the
United States by
Silver Burdett Company
Morristown, N.J.
1980 Printing
ISBN 0-382-06412-7

World of Knowledge

This book breaks new ground in the method it uses to present information to the reader. The unique page design combines narrative with an alphabetical reference section and it uses colourful photographs, diagrams and illustrations to provide an instant and detailed understanding of the book's theme. The main body of information is presented in a series of chapters that cover, in depth, the subject of this book. At the bottom of each page is a reference section which gives, in alphabetical order, concise articles which define, or enlarge on, the topics discussed in the chapter. Throughout the book, the use of SMALL CAPITALS in the text directs the reader to further information that is printed in the reference section. The same method is used to cross-reference entries within each reference section. Finally, there is a comprehensive index at the end of the book that will help the reader find information in the text, illustrations and reference sections. The quality of the text, and the originality of its presentation, ensure that this book can be read both for enjoyment and for the most up-to-date information on the subject.

Contents

South-west Asia   3
South-west Asia, the home of great early civilizations and the
birthplace of three great religions, has recently assumed
tremendous power in world affairs, largely because of the huge
oil deposits which lie beneath the desert sands.

Southern Asia   10
Southern Asia is one of the world's most densely-populated
regions. It has considerable natural resources, but the
population explosion and ancient traditions have made it
difficult for governments to raise living standards.

Eastern Asia   17
Eastern Asia is dominated by two contrasting nations, the
industrial colossus of Japan and the world's most populous
nation, communist China. Both nations are now adjusting to
their vital roles in world affairs.

South-east Asia   26
South-east Asia has been the scene of tremendous upheavals
since the withdrawal of European colonial administrations. War
has scarred the faces of several South-east Asian countries.

Africa   33
Africa, formerly called the 'Dark Continent,' has emerged into
the light of independence in the last 30 years. However, political
independence has left many complex problems in its wake.

Oceania   49
Oceania, the smallest continent, contains two young nations,
Australia and New Zealand. Both are lands of opportunity,
which contrast with the beautiful but far less developed Pacific
islands to the north and west.

Polar regions   62
The polar regions offer hostile environments for people. But the
Arctic and, possibly, the ice-covered continent of Antarctica
contain resources which may assume great importance in the
future.

Index   65

Introduction

The peoples of the world are divided by many factors, including language, politics, race and religion. Another fundamental division in the modern world is the rift between the 'haves' in the developed world and the 'have-nots' in the developing world. This rift is reflected in stark contrasts in standards of living, opportunities, life expectations, health and so on. And many experts believe that, despite aid to and investment in developing countries, the gap between the developing and the developed worlds is becoming even wider, a fact which may have grave consequences for our future. **Peoples and Places** contrasts Asia and Africa, which largely belong to the developing world, with the developed nations of Australia and New Zealand in Oceania. There is also a chapter on the polar regions — the thinly-populated Arctic and the bleak continent of Antartica, which has no permanent population. Population figures for countries are 1980 estimates based on United Nations' statistics. Populations of other political divisions, cities and towns are the latest available figures.

South-west Asia, the home of great early civilizations and the birthplace of three great religions, has recently assumed tremendous power in world affairs, largely because of the huge oil deposits which lie beneath the desert sands.

South-west Asia

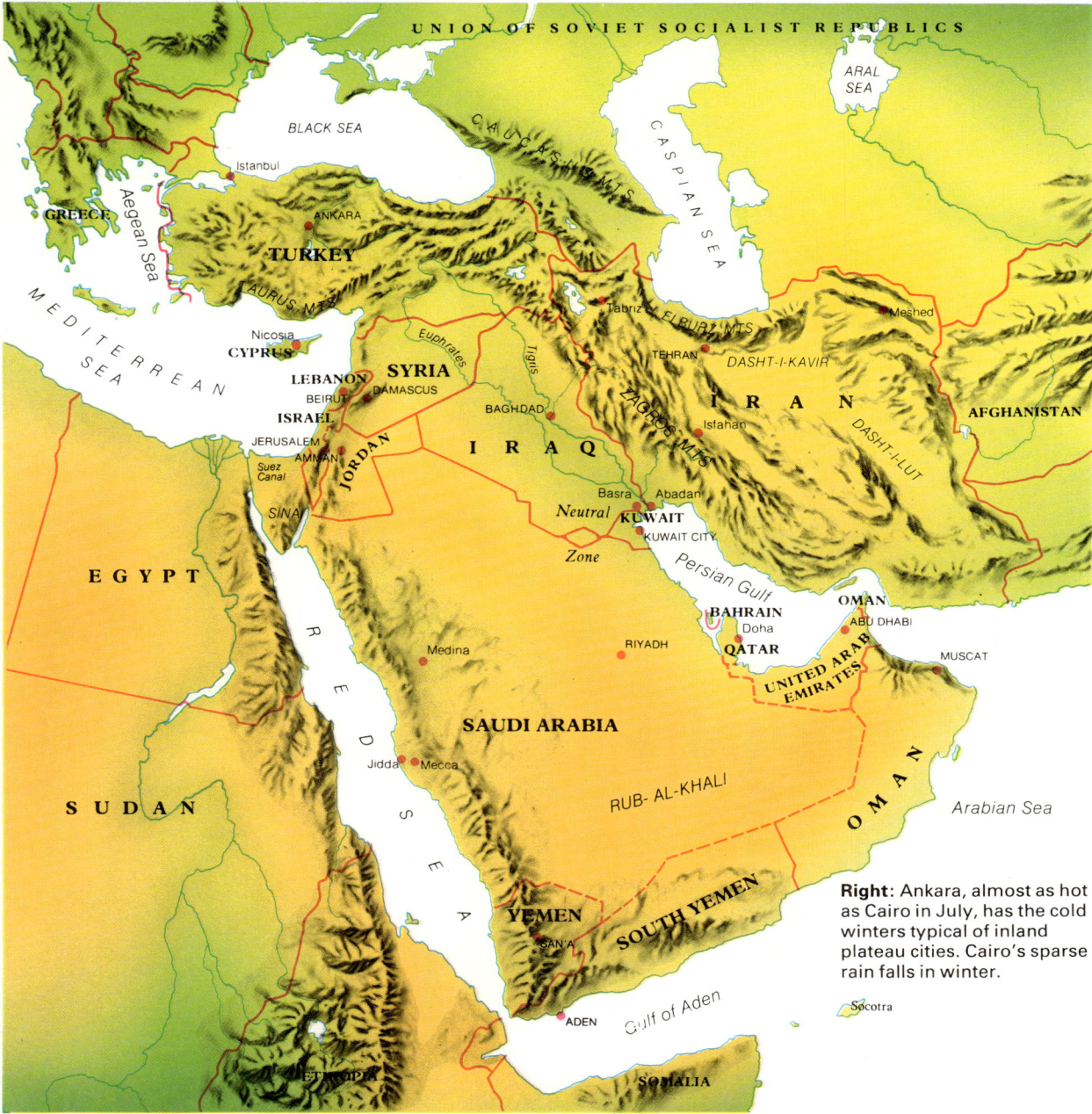

Key to colour range

- Tundra
- Coniferous forest
- Mountains and hills
- Forest
- Woodland
- Grassland and farmland
- Scrub
- Semi-desert
- Desert

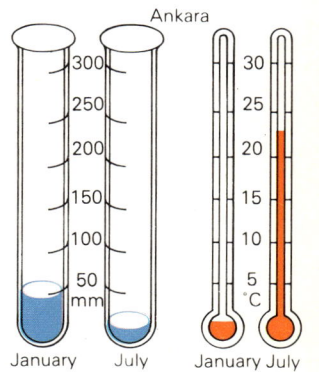

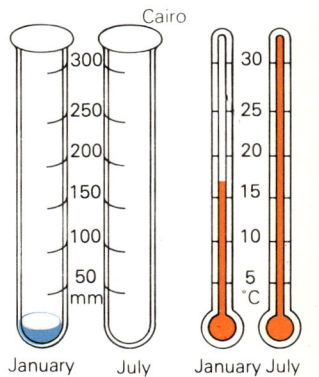

UNION OF SOVIET SOCIALIST REPUBLICS

ARAL SEA

BLACK SEA

Istanbul

CAUCASUS MTS.

CASPIAN SEA

GREECE

Aegean Sea

ANKARA

TURKEY

TAURUS MTS.

Tabriz

ELBURZ MTS.

Meshed

TEHRAN

DASHT-I-KAVIR

Nicosia

MEDITERRANEAN SEA

CYPRUS

SYRIA

Euphrates

DAMASCUS

Tigris

BAGHDAD

I R A N

AFGHANISTAN

LEBANON

BEIRUT

ZAGROS MTS.

Isfahan

DASHT-I-LUT

ISRAEL

JERUSALEM

AMMAN

JORDAN

I R A Q

Basra

Abadan

Suez Canal

SINAI

Neutral Zone

KUWAIT

KUWAIT CITY

Persian Gulf

OMAN

BAHRAIN

ABU DHABI

EGYPT

Doha

QATAR

UNITED ARAB EMIRATES

MUSCAT

Medina

RIYADH

RED SEA

Jidda

Mecca

SAUDI ARABIA

RUB-AL-KHALI

Arabian Sea

O M A N

SUDAN

YEMEN

SAN'A

SOUTH YEMEN

ADEN

Gulf of Aden

Socotra

ETHIOPIA

SOMALIA

Ankara

300 / 250 / 200 / 150 / 100 / 50 mm — January / July
30 / 25 / 20 / 15 / 10 / 5 °C — January July

Cairo

300 / 250 / 200 / 150 / 100 / 50 mm — January / July
30 / 25 / 20 / 15 / 10 / 5 °C — January July

Right: Ankara, almost as hot as Cairo in July, has the cold winters typical of inland plateau cities. Cairo's sparse rain falls in winter.

Reference

A **Aden**, capital of SOUTH YEMEN, declined as an international port after independence in 1972. Population: 290,000.

Aleppo is an important city in north SYRIA. Population: 885,000.

Amman is the capital of JORDAN and the site of the ancient city of Philadelphia. Population: 770,000.

Anatolia is a plateau of Asia Minor and covers most of TURKEY.

Street scene, Aden

Ankara, once a small town in Angora, was developed into TURKEY'S modern capital by Kemal Ataturk, who ruled the country from 1923 to 1938. Population: 1,900,000.

B **Baghdad**, the present capital of IRAQ, dates only from the early 1800s, when the famous historic city was destroyed by fire. Population: 3,000,000.

Bahrain, a tiny oil-producing independent emirate off the east coast of the Arabian peninsula, is an archipelago. The main language is Arabic. Area: 622 sq km; population: 294,000; capital: Manama (120,000).

Basra is IRAQ's only important port. Population: 450,000.

Beirut is the capital of LEBANON and was a leading commercial and cultural centre of the Middle East before civil war began in the late 1970s. Population (not allowing for war casualties and migration): 845,000.

C **Cyprus** is an island republic in the eastern Mediterranean. It had about an 80% Greek population in 1974 when a coup failed to unite the republic with Greece against the wishes of the 20% Turkish minority.

Civil war followed between Orthodox Christian Greeks and Muslim Turks backed by Turkey, which landed 40,000 troops. Following this, the northern 40% of the island became a quasi-independent Turkish state, and the southern 60% a quasi-independent Greek state. Area: 9,251 sq km; population (not allowing for migration and Turkish soldiers): 663,000; capital: NICOSIA.

D **Damascus** is the capital of Syria and one of the world's most ancient

South-west Asia includes TURKEY, IRAN, 12 Arab states, ISRAEL and CYPRUS. The region covers 4.6 per cent of the world's land area and contains three per cent of its population.

Cyprus, Turkey and Iran

The island of CYPRUS is situated in the eastern Mediterranean south of TURKEY and west of Syria. The terrain is mountainous, with the wooded Kyrenia mountains in the north and the higher Troodos mountains to the west of centre. There is a low-lying plain along the east coast. The climate is warm and dry, with some light rainfall, and is suitable for growing cotton, barley, vines and fruits.

Turkey lies at the crossroads of Europe and Asia. Most of the country is in Asia on a large peninsula between the Black, Aegean and Mediterranean seas. This comprises the large central plateau of ANATOLIA, the TAURUS mountain range in the south and the Pontic range in the north-east. European Turkey lies across the Sea of Marmara which connects northwards, through the Bosporus, to the Black Sea and southwards, through the Dardanelles, to the Aegean Sea. Along the coasts, the climate is mild and moist with temperatures ranging from 4°C in January to 27°C in July. In contrast, conditions inland are harsh and dry. January temperatures for the central plateau, for example, average

Above: Nomads spread cooking pots in front of their tents near the border of Luristan and Kurdistan in western Iran. Their tribal loyalties extend beyond national boundaries. Life in much of rural Iran remains unaffected by the country's oil-based prosperity.

Left: Nomadism results from the need of herdsmen to find pasture for their livestock. Tribal wanderings are governed by climate and vegetation patterns well understood by the nomads. The map shows the pattern of migration followed by groups of the Bedouin Ruala tribes. The nomads normally wintered their herds in the places marked **1**. If winter rain was insufficient there, they wintered at the place marked **1a**. If, however, the rains failed there, they wintered in the area marked **1b**. Wherever they wintered, the herdsmen made for the area marked **2** in spring. They moved on in summer to area **3**. By inter-tribal agreement, the Ruala could move only within the desert area shaded. They moved across 4 countries (Syria, Jordan, Iraq and Saudi Arabia), ignoring political frontiers which are still largely unpoliced except the motorized vehicle routes.

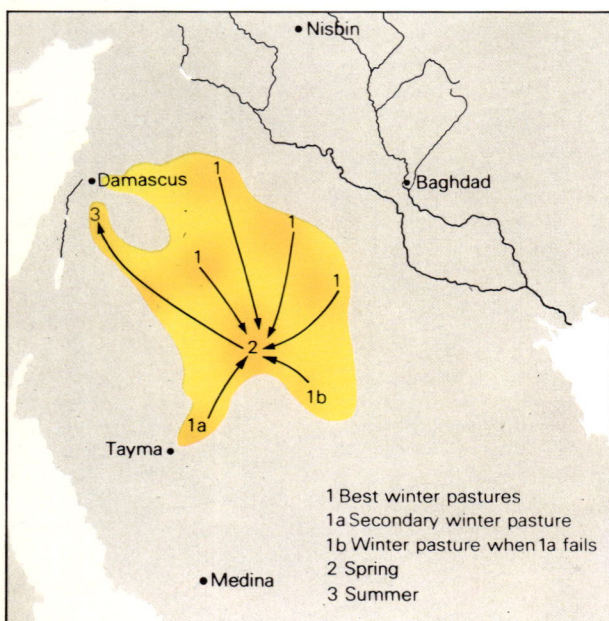

1 Best winter pastures
1a Secondary winter pasture
1b Winter pasture when 1a fails
2 Spring
3 Summer

−11°C. Vegetation reflects the pattern of climate. The west, especially along the Mediterranean, is naturally forested. Here pines give way to deciduous trees, grassy steppe and semi-desert eastwards towards Iran.

Most of Iran is a plateau over 1,200 metres above sea level bordered by high mountain chains. They include the rugged ZAGROS in the west and the snow-capped Elburz range to the north which rises to 5,775 metres. Natural forests cover parts of the northern and western uplands, but between them lie two vast, barren and uninhabited areas — the salt desert of Dasht-I-Kavir and to the south-east the sand desert of Dasht-I-Lut. Several small rivers flow from the mountains on to this central plateau, where most dry up in the intense heat. Temperatures may reach 55°C on summer afternoons although in parts of the country night temperatures drop below freezing even in summer. Annual rainfall varies from 100 millimetres along the Caspian coast to only 12 millimetres in the deserts. Here, violent winds often swirl the salt and sand into dangerous storms. The population lives mainly in farming settlements or towns in the long, narrow, fertile valleys between the mountains. A fertile strip of coastland also borders the low-lying Caspian Sea.

The Arab lands and Israel

The Arab territories of Asia seldom rise more than 1,000 metres above sea level. They comprise

cities, being more than 4,000 years old. Population: 835,000.
Dead Sea, a salt lake on the Jordan-Israel border, lies 397 metres below the level of the Mediterranean. Area: 1,020 sq km.

E Euphrates River is an important river of South-west Asia formed by the confluence of the East and West Euphrates in eastern Turkey.

G Gaza is a small strip of PALESTINE on the Mediterranean coast north

of Egypt. It came under Israeli occupation in 1967.
Golan Heights, a hill region of south-west Syria, came under Israeli occupation in 1967.

I Iran (formerly Persia) is mostly a vast plateau over 1 km above sea level, surrounded by high mountains. Much of the country is desert or too mountainous for cultivation, but it has large oil reserves. When world petroleum prices rose steeply in 1973, the country's overseas earnings soared. The resulting wealth

remained largely in the

Carpet weaving, Iran

hands of the Shah whose ambition was to make Iran a great nation again by industrialization and building up military strength. Resentment against the Shah's policies, especially by devout Muslims opposed to westernization, exploded into open rebellion in 1978-79. Only about 55% of the people are Persian, while some 35% are of Turkic origin, such as the Kurds. The main language is Persian written in Arabic script. Area: 1,648,000 sq km; population: 37,859,000; capital: Tehran.

Iraq is a mostly desert Arab republic. It has a fertile region between the EUPHRATES and TIGRIS rivers which was the site of 3 great civilizations (Sumer, Babylonia and Assyria). The country has a varied economy which is dominated by its income from petroleum. Over 60% of Iraqis are Sunnite Muslims and 30% Shi'ite; some 3% are Christians of various sects. Politically the country has been unstable since the assassination of its last king in 1958. It is a strong supporter of the Arab cause against

the Arabian peninsula and its borderlands northwards to the Mediterranean and Mesopotamia (which lies between the EUPHRATES and TIGRIS rivers). Arabia is mostly an arid, barely populated sand desert with grassland and palms in the more fertile areas. The RUB AL KHALI, a desert in the south, is called the 'Empty Quarter'. SAUDI ARABIA occupies the bulk of the peninsula, with NORTH YEMEN and SOUTH YEMEN in the south-west, OMAN in the south-east and the smaller UNITED ARAB EMIRATES, QATAR, BAHRAIN and KUWAIT in the east.

From this austere heartland the early Arabs pushed northwards to enter a comparatively fertile, crescent-shaped belt of grasslands and date palms. Along this 'fertile crescent' the northern Arab states of IRAQ, JORDAN, SYRIA and LEBANON later developed. ISRAEL, like PALESTINE

Above: Riyadh, the modern capital city of Saudi Arabia, has developed in 2 generations from a desert outpost to one of the world's most important commercial centres. Skilled workers from many countries have gone to work in Saudi Arabia on short-term contracts, attracted by high pay.

Left: Irrigation and scientific farming have restored fertility to barren areas of the Middle East, once part of the ancient 'fertile crescent'. The picture shows an Israeli experimental site near the River Jordan.

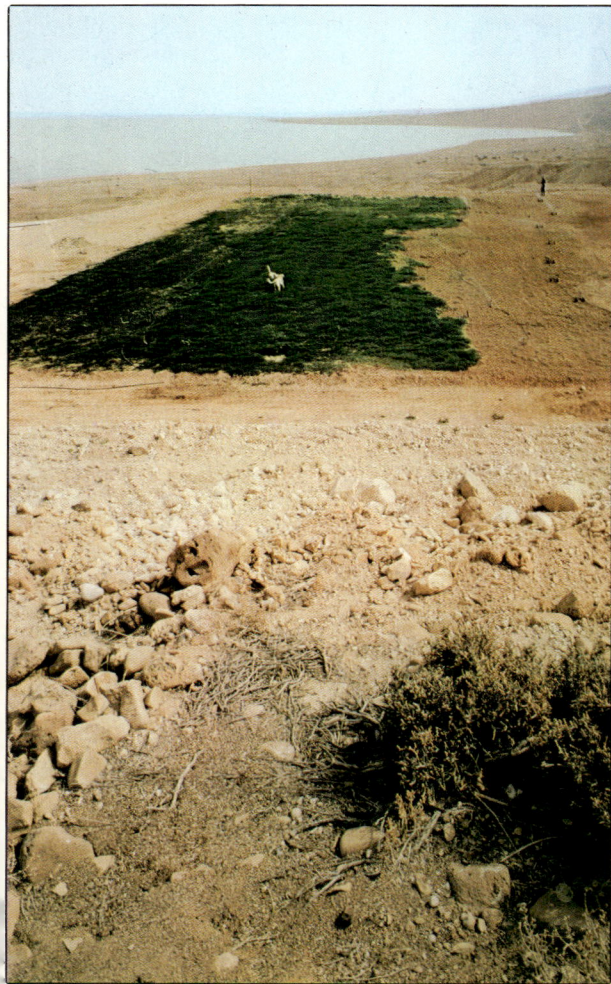

and Canaan before, lay along this belt between the Mediterranean and the Jordan Valley.

The dominating climatic feature of the Arab lands is the general lack of rain. July day temperatures may rise to 52°C inland, then fall drastically at night. In winter, inland temperatures often fall below zero at night.

Peoples of South-west Asia
Almost the whole of South-west Asia is Islamic in religion except for Israel which is mainly Judaist and southern Cyprus where people practise Orthodox Christianity.

The Cypriots
The southern 60 per cent of CYPRUS is occupied by Greek Cypriots who in 1973 comprised 79 per cent of the population. Most of the rest are Turkish Muslim Cypriots, and due to friction between these two communities they have been rigidly separated since 1974. Farming is the main activity for about 35 per cent of the people. Village houses are simple, but the towns have new buildings and often luxury tourist hotels. The trend is towards a more modern way of life. This is seen most clearly in the style of dress the younger people are now adopting. They have largely discarded the old-style Greek and Turkish costumes of their parents and grandparents.

Turks and Iranians
The Turks are mostly a Mongoloid people

Israel, but was much preoccupied in the 1970s by an internal war between its Arab and Kurdish peoples. The main language is Arabic, with Kurdish the chief minority language. Area: 434,924 sq km; population: 13,150,000; capital: BAGHDAD.
Isfahan was the 16th century city of Shah Abbas I. Despite industrialization, the old architecture still survives. Population: 570,000.
Israel, being mainly non-Arab, non-Muslim, and having only small known petroleum deposits, is the

'odd man out' among the mainland states of South-west Asia. The Israeli republic came into being in 1948 after Britain acknowledged the demands of the Jews for an independent homeland in PALESTINE. Four wars with surrounding Arab states (1948, 1956, 1967 and 1973), with intervening periods of 'no war no peace', have dominated the country's brief history. Jews make up 90% of the population of pre-1967 Israel. The other 10% is mostly Muslim Arab, with some Christians. The main languages are Hebrew,

Arabic and English. Area: 20,770 sq km (but another 68,600 sq km of Arab territory was occupied by Israel

Mosque, Isfahan.

after the 1967 war); population: 3,900,000; capital: Jerusalem.
Istanbul (in Europe) is Turkey's biggest city. As Byzantium it was once the capital of the Byzantine empire. Later, as Constantinople, it became the capital of the Turkish empire. Population: 2,930,000.

Jerusalem, holy to Jews, Christians and Muslims, is the capital of Israel, which took control of the old part of the city only in 1967. Population: 330,000.
Jidda (Jedda) is the main

business city of SAUDI ARABIA. Population: 670,000.
Jordan is an Arab kingdom in South-west Asia. It expanded in 1948 to absorb the region of PALESTINE known as the WEST BANK (of the Jordan River). The country has borne much of the brunt of the Arab-Israeli conflict. The West Bank, for example, was occupied by Israel following the 1967 war. AMMAN, the capital, is the only major city. Area: 97,740 sq km; population: 3,153,000; capital: Amman.
Jordan River separates the WEST BANK from Jordan's

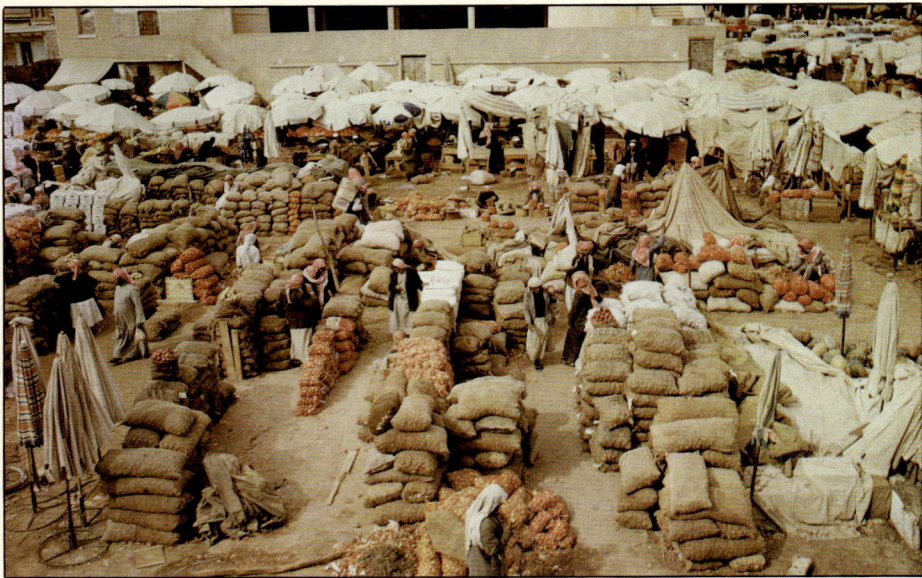

related to the medieval Tartars, but they are intermixed with earlier inhabitants of Asia Minor such as the Hittites and the Greeks. Kurdish tribes occupy a region called Kurdistan which straddles the borders of TURKEY, IRAN and IRAQ, and make up about seven per cent of Turkey's population. Arabs, Armenians, Greeks, Georgians, Jews and Circassians form smaller minorities.

During the 1900s, Turkey has undergone some dramatic changes. From an oriental empire, it has developed into a westernized state. Western dress was promoted and women officially discouraged from wearing the veil. In modern cities, such as ISTANBUL, ANKARA and Izmir, women now have near equality with men. About 60 per cent of all workers are still farmers. One of the most significant changes to the country came in 1928 when the Turks replaced the Arabic script with the Roman alphabet. The language therefore became easier to write, so this was a great boon to education.

Like Turkey, Iran has undergone considerable social change in the 1900s. But the great size of the country and the remoteness of many settlements have slowed the pace of development. There are several modern western-style cities such as TEHRAN, ISFAHAN and Abadan, but nearly half of the population lives outside towns, often in mud-built houses. The same proportion are either farmers or nomadic herdsmen. Islam is

Above: An open-air *souk* (market place) in Saudi Arabia serves as the main market for locally-produced commodities such as dates, wheat and wool.

Below: Turkey, once the overlord of Arabia, has fallen behind in prosperity. Here farmers beat out linseed by hand. Many men have emigrated from Turkish farms to find work in western Europe.

much stronger than in Turkey and only four per cent of the people are Christians, Jews or Zoroastrians. The Arabic script has been retained for the Persian language. Persians are of Indo-European descent and the name Iranian means Aryan. But only about 60 per cent of Iranians are Persians, the rest are mainly Turks with some Kurds and Arabs who live along the borders.

The Arabs

North of Arabia, the Arabs have intermixed with other peoples, especially in Syria and Lebanon, while in the south there has been a Negroid admixture. Up to 1900, the Arabs were mainly nomadic herdsmen living a primitive life under Turkish rule. Permanent settlements were few and small in scale away from bustling cities such as DAMASCUS, ALEPPO, BEIRUT, AMMAN, BAGHDAD and BASRA. Bedouin tribes wandered from oasis to oasis in search of water and pasture for their herds. Women held a very low position in Arab society. Diet was poor and disease ensured that people did not live long. But the discovery and exploitation of petroleum beneath the sand transformed this way of life – gradually at first, then with remarkable speed. Arab states are now among the wealthiest in the world. They have embarked on a programme of rapid modernization, buying expertise from industrial nations. Standards of living have gone up, education increased and the position of women improved.

East Bank. It rises in SYRIA and flows 600 km to empty into the DEAD SEA.

K **Kurdistan**, a mountainous area with no clearly defined borders, covers about 190,000 sq km where south-east Turkey, northwest Iraq, and north-east Iran come near together. It is the homeland of the Kurds, whose repeated efforts to found an independent state have been unsuccessful.

Kuwait was one of the first of the small Arab emirates to rise from poverty to riches on its income from pet-

roleum. The transformation took place between 1946 and 1961, in which year it gained independence from Britain. Then holding 20% of the world's known oil reserves, Kuwait had already become the world's richest country, even before the vast increase in oil prices began in the 1970s. Two areas called the Neutral Zone, totalling 5,698 sq km, were created in 1922 along the Kuwaiti-Saudi Arabian border. But they were divided between the 2 countries in 1966. It is now known as the Partitioned Zone. The main lan-

guage of the country is Arabic, although English is also spoken. Area without the Partitioned Zone: 17,818 sq km; population: 1,282,000; capital: Kuwait City (population 250,000).

L **Lebanon** is a small republic in South-west Asia. It has a mainly Arab population divided almost equally into Muslims and Christians. The Christians are subdivided into Maronites, Greek Orthodox, Armenians, Greek Catholics and Protestants. Muslims are subdivided into Sunnites

and Shi'ites. There are also Druses, a group whose secret religion is based on aspects of Islam and Christianity. The country occupies

Beirut, Lebanon

roughly the same area as ancient Phoenicia. It has a mixed economy and 26% of the gross national product normally comes from finance and commerce. The varied religions, corresponding roughly to cultural groups, have given the Lebanese a vigorous society. However, group rivalries, worsened by the presence of Palestinians in the country, exploded into multi-sided civil war in the late 1970s. In the capital, BEIRUT, some 50,000 lives were lost. Lebanon's second city, Tripoli has some 210,000 people

However, these changes have sometimes come into conflict with traditional Islamic beliefs.

The Israelis

Since 1948 the Israelis have created a Western-style state superimposed on the more traditional Palestinian way of life that had much in common with Syrian and Lebanese society. Because most of the Arab Palestinians left the country when Israel gained independence, 85 per cent of the population are Jews. The rest are Muslims, with a few Christians and Druses. Hebrew and Arabic are the official languages.

The economy

Petroleum dominates the economy of South-west Asia although not all countries possess deposits. SAUDI ARABIA, IRAN, KUWAIT, IRAQ, the UNITED ARAB EMIRATES, QATAR, OMAN and BAHRAIN all have substantial reserves of petroleum which account for about 75 per cent of their income. LEBANON, JORDAN, NORTH YEMEN, SOUTH YEMEN and CYPRUS have not found oil, but SYRIA, TURKEY and ISRAEL each possess small reserves.

The importance of oil

Towards the end of June 1978, world petroleum production totalled 22,373 million barrels. (As defined by OPEC a barrel equals 35 imperial gallons or 159 litres.) OPEC is the Organization of Petroleum Exporting Countries to which many oil exporting countries, especially in south-west Asia belong. South-west Asia produced about 30-34 per cent of this total, the USA and the USSR another 35 per cent and the rest of the world produced the remainder. The Americans consumed all their own output and imported much more, while the Russians consumed about 75 per cent and exported most of the rest to communist countries. Consequently Japan and the major western powers relied heavily on Iranian and Arab oil to maintain the economies of the chief non-communist industrial nations. Understandably, the Iranians and Arabs had different interests than their customers. The Iranians especially took account of the fact that their oil reserves were limited. (At the 1978 level of production, their known petroleum reserves would run out by about the year 2010.) When in power, the Shah of Iran proposed to use the oil wealth to industrialize his country, thereby

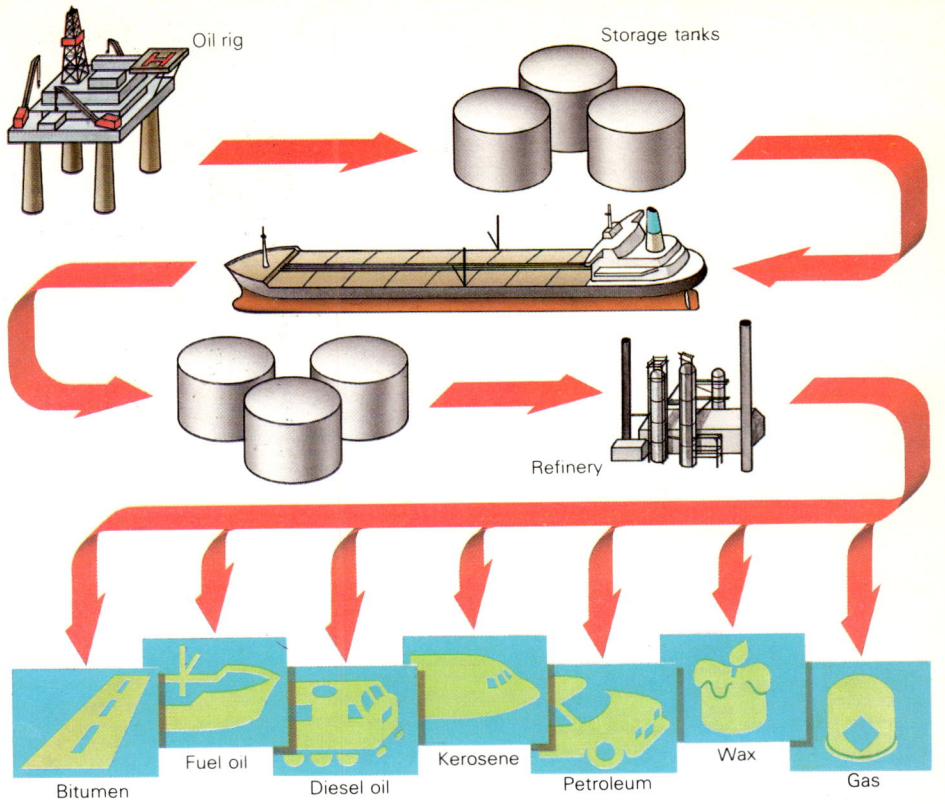

Oil rig · Storage tanks · Refinery · Bitumen · Fuel oil · Diesel oil · Kerosene · Petroleum · Wax · Gas

Above: Petroleum, the main commodity of South-western Asia, is extracted from ocean or inland oilfields. Once extracted, it is stored in tanks locally, awaiting transport by tanker to storage tanks in the importing country. From there it goes to the refinery, where it is broken down by distillation in fractioning towers. There, crude oil, heated to a vapour, rises through the towers. Differing kinds of oil condense at varying levels, and are piped off for further refinement or processing. The plan shows the different qualities of oil. Light fuel gas is at the top of the tower; heavy bitumen at the bottom.

Below: The burning off of surplus gases gives colour to desert oilfields. Petroleum from this site at Ras Tanuna, near Bahrain, contributes towards making Saudi Arabia the world's third largest petroleum producing nation after the USSR and the United States.

The main language is Arabic, but French and English are widely used. Area: 10,400 sq km; population (not allowing for war deaths and migration): 3,347,000; capital: BEIRUT.

M Mecca, along with Riyadh, is the joint capital of SAUDI ARABIA. It is the birthplace of Muhammed and the focal point of the Islamic religion. Each year thousands of pilgrims visit the Kaaba — a small, stone building in the Great Mosque. Population: 438,000.

Medina, SAUDI ARABIA, is the second holiest city of Islam. Muhammed lived and died here after he fled Mecca in AD 622. Population: 235,000.

Pilgrims' tents, Mecca

N Nicosia is the capital of Cyprus. Population (before the Greek coup and Turkish invasion of Cyprus in 1974): 147,000.

North Yemen, a little-visited Arab republic in the south-west corner of Arabia, has an almost 100% Muslim Arab population about equally divided between the Sunnite and Shi'ite sects. The people along the coastal strip are partly Negroid. Asn'a and Taiz are the only large towns. The economy is mainly agricultural. Area: 195,000 sq km; population: 7,732,000; capital: SAN'A.

O Oman (formerly Muscat and Oman) is an independent sultanate in the south-east corner of the Arabian peninsula. Until 1970, it was socially and economically among the world's least advanced countries. In that year, the sultan was replaced by his son, who began to use the income from petroleum for the advancement of the nation. Oman is barren except for its narrow fertile coastal plain. The Arab population is descended equally from north and south Arabians. Black Africans live along the coast,

and there are also important Iranian, Pakistani, Indian and European minorities Nearly everybody is a Muslim. The main language is Arabic although Urdu, Baluchi, Hindi and English are spoken. Area: 212,457 sq km; population: 894,000; capital: Muscat (Masqat) (14,000).

P Palestine is the homeland of the biblical kingdoms of Israel and Judea. It was largely occupied by modern Israel following 4 Arab-Israeli wars (1948, 1956, 1967 and 1973). The dispossessed Palestinians

creating the basis of a sound economy after the oil had run out. The Arabs put as their priority the conflict with Israel. In 1973 their oil was used as a weapon against the industrial nations to try to force them to give more political support against the Israelis. Simultaneously with the outbreak of the fourth Arab-Israeli War in October 1973, petroleum prices soared. During the next year prices quadrupled and by the end of 1978 they had increased sevenfold. However, the Arabs were paid in American dollars that had lost over half their purchasing power through world inflation, caused largely by the rise in oil prices. Nevertheless, the increase in wealth that had come to Arab rulers was enormous. But it remains to be seen how effective the plans to develop their countries prove.

Countries outside the oil-rich belt

Those countries which produce little or no oil have considerable problems in balancing their economies. Usually they have to be supported by a range of activities. Syria receives 'rent' for the Iraqi pipeline that crosses the country to take oil to the Mediterranean. Jordan exports phosphates, potash and cement, while Lebanon's income derives mainly from commerce and finance. Exports of fruit and vegetables, wines, cement, clothing and footwear are important to the Cypriot economy. However, both Lebanon and Cyprus were seriously disrupted by civil war in the 1970s. Turkey endures particular problems in that exports of cotton, fruits, minerals and cereals pay for only about 30 per cent of its imports. Fortunately, money sent home from migrant workers in Western Europe helps to balance the budget. North Yemen produces salt, cotton and farm products, and nearly half its exports go to China. South Yemen is also mainly agricultural, but Aden is still a transit port for the trade of nearby countries.

Despite its lack of petroleum, Israel is comparatively rich, however, about 30 per cent of its income is spent on defence. The Israelis have achieved remarkable progress economically. Between 1955 and 1977 the area of cultivated land was doubled through irrigation, and atomic energy has been developed and minerals worked. But exports pay for only 47 per cent of imports so tourism and money from Jews living abroad help to keep the country solvent.

Above: Many Iranian women continued to wear the veil outside their own homes despite the efforts of the last 2 Shahs to westernize the country between 1925 and 1978. In 1979, followers of Ayatollah Khomeini tried to persuade Westernized women to go back to the veil.

Below: Jerusalem's 'Wailing Wall' is a remnant of King Herod's temple. The wall has strong emotional significance for Jews. It is grooved horizontally where generations of Jews have gashed their foreheads to bewail the destruction of the temple.

History and culture

Some 2,500 years ago Persia became the first of the great empires. It reached a peak of Islamic culture under Shah Abbas in the early 1600s, then declined. By 1907, Persia was practically under the control of Russia and Britain and soon after, the British Anglo-Persian Oil Company began developing the country's petroleum. This foreign occupation speeded political change and the collapse of the dynasty. In 1925, Reza Khan, commander of the Persian Cossack brigade, became the first shah of a new dynasty. During World War II, Persia suffered another British-Russian occupation. This resulted in the forced abdication of Reza and the succession of his son, Mohammed Reza Pahlavi. Under this shah, Persia (renamed IRAN), nationalized its oil and from 1973 accumulated the great wealth with which the shah proposed to industrialize the country. The social changes which wealth brought were resisted by Muslim leaders who organized rebellion against the shah's economic and foreign policies in 1978-79. The Shi-ite Muslim leader Ayatollah Khomeini returned from exile in 1979 to establish an Islamic republic.

Turkey and its successor states

The Turkish empire spread across three continents to reach its height under Suleiman the Magnificent in 1520-66. Although Turkey declined, it held the whole of south-western Asia

---

and their descendants have been a major international problem since 1948.

Q **Qatar** is a small, oil-rich, independent sheikdom on the east coast of Arabia. It has an almost entirely Arab Muslim population which lives in and around the booming capital, Doha. The main language is Arabic. Area: 11,000 sq km; population (including migrant workers): 235,000; capital: Doha (130,000).

R **Rub 'al-Khali** is a huge sandy and stony desert

in southern Arabia. Area: 650,000 sq km.

S **San'a** is the capital and largest town of NORTH

Street scene, San'a

YEMEN. Population: 150,000. **Saudi Arabia** is a traditionally-governed Arab monarchy and the homeland of Islam. Its holy cities of MECCA and MEDINA are more widely known than its political capital, Riyadh. JIDDA is the main port. Slavery became illegal only in 1962. Petroleum is the mainstay of the country's wealth, but its international influence stems also from Mecca as it is the world centre of Muslim pilgrimage. Most of the people are descended from Arab tribes with an admixture of Black Africans.

Arabic is the universal language. Area: 2,149,690 sq km; population: 10,400,000; capital Riyadh.

South Yemen came into being in 1967 by the union of the British colony of Aden with 23 tribal sheikdoms then under British protection. The republic includes the island of Socotra, 400 km offshore. Most of the population are Muslim Arabs, with Indian, Pakistani and Somali minorities. The main languages are Arabic and English. Area: 332,968 sq km; population: 2,000,000; capital: ADEN.

Syria is a republic situated south of Turkey and west of Iraq. Most Syrians are Arabs, but there are Alwi, Armenian, Turkish and Kurdish minorities. About 87% are Muslim and 13% Christian. The economy is basically agricultural with cotton an important crop. Revenue from oil-carrying pipelines which cross the country from Iraq to the Mediterranean is another source of income. DAMASCUS and ALEPPO are the only major cities. Area: 185,180 sq km; population: 8,649,000; capital: DAMASCUS.

west of Persia. Further decline saw Cyprus lost to British rule in 1878, and defeat in World War I finally destroyed its empire. France took SYRIA and LEBANON and Britain took PALESTINE, JORDAN and IRAQ. By 1924, Ibn Saud, head of a family allied to the Muslim Wahhabi sect, had hammered most of Arabia into the kingdom of SAUDI ARABIA. World War II speeded the departure of France and Britain from South-west Asia and brought independence to the northern Arab states. The last remaining sultanates of the Arabian peninsula became fully independent by 1971. The Bedouin nomadic shepherds were fast disappearing into the prosperous towns, while trucks and aircraft replaced camels. Despite social change, the Islamic religion strengthened.

Palestine and the emergence of Israel

The Jews had been scattered as minority groups in many countries for 1,800 years when a movement began in the late 1800s to set up a Jewish national home in PALESTINE – their Biblical homeland. Little came of this idea until World War I. Then, having secretly promised the Arab's independence to gain their support against the Turks, the British further agreed to Jewish settlement in Palestine, which was then populated mainly by Arabs. Matters came to a head after World War II. Many of the surviving Jews in Europe made their way to Palestine. They endured barely tolerable conditions in 'hell ships' which managed to smuggle them into the country past the British blockade. As the last British soldiers left Palestine in 1948, the first Arab-Israeli War began. Israel survived this war and three others in 1956, 1967 and 1973, despite the overwhelming numbers of their Arab opponents. The 'Palestinian problem' has continued to dominate South-west Asian affairs politically as oil has done economically. In 1979 Egypt became the first Arab country to sign a peace treaty with Israel, but other Arab states condemned Egypt and a permanent peace is still sought. Israel and the territories it captured in the 1967 war, has a sizeable Arab Muslim minority. On its borders, particularly with Jordan and Lebanon, live the dispossessed Arab Palestinians whose families fled from Israel in 1948. They continue to fight a guerrilla war against Israel in the hope of retrieving some of their former lands.

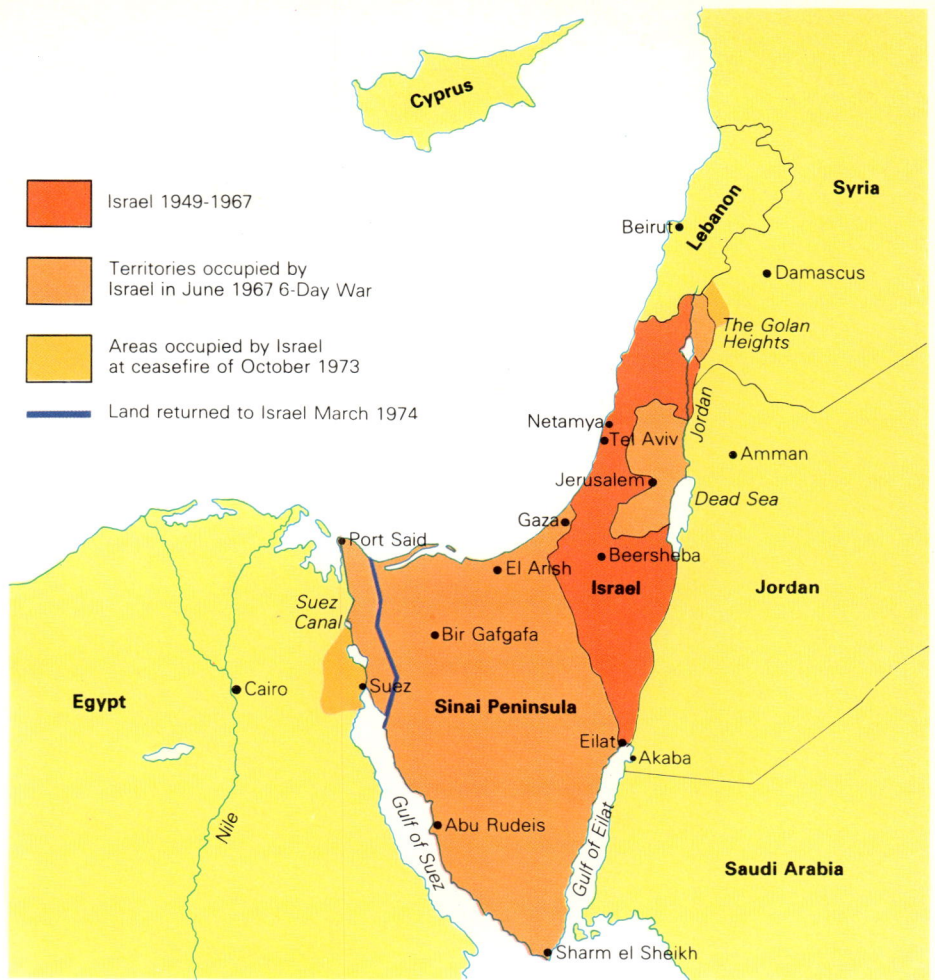

Israel 1949-1967

Territories occupied by Israel in June 1967 6-Day War

Areas occupied by Israel at ceasefire of October 1973

Land returned to Israel March 1974

Above: The first Arab-Israeli war (1948) left Israel in possession of roughly the old Palestine area except the West Bank (of the Jordan River). In the third Arab-Israeli war (1967), Israel occupied the West Bank, the Golan Heights, and the Sinai Peninsula.

Right: Following the Israeli invasion of Egypt in 1967, the Suez Canal was blocked by sunken ships. Egypt claimed Israeli bombers sank the ships; Israel charged Egypt with deliberately sinking them along with floating docks.

Taurus Mountains, a range in southern Turkey, rise to over 3,600 km.

Tehran is the capital of IRAN. It is a modern city of international importance, as well as being an industrial and railway centre. Population: 4,300,000.

Tel Aviv is ISRAEL's biggest city and an important centre of business and industry. A modern town, dating back only to 1906, it has absorbed the city of Jaffa. Population: 440,000.

Tigris River rises in Turkey and flows 1,900 km through Iraq to unite with the EUPHRATES RIVER and finally empties into the Persian (Arabian) Gulf.

Turkey, situated partly in Europe but mainly in South-west Asia, occupies the region once known as Asia Minor. Turkey's varied economy has not achieved the prosperity of most European states and many people leave the country to find work abroad. The main language is Turkish, and Kurdish and Arabic are the minority languages. Area: 780,576 sq km; population: 44,160,000; capital: ANKARA.

Kemal Ataturk and wife

United Arab Emirates became an independent emirate in 1971 following British withdrawal from the 6 emirates of Abu Dhabi, Dubai, Sharjah, Ajman, Umm al Qaiwain and Fujairah. A seventh emirate, Ras al Khaimah, joined in 1972. Petroleum dominated the economy of this rich federation, which is governed by its leading families. The mainly Arab population has important Iranian, Pakistani and Indian minorities. Area: 83,600 sq km; population: 229,000; capital: Abu Dhabi.

West Bank is that part of PALESTINE west of the JORDAN RIVER taken by JORDAN in 1948 and occupied by ISRAEL in 1967.

Zagros Mountains run north to south-east along the borders of IRAN with TURKEY and IRAQ. The peaks rise from 2,750 to 4,550 metres above sea level.

Southern Asia is one of the world's most densely-populated regions. It has considerable natural resources, but the population explosion and ancient traditions have made it difficult for governments to raise living standards.

South Asia

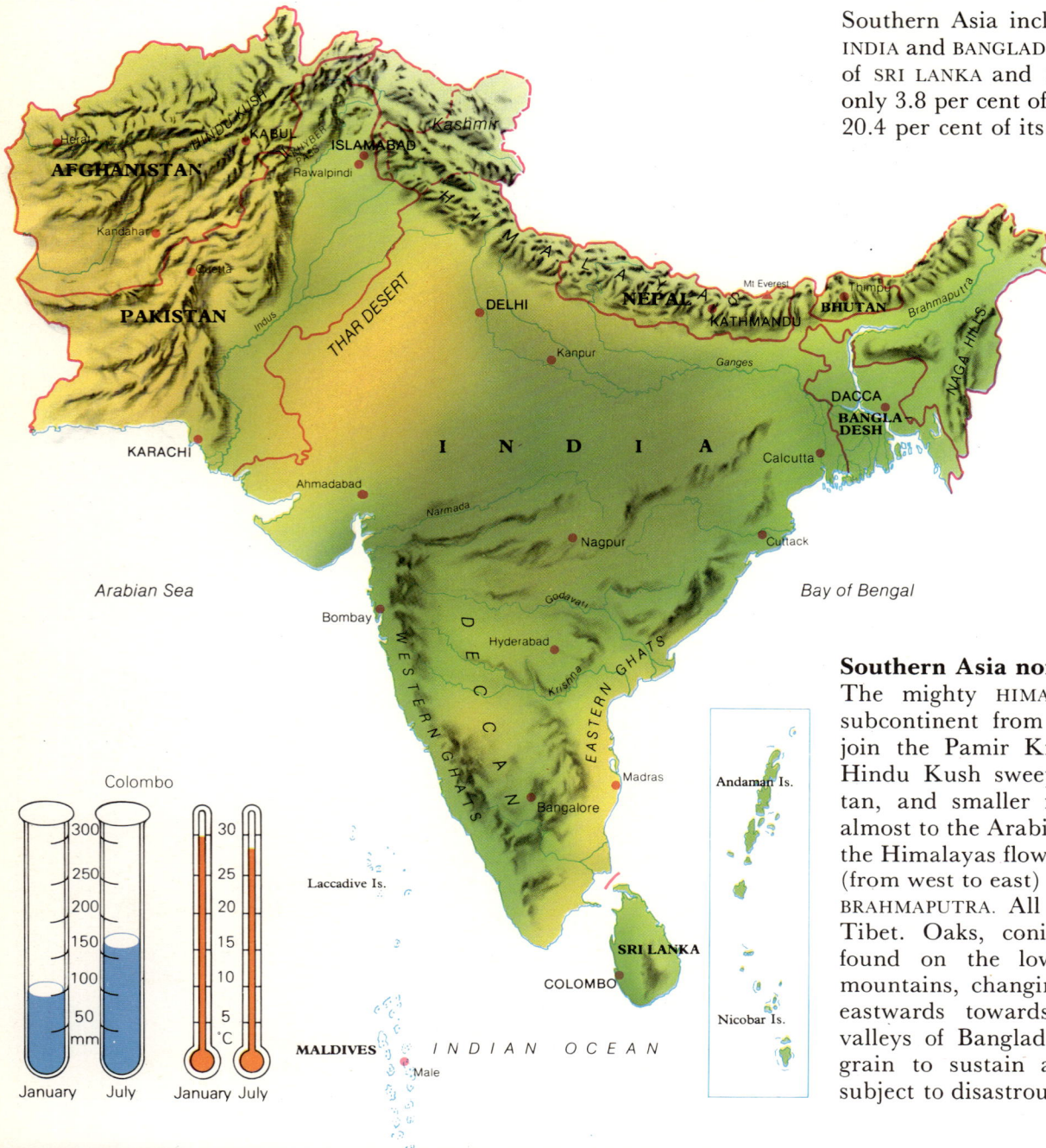

Southern Asia includes AFGHANISTAN, PAKISTAN, INDIA and BANGLADESH; and the southern islands of SRI LANKA and MALDIVES. The region covers only 3.8 per cent of the world's land area but has 20.4 per cent of its population.

Below and **below left:** Karachi has more extreme day temperatures than Colombo, which has a heavier rainfall.

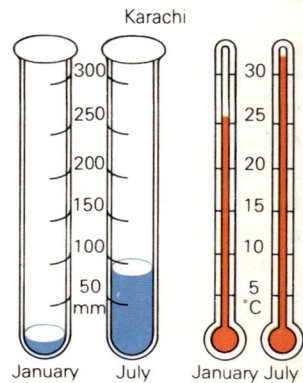

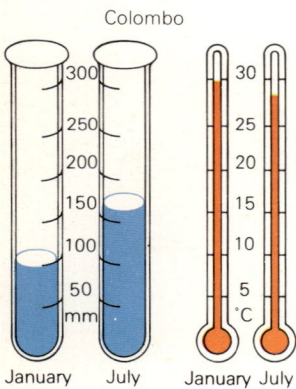

Karachi

January   July   January July

Colombo

January   July   January July

Southern Asia north of the tropics

The mighty HIMALAYAS separate the Indian subcontinent from the plateau of Tibet. They join the Pamir Knot, from where the barren Hindu Kush sweeps south-west into Afghanistan, and smaller ranges extend into Pakistan almost to the Arabian Sea. In the plains south of the Himalayas flow several great rivers including (from west to east) the INDUS, Sutlej, GANGES and BRAHMAPUTRA. All except the Ganges rise in Tibet. Oaks, conifers and rich meadows are found on the lower slopes of the northern mountains, changing to dense evergreen forests eastwards towards Assam. The fertile river valleys of Bangladesh and India grow enough grain to sustain a dense population but are subject to disastrous flooding. Bangladesh grows

Reference

A **Adam's Bridge** is a chain of shoals between south-east India and north-west Sri Lanka, nearly 50 km in length. In Hindu mythology, the 'bridge' was built by the divine hero Rama to enable his Indian armies to attack Sri Lanka.
Afghanistan, a landlocked republic, lies between IRAN (*see page* 4), PAKISTAN and the USSR. The Hindu Kush, together with other ranges and barren plains, cover

most of the country. Only the valleys are fertile. Consequently, Afghanistan is a poor country. In origins the people are about 50% Pathan, a tall Caucasoid people, and 50% Mongoloid, especially Uzbek, Hazara and Tadzhik. About 72% of the gross national product comes from agriculture and 85% of the people live outside towns. Previously stable, Afghanistan had 2 coups in the 1970s and by 1979 was in a state of insurrection. The chief cities include KABUL, the capital, Kandaha, Herat and Mazar-i-

Sharif. The main languages are Pushtu, spoken by the Pathans, and Dari, a Persian dialect spoken by Tadzhiks and Hazaras. Uzbeks speak a

Golden Temple, Amritsar

form of Turkish. Area: 647,497 sq km; population: 21,858,000; capital: Kabul.
Ahmedabad is the capital of Gujarat state, INDIA. Population: 1,850,000.
Ajanta, site of 30 Buddhist rock-hewn caves from 1,200 to 2,200 years old, is an important tourist site in west-central India.
Amritsar in north-west India is the site of the Golden Temple of the Sikhs. Population: 540,000.

B **Bangalore** is the capital of Karnataka state, India. Population: 1,250,000.

Bangladesh, a republic surrounded by the Bay of Bengal and INDIA, was the province of East PAKISTAN until independence came following civil war with the West Pakistanis in 1971. The revolt against the Pakistan government had been sparked off by a devastating tidal wave caused by a cyclone that killed about 250,000 people. Climatic misfortunes have dominated this small state, 50% of which is covered by the deltas of the GANGES and BRAHMAPUTRA rivers. The rivers cause disastrous

Above: Rice farmers protect themselves from India's monsoon rains by wearing short straw 'coats' to cover their heads and backs.

Below: Despite the high altitudes, valleys in the Nepalese Himalayas benefit from good soil, regular rainfall, and generous sunlight. Farmers grow rice in the monsoon season and wheat in the dry season.

mainly rice, but as the soil becomes drier westwards towards Pakistan and Afghanistan, wheat becomes the main crop. Only two per cent of Afghanistan can be cultivated and only the southern 25 per cent of Pakistan – the plain formed by five rivers – is fertile. East of the Indus and north of the Tropic of Cancer, lies the dry, sandy THAR DESERT, covering more than 250,000 sq km of Pakistan and India. The rain-drenched southern slopes of Bhutan's mountains are thickly forested. Despite their height, the fertile valleys of Nepal are sunny and warm for much of the year.

Tropical Southern Asia

The DECCAN, a fertile plateau where crops are grown and animals grazed, covers most of tropical India south of the NARBADA RIVER. Its western edge rises from 900 to 1,500 metres as the Western Ghats, a mountain range that borders the coastlands along the Arabian Sea. Here the chief city and port is BOMBAY. Several rivers flow from the Western Ghats eastwards into the Bay of Bengal notably the GODAVI. Although dry for much of the year, they often flood the country during the rainy season, especially in mid-June to September. The Eastern Ghats of north-eastern Deccan rise to between 450 and 600 metres. The Malabar coast of south-western India contains evergreen rain

forest. The island of Sri Lanka lies 70 kilometres across the Gulf of Mannar, almost connected to south-eastern India by ADAM'S BRIDGE. Once all forested, it now has large areas of savanna, grasslands and fernlands. The low-lying triangular-shaped island rises to over 2,400 metres south of the central area, and several small rivers flow seaward passing through forests and rubber and tea plantations.

The 2,000 mainly uninhabited coral atolls (islands) of Maldives are grouped into 12 clusters. They lie only two to 24 metres above sea level but are protected from the Indian Ocean by barrier reefs. Islanders grow coconut palms, fruit trees and millet and are excellent fishermen.

Climate of Southern Asia

Most of Southern Asia has a monsoon climate. Westerly winds bring a wet season, lasting in places from May to October, and a 'dry' season from November to April. However, this dry season's rain can be heavy at times, especially in Assam and Bangladesh in the north, and in Sri Lanka in the south. The rain gradually phases out as the peak of the dry season approaches. The sub-continent has great variations in rainfall. For example, Jacobabad near Quetta in Pakistan has only 100 millimetres of rain a year, but Cherrapunji in Assam, north of Bangladesh, has over 100 times as much. The populated areas of Afghanistan have a dry, healthy climate, with about 300 millimetres of rain annually.

The coastal areas of Bangladesh and West

floods, yet also provide the fertility to grow rice, tea and jute, which are the mainstays of the economy. Bangladesh has a population density of about 625 people to the sq km, 7 times the world average. DACCA, the capital, and CHITTAGONG are the largest cities. Nearly all the people are Bengali; 87% are Muslim and 12% Hindu. Bengali is the language spoken. Area: 143,998 sq km; population: 90,670,000; capital: Dacca.
Benares, see Varanasi.
Bhutan, lying between India and China, is a remote coun-

try. The southern plains, only 50 metres above sea level, rise northward to the HIMALAYAS, where mountain peaks reach 7,300 metres. It has been dominated politically in the past by India, but Bhutan's king began to open his land-locked Buddhist kingdom to the rest of the world in the mid-1970s. Most of the people are Bhutanese (Bhotias) of Tibetan descent, although about 25% are Nepalis. There are few towns and nearly all the inhabitants live in the countryside. The main language is Dzongka, with Nepali and

tribal dialects also spoken. Area: 47,000 sq km; population: 1,311,000; capital: Thimpu (population 9,000).
Bombay is INDIA'S main port to the West and capital of the Maharashtra state. Population: 7,000,000.
Brahmaputra River rises in south-west Tibet, where it is called Tsangpo, and flows about 2,900 km through northern India and Bangladesh. Here it becomes the River Jamuna, and merges with the GANGES.

C **Calcutta** is the capital of West Bengal State

and is the largest city in INDIA. With access to the Bay of Bengal along the Hooghly River, it is a major port, handling jute and iron

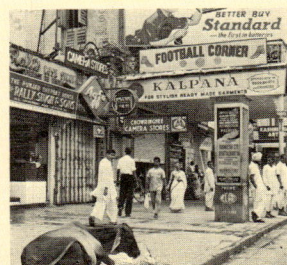

Chowringhee, Calcutta

among other products. With Howrah, its satellite town, it is also a major industrial centre. Road and rail routes converge on the city. Population: 8,500,000.
Chittagong is the second city and principal port of BANGLADESH. Its annual rainfall is one of the heaviest in the world. Population: 580,000.
Colombo is the capital, business centre and chief port of SRI LANKA. Population: 725,000.

D **Dacca** is the capital of BANGLADESH. It is situated

Bengal, India, comprise the Brahmaputra-Ganges delta region, which is very fertile but prone to devastating floods and cyclones (vast, inward-spiralling winds of great force). The Maldive islands near the Equator, are hot and humid.

Temperatures in KABUL, Afghanistan, range from about 3°C in January to 25°C in July. In the Kathmandu Valley region of Nepal, temperatures range from 10°C in January to 26°C in July. But they can drop to −40°C in Nepal's highest Himalayan peaks. In Pakistan, northern India and Bangladesh, January temperatures usually exceed 17°C and July temperatures go well above 27°C. Temperatures range between these extremes in tropical India and Sri Lanka.

Right: Highly-decorated heavy vehicles ford a shallow waterway by the Indus River, near Islamabad, capital of Pakistan. Decoration of vehicles, especially with religious motifs, is common in Pakistan. A favourite symbol is the hand of Fatima, believed to ward off the evil eye.

Left: India's hereditary caste system takes 2 forms. *Jati* divides society into hundreds of castes based on occupations. Alongside it, *Varna* divides people into *brahmans* (priests), *kshatriyas* (rulers and warriors), *vaisyas* (merchants and craftsmen), and *sudras* (unskilled labourers). 'Outcastes' or 'untouchables' are outside the caste system.

Peoples and ways of life

INDIA is the giant of Southern Asia, occupying 64 per cent of its land area and containing 76 per cent of its people. About 63 per cent of all Southern Asians are Hindus and most of the rest are Muslim. Other religions (roughly in order of numbers) include Buddhists, Sikhs, Christians, Jains, Lamaists, Zoroastrians and Jews. Nowhere else in the world is there such a variety of active religions practised as part of daily life. Farming is the dominant occupation of the region where most people live in villages. Incomes are low but money matters much less in Southern Asia where much of what is consumed is either home produced or obtained by barter.

Styles of dress

The cultural heartland of Southern Asia is the territory once contained in the Indian Empire which lasted for over 2,000 years until 1947. Despite the antagonism of Hindus and Muslims, the old empire had a cultural unity still evident in its ways of dress. Women generally wear the *sari,* an unsewn length of coloured cloth, except for special groups such as the trouser-wearing Sikh women of the Punjab. Richer women also wear a *choli,* a blouse-like garment. In contrast most men wear a cotton turban and a *dhoti,* a single length of white cotton cloth worn as a loincloth that can also be thrown over the shoulders. These styles of dress are prevalent in the million villages that house 80 per cent of India's population. They are also worn in Sri Lanka, but to a lesser extent in the colder,

---

on the Burhiganga River with an outport at Narayanganj. Population: 1,200,000.
Darjeeling is a hill station in West Bengal, India, and the surrounding area is famous for its tea. It lies 2,165 metres above sea level. Population: 55,000.
Deccan is a large plateau in INDIA between the NARMADA and Krishna rivers, and more generally the area south to the sea. The plateau rises to the west where it is bounded by the Western Ghats (1,500 m). In the north-east, the Eastern Ghats rise to 600 metres, while to the north

the Vindhya, (1,200 metres) and other mountain ranges separate the Deccan from the northern plains.
Delhi, capital of INDIA, is situated on the Jumna River.

Lutyens building, Delhi

It comprises Old Delhi which was largely rebuilt in the 17th century and New Delhi which was designed mainly by Sir Edward Lutyens and completed in 1929. Population: 5,000,000.

E Eastern Ghats *see* Deccan.
Ellora is the site of 34 Buddhist, Hindu and Jain cave temples 1,000 to 1,500 years old. It lies in west central India The site has a complete rock-cut temple.

G Ganges River rises in the Indian HIMALAYAS and

flows south and east through India, where it is regarded as sacred, especially at VARANASI. It flows through West Bengal and Bangladesh, forming a vast delta before emptying into the Bay of Bengal. Its total length is about 2,500 km.
Godavari River rises in north-east Maharashtra, India, and flows about 1,450 km southeast across the DECCAN to empty into the Bay of Bengal through several tributaries.

H Himalayas (Himalaya), a huge mountain range

forming the northern border of the Indian subcontinent extends for 2,400 km from Kashmir in the west to Assam in the east. The range covers most of Nepal, Sikkim, Bhutan and south Tibet. Its average height is 6,000 metres, but Mount Everest, the world's highest mountain, towers 8,848 metres. K2 (also called Godwin-Austen or Dapsang), the world's second highest mountain rises to 8,616 metres.
Hyderabad is the largest city of Andhra state, India Population: 1,400,00.

landlocked countries of the north. Many Pakistani women wear trousers like the Sikhs, especially in cities, or, like Afghan village women, a black garment with small eyeholes that covers them from head to toes. Orthodox Muslims believe that women should always be hidden from men except their near relatives. In the cities of Southern Asia, most men now wear western dress. More distinctive styles of dress are worn in Bhutan and northern Nepal, which come under Tibetan influence.

Villagers and city dwellers

In the villages, houses are often built of mud, in a square, windowless style, but brick or stone may be used in some areas. Streets are unpaved and usually unlit except in the more prosperous areas. Women still carry water on their heads for a kilometre or more in some parts. In areas remote from towns, villagers have been used to looking after themselves for many generations and continue to do so. Indian villages have the *panchayet* (rule by five) system whereby a group of elected councillors (ideally five) meet and decide communal matters in the village. The Indian state governments often support the *panchayets*, giving them money perhaps to buy a radio or install oil lamps to light village meeting places at night. The most precious possessions of village families are often their cooking pots and brass water containers, which may be inherited.

City life is a world apart, where newcomers from the villages fight for jobs that will bring a

Above: Colourful religious festivals are frequent throughout India. In the Hindu festival shown, worshippers fly pennants bearing sacred signs such as the swastika—one of the earliest-known symbols of several Asian religions.

Left: Houses built of mud and straw accommodate many millions of Indian villagers. When a village is near a town, some members of the family may work in the town to increase their income, which can be used to buy a radio, a bicycle, or other factory-made goods.

little money to ward off starvation. Home for many in the cities is a pitch on the pavement at night, sufficiently big to lay a bedding roll and perhaps play a game of cards with a neighbour before trying to sleep through the all-night bustle. The caste system that once decided a Hindu's status in life from birth, is fast breaking down in the turmoil of city life. High caste Brahmins and outcast 'untouchables' stand crushed together in the packed trains that carry them from the cheaper suburbs to their jobs in the centres of great cities such as Calcutta and Bombay. For many families, city life holds only the promise of a room in a slum with half the food eaten by a village family. However, with caste discrimination long banned by law, there is now the chance of rising by merit into the growing

India is the world's second most populous country. It is a federal republic of 22 states and 9 territories of vastly different size. Nagaland state has only 20,000 people while Uttar Pradesh has 106,000,000. Indians range from the light-skinned Kashmiris of the north to the dark Tamils of the south. About 83% of Indians are Hindus, 11% Muslims, 2% Sikhs, 2% Christians, and 0.5% Jains. Other communities include Zoroastrians, Buddhists and Jews. The Hindu caste system, once dominant, is

Village barber, India

now breaking down. Despite its very great population, India is not so crowded as some other Asian countries. Although its people are among the world's poorest, India is rich in potential resources. Food production could probably be doubled by the use of fertilizers, the adoption of better methods of agriculture and the implementation of hydro-engineering projects to prevent disastrous flooding. Until recently, economic progress has been severely hampered by the passive opposition of traditionalists. Over 80% of India's people live in some 750,000 villages, yet the country has some of the most populous cities and biggest industries

in the world. It has the largest steelworks in the Commonwealth and the world's most productive film industry. Few go hungry in the villages, but in the cities, workless people may starve. Indian cities with over a million people include CALCUTTA, BOMBAY, DELHI, the capital, MADRAS, HYDERABAD, BANGALORE, AHMEDABAD and Kanpur. About 44% of India's gross national product comes from agriculture, 23% from mining and manufacturing, and 16% from commerce and communication. It has the most exten-

sive rail system in Asia. There are 14 official languages: Assamese, Bengali, Gujarati, Hindi, Kannada, Kashmiri, Malayalam, Marathi, Oriya, Punjabi, Sanskrit, Tamil, Telegu, and Urdu. However, English is the general language of communication between educated Indians. Hundreds of local languages and dialects are spoken. Thirty years of rule by the Congress Party ended in 1977, when Indira Gandhi, daughter of Jahalawal Nehru, India's first prime minister, was defeated in a general

Left: Cows, especially sacred to the Hindus, roam freely through the streets of India's great cities. Few cows are sufficiently nourished to produce milk. These brahmin humped cattle seek food in a Bombay street.

maize and barley crops while India and Pakistan are leading cotton countries. With Bangladesh they produce much tobacco for home consumption. Nepal grows rice in the monsoon season and wheat in the dry season. Bangladesh produces much of the world's jute and Sri Lanka and India a large percentage of the world's rubber and tea. Mechanization is improving. India, for example, has some 220,000 tractors, but Bangladesh has only 2,500.

The region has over 500 million domesticated animals, 50 per cent of which are cattle found mainly in India. Water buffaloes, for example, are widely spread, especially in rice-growing areas. And India, Pakistan and Afghanistan raise most of the 80 million sheep kept. Pigs are reared in India and Nepal, but not in Muslim countries. Poultry are kept everywhere.

Southern Asia produces very little petroleum

middle class. Education too, can be bought cheaply by those who have the stamina to cram in the many night classes run by poor teachers.

Economy

The economy of Southern Asia is fairly uniform, though patterns change in the mountain regions of the north where crop farming is difficult. But differences are determined as much by the differing lifestyles of Hindus and Muslims as by geography.

Crops, animals and industry

Small-scale agriculture dominates the economy except in SRI LANKA, where the rubber and tea estates have been brought under government control. The average Indian farm, for example, comprises only two hectares compared with 45 hectares in Britain and 150 hectares in the USA. INDIA and BANGLADESH lead in rice production, and India, PAKISTAN and AFGHANISTAN in wheat.

India and Afghanistan also grow important

Above: India desperately needs more dams such as the Tungabhadra Dam on the Deccan Plateau in Karnataka state, which irrigates over 750,000 hectares and controls floods. The 600-km long Tungabhadra River is formed by the confluence of the Tunga and Bhadra rivers.

and outside India has few large industries. Reflecting its size, India ranks as an important producer of coal, iron ore and steel. A giant steel mill near CALCUTTA is among the world's biggest and the country has the largest chemical fertilize plant in Asia. India also makes its own vehicles has the most extensive rail system in Asia, and has a nuclear power station near BOMBAY. The

election that was fought with much bitterness. Area: 3,287,590; Population: 662,961,000; Capital: Delhi.
Indus River rises in south-west Tibet and flows 2,900 km through Kashmir and Pakistan into the Arabian Sea. Its river basin is nearly 1,000,000 sq km in area. The Indus Valley civilization developed within this basin about 4,500 years ago and lasted for about 1,000 years.
Islamabad, the newly-built capital of PAKISTAN, was planned as a city of outstanding modern architecture. Population: 75,000.

K **Kabul** is the capital of Afghanistan. It once commanded the strategic mountain passes through which many invaders gained entrance to the Indian subcontinent. Population: 650,000.
Kanpur, India, is an industrial city and transportation centre on the GANGES RIVER in Uttar Pradesh. Population: 2,400,000.
Karachi, the former capital of PAKISTAN is the country's biggest city and main port. Population: 4,700,000.
Kashmir, borders Tibet and Sinkiang-Uighur and is the

northernmost region of the Indian subcontinent. In area, it is the size of France. It was claimed by both India and Pakistan at independence in 1947. After war in 1947–49,

Kashmiri with hookah

Pakistan occupied the west and India the east. Area: 222,800 sq km; population: 5,500,000.
Kathmandu the capital of NEPAL, is an unmodernized town with many temples of unique architecture. The similar towns of Patan and Bhadgaon lie nearby. Population: 185,000.
Khyber Pass was for hundreds of years the gateway to the Indian subcontinent for invading armies. About 53 km long, it is situated on the Afghan-Pakistan border in the Safed Ko range, an offshoot of the Hindu Kush.

L **Laccadive Islands**, with Minicoy and Amindiv form an Indian territory 32 km off the south-west coast of India. Area: 28 sq km population: 30,000.
Lahore is the capital o Punjab province and a leading cultural centre in north east PAKISTAN. Population 2,500,000.

M **Madras** is the bigges city of southern IND and is the capital of Tam Nadu state. Population 2,500,000.
Maldives is an independent republic in the Indian Ocean

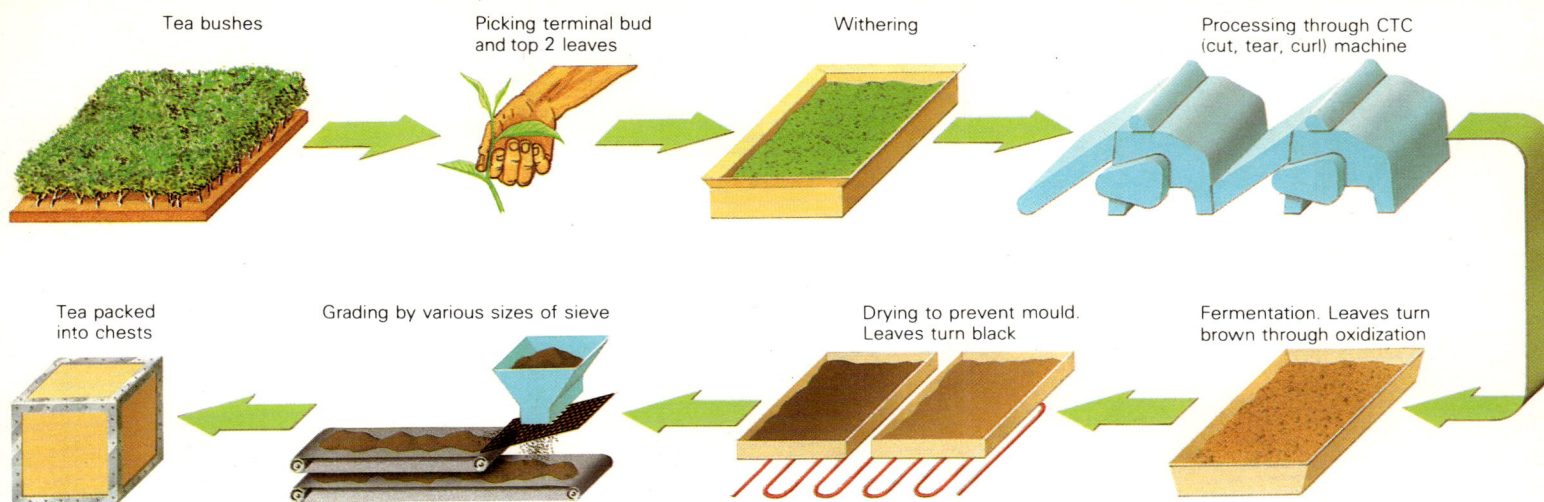

Tea bushes → Picking terminal bud and top 2 leaves → Withering → Processing through CTC (cut, tear, curl) machine

Tea packed into chests ← Grading by various sizes of sieve ← Drying to prevent mould. Leaves turn black ← Fermentation. Leaves turn brown through oxidization

great rivers of the subcontinent have been harnessed to provide irrigation, produce electricity and reduce flooding. In 1979, India sought Russian aid in an ambitious project to link India's waterways by a huge canal network.

The problem of population

India, Pakistan, Bangladesh and Sri Lanka are bedevilled by a basic problem that troubled countries such as Britain during the time of their early industrialization. As the standard of living rises, more babies survive to swell the population, so consuming the extra production that brings about the higher standard of living in the first place. Indian governments, for example, have tried to solve this problem by persuading people to have less children. In fact India's annual rate of population increase slowed from 2.4 per cent to 2.1 per cent in the ten years ending 1976, representing two million less mouths to feed each year. However, except for Bangladesh, Southern Asia is less densely populated than either Japan or South Korea, which have much higher standards of living.

The potential wealth of India

Despite Southern Asia's poverty, it has the resources to become a prosperous region. It has a wealth of fertile land and rich mineral reserves. Food production could certainly be doubled because tradition often stands in the way of

Above: Stages in the processing of tea are shown. The best quality tea comes from leaves picked from the end of the branch; the very best tea, 'pekoe tip', comes from the leaf bud at the end of the branch. Picked leaves are left on trays in racks for 1 or 2 days to dry—a process called 'withering'. The leaves are then crushed to bring out the flavouring juices. Some tea is then allowed to ferment before drying to become black tea. Green tea is unfermented. After drying the tea is graded and packed into tea chests for export. Indian and Sri Lankan teas are sent to London for the skilled process of blending.

Right: Salt, excavated by simple machinery, lies ready for processing at a mine head in Pakistan. The mineral has played an important part in the history of the Indian subcontinent. Taxes were sometimes levied in salt during the time of the British Raj.

progress. For example, India has millions of cows which, being holy to Hindus, wander freely even into city streets. These half-fed animals consume valuable food but are too undernourished to produce much milk and too sacred to be eaten. The cow dung, which if applied to the land could increase fertility, is instead collected and patted into 'cakes' to provide fuel to burn under domestic cooking pots.

t comprises some 2,000 coral islands situated nearly 600 km off south-east India. About 220 islands forming 12 clusters are inhabited. Fishing is the mainstay of the economy. The people are mainly Muslims of mixed Indian, Sinhalese and Arab descent, and they gained independence from Britain in 1965. Area: 298 sq km; population: 134,000; Capital: Malé (15,000).

N Naga Hills border the Indian state of Nagaland and north-west Burma and rise about 3,000 metres.

Narbada (Narmada or Nerbuddha) River, which rises in the Maikala Range of Madhya Pradesh, divides north INDIA from the DECCAN. It flows 1,290 km roughly east to west to empty into the Gulf of Cambay. The river is sacred to Hindus.

Nepal is a landlocked Hindu-Buddhist mountain kingdom lying between India and Tibet. It was cut off from the rest of the world until the 1950s. The Nepalese are mainly descended from migrants from India, Tibet and Central Asia. Only 4% of the people live in

towns, which include KATHMANDU, Patan and Bhadgaon, all in the fertile Kathmandu Valley. The main

Patan, Nepal, fruit stall

language is Nepali but there are also Tibeto-Burman and Indian languages and dialects. Area: 140,797 sq km; Population: 14,082,000.

P Pakistan broke away from INDIA at independence in 1947 because its 86% Muslim population feared Hindu domination. The Islamic Republic of Pakistan was first divided into western and eastern regions, separated by 1,600 km of India. The two regions separated following civil war in 1971, East Pakistan becoming BANGLADESH. In the

past, Pakistan was the northwestern frontier of the Indian subcontinent through which many invaders passed. Consequently, Pakistanis are of mixed origins. Like India, Pakistan is a poor country. Much of the land is too dry or too mountainous to be productive and 80% of the people live in villages. Leading cities of Pakistan include KARACHI, LAHORE, Shah Faisalabad, HYDERABAD, Rawalpindi and the small adjacent newly-built town of ISLAMABAD, the capital. In its first 30 years of independence Pakistan ex-

Above: The Khyber Pass now has a good road connecting Pakistan to Afghanistan. This narrow ravine, forms the strategic gateway to the plains southward.

Agricultural inefficiency is bound up with the land system. Many farmers have inherited family debts. Apart from owing money to landlords and moneylenders, they also have to borrow from them at very high interest rates in order to buy the vital seeds and tools needed to carry on working the land. New hope came in the mid-1970s when the governments of India and Pakistan promised land reform. The first groups of tenant farmers were given possession of the land they tilled and the opportunity to borrow the capital needed at reasonable rates of interest from government agencies.

History and culture

Southern Asia has been the home of several great civilizations. The earliest, the Indus Valley culture, flourished some 4,000 years ago in what is now PAKISTAN. A Buddhist-Hindu-Jain-based civilization reached its height about 2,300 years ago and has left many traces, especially at ELLORA and AJANTA. Beginning in the AD 700s, Islam dominated the area for 1,000 years as a

Below: Mrs Sirimawo Bandaranaike, the world's first woman prime minister, led the government of Sri Lanka during 1960-65 and again during 1970-77.

result of several invasions of India from the direction of Afghanistan, through the strategic KHYBER PASS. For about 200 years up to 1947, Britain controlled much of the area, often through local rulers. The many religions of the subcontinent have been mainly responsible for moulding its deep and diverse culture.

Political problems of the new states

At independence in 1947, the Indian empire split into India, where Hindus predominated, and Pakistan, which was mainly Muslim. The multiracial island of SRI LANKA (then Ceylon) gained independence in 1948. Pakistan comprised a western region and a smaller, eastern region, separated by 1,600 kilometres of Indian territory. Control of the northern region of KASHMIR, with its mainly Muslim population but Hindu ruler, was disputed by INDIA and Pakistan and eventually led to war in 1947–49. A cease-fire arranged by the United Nations left Kashmir divided between the two countries. India lost a brief border war with China in 1962 and fought another inconclusive war against Pakistan over Kashmir in 1965–66. Resentment in East Pakistan over its alleged exploitation by West Pakistan increased in 1971 following a disastrous cyclone that hit the East Pakistan coast in late 1970. Disease and famine followed, and between 200,000 and 500,000 died. The East Pakistanis claimed that most of these deaths happened because the western-based Pakistani government neglected its duty to arrange speedy relief. Anger exploded into rebellion, military repression and finally civil war. Following a third Indo-Pakistani war, East Pakistan became the independent republic of BANGLADESH in late 1971. Following a coup, General Zia assumed power in Pakistan in 1977. The former prime minister, Zulfikar Ali Bhutto, was executed in 1979, allegedly for complicity to murder.

In Sri Lanka, Mrs Bandaranaike, became the world's first woman prime minister, ruling in 1960–65 and again in 1970–77. In India, Mrs Ghandi, the daughter of the country's first prime minister, Jawaharlal Nehru, headed the government from 1966 to 1977 when she was replaced by the Janata Party government led by the veteran politician Morarji Desai. BHUTAN moved towards full independence and Maldives became independent from Britain in 1965.

perienced several military takeovers of government and fought 3 wars with India. KASHMIR remained in dispute between the two countries, but agreement was reached on the disposal of the vital Indus Valley waters in 1960. The main languages are Urdu and English, Punjabi, Sindhi and Baluchi are spoken regionally. Area: 803,943 sq km; population: 81,450,000; capital: Islamabad.

Poona, India, is a main centre of Marathi culture. It is a commercial centre. Population: 900,000.

S **Sri Lanka,** formerly Ceylon, is an island republic off the south-east coast of India. About 66% of Sri Lankans are Buddhist Sinhalese and most of the rest are Tamils who are mainly Hindu. However, Christians form about 8% of the population. Minorities include the Muslim Moors (descended from Arabs), Burghers (Eurasians) and Veddahs (descendants of the earliest known inhabitants) who now live in remote forests. Tea, rubber and coconuts are the mainstay of the country's economy. The

main languages in Sri Lanka are Sinhalese, English and Tamil. Area: 65,610 sq km; Population: 15,568,000; Capital: COLOMBO.

T **Thar Desert** (Great Indian Desert) is a sandy wasteland in north-west India and south-east Pakistan. It is bounded by the Aravalli Hills, the Indus and Sutlej rivers, and the Arabian Sea. It covers about 2,600,000 sq km.

Thimpu is the capital and largest town of Bhutan and was established only in 1961 around some old temples. It

stands 2,500 metres above sea level. Population: 9,000.

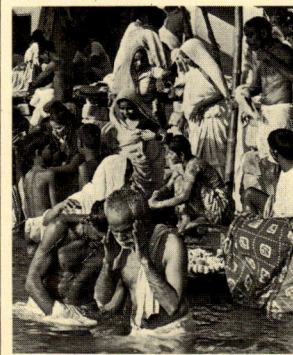

Pilgrims at Varanasi

V **Varanasi** (formerly Benares), the holiest city of Hinduism, is a centre for pilgrims. It stands on the GANGES RIVER in north-east INDIA. Population: 750,000.

W **Western Ghats** (see DECCAN).

Eastern Asia is dominated by two contrasting nations, the industrial colossus of Japan and the world's most populous nation, communist China. Both nations are now adjusting to their vital roles in world affairs.

Eastern Asia

USSR

MONGOLIA

ULAN BATOR

GOBI

Inner Mongolia

TIEN SHAN

Sinkiang-Uighur

KURLUK

CHINA

PEKING

Shenyang

Harbin

NORTH KOREA

Pyongyang

SEOUL

SOUTH KOREA

Pusan

Kitakyushu

Lu-ta

Tientsin

Taiyuen

Lanchow

Sian

Kwang Ho

Tsingtao

Nanking

Shanghai

Wuhan

Yangtze Kiang

Chengtu

Chungking

Tibet

Mt Everest

HIMALAYAS

BANGLA-DESH

INDIA

BURMA

Kunming

Si Kiang

Canton

MACAO

HONG KONG

KWANGCHOW

TAIPEI

TAIWAN

Ryukyu Is.

East China Sea

Yellow Sea

JAPAN

Honshu

TOKYO

Hokkaido

Sapporo

Kyoto

Kobe

Osaka

Nagoya

Shikoku

Kyushu

PACIFIC OCEAN

PHILIPPINES

South China Sea

LAOS

THAILAND

VIETNAM

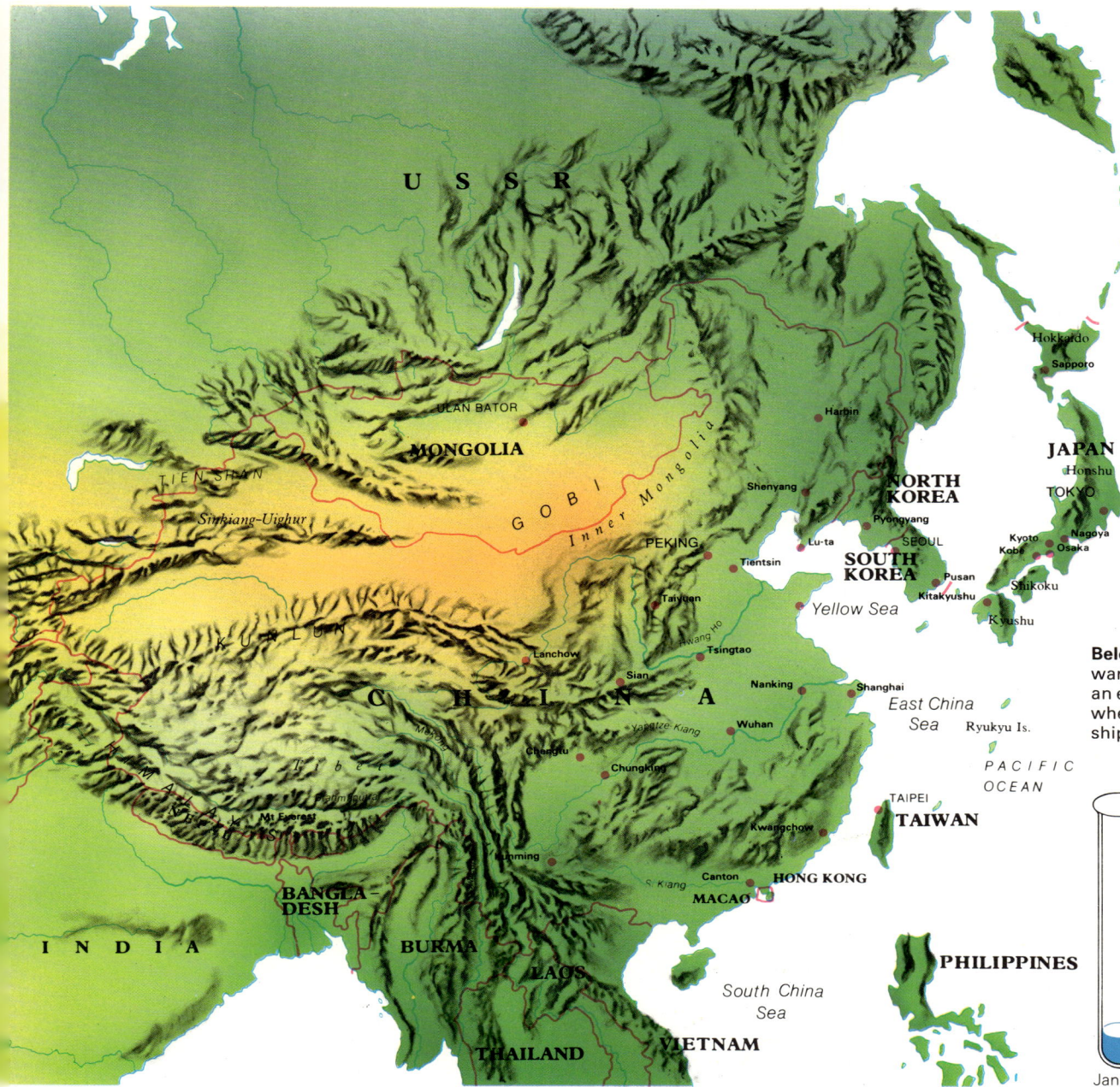

Below: Hong Kong has a warm, moderate climate but an excess of rain in summer, when typhoons endanger shipping.

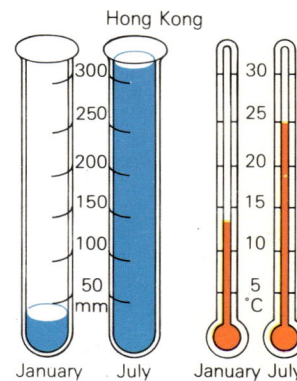

Hong Kong

January July (rainfall mm: 300 250 200 150 100 50)

January July (temperature °C: 30 25 20 15 10 5)

Reference

A Ainu people, numbering about 16,000, are the survivors of a white people of Caucasoid race who may have been the original inhabitants of JAPAN. They are now confined to north-east Japan.

C Canton, see KWANG-CHOW.

China is the world's most populous country and also the third largest in area. The People's Republic of China is bigger than all Europe and is divided into 21 provinces and 5 autonomous (self-governing) regions. Szechwan province alone is larger than France and has more people than France, Belgium and the Netherlands combined. Yet the population density of China is less than the average for Asia and its annual rate of increase is well under the world average. China's age-old culture is rooted in the Confucian-Taoist and Buddhist traditions, but some 5% of the population is Muslim. However, religion as such now has little influence on Chinese affairs. China's economy — once among the world's poorest — has improved considerably since the ending of over 20 years of civil and foreign wars in 1949. In that year, a communist government was established under Mao Tsetung. Mao was revered almost as a god, especially during the 'cultural revolution' in 1966-69. Opponents of his policies were attacked as 'revisionists'. But reverence for his inward-looking objectives declined rapidly after his death in 1976. China then increased its contacts with the non-communist world and gave priority to the modernization of its economy. Although China's industry is growing rapidly, agriculture is still the basis of the economy. Steel production, for example, had by 1978 reached only 30% of Japan's output. About 94% of China's people are 'Han' Chinese and the remainder include Tibetan, Manchu, Mongol, Korean, Uighur, Hui, Yi Chuang and Maio

Great Wall of China

Eastern Asia comprises the mainland countries of CHINA, MONGOLIA, NORTH KOREA and SOUTH KOREA; the European enclaves of HONG KONG and MACAO; and the island countries of JAPAN and TAIWAN. The region covers 8.85 per cent of the world's land area but holds 26 per cent of its population.

China, Mongolia and Korea

The Manchurian Plain, east of the Great Khingan Mountains in north-east China, and the North China Plain in the valley of HWANG HO southeast of PEKING, comprise China's best agricultural land. Westwards lies the Loess Highlands, an area made fertile by loess, yellow dust blown by winds from Central Asia. Loess washed away by the Hwang Ho (Yellow River) accounts for the name of that river and of the Yellow Sea into which it empties. Southwards, across the Tsinling Mountains, lies the vast, fertile Yangtze Plain where about seven per cent of the world's people live in the basin drained by the YANGTZE KIANG. Southwards again, the land becomes hilly. Westwards lies the great black plateau of TIBET, source of the Hwang Ho and

Yangtze Kiang. The Himalayas tower along the southern edge of the plateau, forming a mighty wall against the Indian subcontinent. West of Tibet, the Karakoram Range runs through Jammu and Kashmir to join the PAMIR KNOT, from where the TIEN SHAN range branches northeast into China's Autonomous Region of SINKIANG-UIGHUR. The Tien Shan forms the northern edge of the Takla-Makan, which extends to the KUNLUN SHAN and Altyn Tagh ranges that rise along the northern fringe of the Tibetan Plateau. North-east of the Takla-Makan, across the Turfan depression, which is over 150 metres below sea level, lies the Dzungarian basin. North-east again, extending into Mongolia, lie the Altai Mountains. This range extends into the Plateau of Mongolia, and south of this lies the bleak GOBI. This desert extends into China's autonomous region of INNER MONGOLIA. North and South Korea form a peninsula off north-eastern China, extending almost to Japan. The YALU RIVER, which rises in the Chang-pai Shan range in China, forms most of the border between North Korea and China before emptying into Korea Bay.

Below left: The bleak steppes of Mongolia can barely sustain settled agriculture, which was almost unknown in the country before 1955. Stockraising is the main occupation.

Below: The 'boat people' of Macao, Portugal's tiny enclave on the Chinese mainland, live mainly by catching and sellng fish. Their fishing boats are also their homes. Often, boat people of Macao continue to live on the waters of the South China Sea from choice rather than from necessity.

(Meo) peoples. China has some of the world's most populous cities, including SHANGHAI, PEKING, TIENTSIN, SHENYANG, CHUNGKING, LU-TA, KWANGCHOW (Canton), WUHAN, HARBIN, SIAN, NANKING and TSINGTAO. These 12 cities have a combined population roughly equal to that of Britain or Italy. About 20 million Chinese live outside China in addition to 4.5 million in HONG KONG and 18 million in TAIWAN — an off-shore state which China claims as part of the homeland. Thirty per cent of the people live in the YANGTZE

KIANG basin. Wheat is the main crop in the north and rice in the south. Chinese is written in a standard non-alphabetical script and spoken in many dialects of which Mandarin is the official one. Minority languages include Tibetan and Uighur (a Turkic language). Area: 9,596,961 sq km; Population (including Chinese residents abroad): 911,573,000; capital: Peking.
Chungking is a city in southern China and the country's former wartime capital. Population: 3,000,000.

G **Gobi** is a windswept, basin-shaped desert in central Asia covering 1,250,000 sq km. A plateau over 1,000 metres above sea level, it straddles south-east Mongolia and north-east China, and is surrounded by mountains. A few nomadic tribes roam the desert and there are a few settlers. The Turk-Siberian railway passes through it to Peking.

H **Harbin**, a city in China's former province of Manchuria, is an important transportation centre. Population: c. 2,000,000.

Hindu Kush, an offshoot of the PAMIR KNOT, divides east Afghanistan from northwest Pakistan. Its highest peak, Tirich Mir, rises to 7,705 metres.
Hiroshima, in west Honshu, Japan, was largely destroyed in 1945 by the first atomic bomb to be dropped on a city. Population: 650,000.
Hokkaido, nothernmost of Japan's 4 main islands, contains only 5% of its population, including most of the AINU people. Area: 78,073 sq km; population: 6,200,000.
Hong Kong is a British colony on the coast of south

China and has a 98% Chinese population. Most of the people live crowded on Hong Kong island or in Kowloon, a city on the mainland. Beyond Kowloon, covering most of Hong Kong's area,

Floating restaurant, Hong Kong

The tiny Portuguese enclave of Macao, a peninsula and two islands, lies on the east side of the Si Kiang (West River) of southern China. Hong Kong, a British enclave on the Chinese mainland and some 230 islands, lies east of Macao on the Chu Chiang (Pearl River).

Japan and Taiwan

Japan is an archipelago off the north-east Asian mainland. It is made up of four main islands which are (north to south) HOKKAIDO, HONSHU, SHIKOKU and KYUSHU. The country is very mountainous and has about 200 volcanoes, some still active. The highest mountains, the Japanese Alps, rise to 3,779 metres at Mount Fuji (Fujiyama) an inactive volcano in central Honshu. Japan is on the 'ring of fire', an earthquake belt that rings the Pacific and has over 1,000 earth tremors a year. A great earthquake that struck Tokyo in 1923, together with the resultant fire and tidal wave, killed over 100,000 people. Nowhere in Japan lies more than 150 kilometres from the sea and the country has no long rivers. Instead, thousands of swift-flowing streams flow down from the mountains to the coasts.

South-west from Japan and part of the same archipelago, the RYUKYU ISLANDS (owned by Japan) extend in an arc towards Taiwan. They are hilly and infertile. Taiwan, like Japan is mountainous and earthquake-prone.

Natural vegetation of Eastern Asia

Forest land forms the natural vegetation of eastern China. Hardwoods and conifers predominate in the extreme north-east (near the USSR border), and the deciduous oaks along the North China Plain. These give way to evergreen oaks towards the south. Tropical rainforest once covered the southern coastal region and Hainan Island. Mountain plants and desert grasses cover much of Tibet below the snow line. Most of the vast area between Kashmir and eastern Mongolia is desert. Grassland, steppe and meadow predominate in the long region extending from the north-eastern border of Tibet north-eastwards through Inner Mongolia to the USSR. Deciduous trees predominate in the north of Korea, giving way to bamboo and evergreens in the south. The natural vegetation of Japan and Taiwan is similar to that of eastern China.

Above: Japan's sacred Mount Fujiyama, an exhausted volcano 100 km south-west of Tokyo, is still the site of Shinto pilgrimages. In the foreground, rice dries within sight of Fujiyama's snow-capped peaks.

The climate of Eastern Asia

China's climate is much affected by monsoons. These winds carry warm, moist air inland from the sea in summer. In winter, they are reversed, blowing cold, dry air seawards from central Asia. Summer temperatures average about 27°C over much of China, rising to over 37°C in the Takla Makan and Gobi desert regions, but averaging only 15°C in Tibet. January temperatures for north and central China and Tibet fall to an average of about –7°C in winter, and on the Plateau of Mongolia drop to an average of about –24°C. China's coastlands vary less than these extremes. Generally, the south-east coast has a warm, subtropical temperature for most of the year; inland extremes are greater between summer and winter and between day and night.

Japan's climate is affected by two ocean currents. The Japan Current, flowing northwards along the southern and eastern coasts of the country, keeps southern Japan and eastern Taiwan warmer than the Chinese mainland opposite. However, the Oyashio Current flows south to bring cold northern waters to the coasts of north-western Japan. July temperatures aver-

---

...e the New Territories, so ...alled because they were ...occupied by the British later ...han Hong Kong island. They ...re due under treaty to be ...eturned to China in 1997. ...ong Kong has a dynamic ...conomy prospering from ...anking, commerce, ship-...ing and manufacturing, ...nd from acting as an outlet ...or Chinese trade. It is large-... dependent upon China for ...ater and food, although the ...nd is intensively farmed. ...he Confucianist-Taoist-...uddhist religion is not a ...trong force. Most of the ...eople are refugees, or

children of refugees, from China. Area: 1,045 sq km; population: 4,689,000; capital: VICTORIA.

Honshu is Japan's largest island and contains about 78% of the country's people. Area: 227,415 sq km; population: 92,030,000.

Hwang Ho (Yellow River) is the second longest river of China. It rises in north-east Tibet and flows about 4,700 km through Chinese territory to the Yellow Sea, draining more than 1,000,000 sq km. The yellow colour of the river and sea results from the presence of loess, a fine

yellow dust, which is carried in the water.

Inner Mongolia is an Autonomous Region of CHINA bordering the Mongolian People's Republic. Area: 1,177,500; population: 16,000,000.

Japan, an island empire in North-east Asia, has within 100 years developed from a medieval state to the world's third greatest industrial nation. Although Japan's density of population is 10 times that of the world average, only 15% of its land can

be cultivated and there are few natural resources. Consequently most of its food, petroleum, coal and timber

Sumo wrestling, Japan

have to be imported. Japan's wealth is based mainly upon the export of vehicles, electronic and telecommunications equipment, instruments, man-made fibres, ships and other manufactures. More than 60% of all Japanese now live in cities, which include TOKYO, the capital, OSAKA, YOKOHAMA, NAGOYA, KYOTO, KOBE, KITAKYUSHU, SAPPORO, Kawasaki and Fukouka. These 10 cities have a population equal to that of Canada's. Despite industrialization, the Japanese still value ancient traditions

Right: Four Chinese villages form a small commune. Besides improving agricultural efficiency, commune members aim to become self-sufficient by setting up manufacturing and repair workshops, and organizing schools and shops.

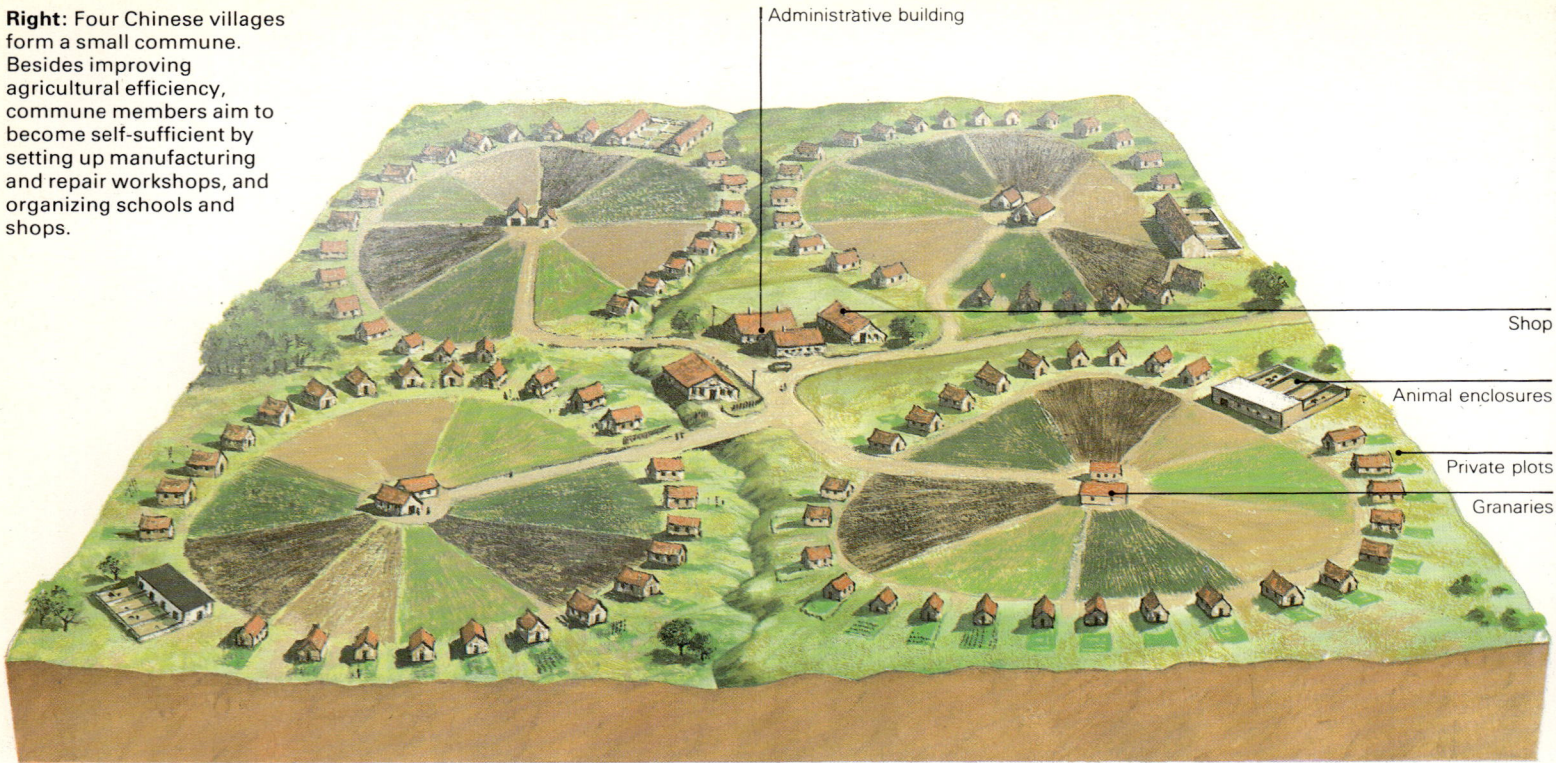

Administrative building

Shop

Animal enclosures

Private plots

Granaries

age 16–22°C in northern Japan, rising above this in the south and up to 30°C in Taiwan. January temperatures of 15–18°C in Taiwan drop to 4–8°C in the southern tip of Japan and fall further northwards to below –6°C in northern Hokkaido.

China receives most of its rainfall in summer. Its annual precipitation (rain and snow) gradually decreases from above 1,500 millimetres in south-east China to about 500 millimetres in central China and below 100 millimetres in Mongolia. Korea's annual precipitation varies from 550 millimetres in the north to 1,400 millimetres in the south. The driest part of Japan, eastern Hokkaido, receives about 1,000 millimetres of precipitation; the wettest part, the south-eastern coast, receives more than 3,000 millimetres a year. Most of Taiwan receives 1,000 millimetres of precipitation annually and mountain areas up to 5,000 millimetres.

Peoples and ways of life
Almost all the 1,100 million people of Eastern Asia are of the Mongoloid race and over 80 per cent are Chinese. Traditionally, Buddhism was

the dominant religion of the whole area, alongside the earlier established religions of Taoism and Confucianism in China and Taiwan, and Shinto in Japan. Koreans practised all four of these religions and others too, including Christianity. About 5 per cent of China's people are Muslims. However, religion now has little influence in the communist republics of China, Mongolia and North Korea.

Life in the Chinese communes
China has always been an agricultural country. It was also once a land where bandits, warlords, oppressive landlords and tax collectors kept the peasants perpetually poor. Although poverty did not disappear after the communist victory in 1949, these four age-old enemies of the peasants did. Also famine and flooding — the twin scourges — were greatly reduced by an urgent programme of public works. At first, the communists seized the land and redistributed it to those that tilled it. During the 1950s, each tiny family farm was merged into a cooperative (a group of farms organized as a larger unit) to gain the benefits of large-scale production. The

Below: To use chopsticks, grip one at the base of the thumb; then the second chopstick is held by the top of the thumb and the forefinger, to be deftly manipulated with the rigidly-held first chopstick.

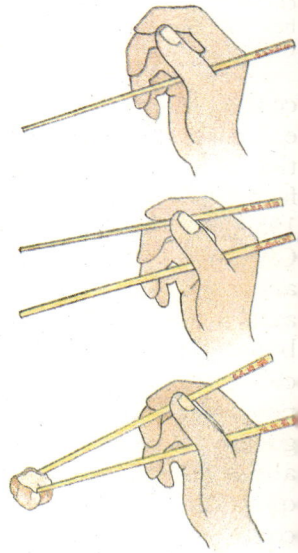

founded upon the national religion of Shinto, which for most people is fused with Buddhism. Following defeat in World War II, Japan retained its monarchy but renounced the claim that its emperor was a god. Over 99% of the people are Japanese and speak Japanese, but some 16,000 AINU people live in the north-east. Area: 372,313 sq km; population: 118,747,000; capital: Tokyo.

K **Kitakyushu** is a city in north KYUSHU, Japan. It was formed in 1963 by combining the former cities of

Kokura, Moji, Tobata, Wakamatsu and Yawata. Population: 1,150,000. **Kobe,** a leading Japanese city, is also the port for OSAKA. Population: 1,400,000. **Kun Lun** is the longest mountain system of Asia, extending over 3,000 km into Tibet from the PAMIR KNOT. It rises over 7,700 metres. **Kwangchow** (formerly Canton) is an important river port in south CHINA. It is situated on the Canton River to the north-west of Hong Kong. Population: 4,000,000. **Kyoto,** the capital of Japan for 1,000 years until 1868, is

a leading cultural centre. Population: 1,580,000. **Kyushu** is the southwesternmost of Japan's 4 main islands. It contains 13% of the total population, to make it the most densely populated island with 420 people to the sq km. But none of the largest Japanese cities are situated here. Area: 36,555 sq km; Population: 15,470,000.

L **Lhasa** is the capital of Tibet and one of the world's most remote cities. It contains the Potala Palace, once the winter residence of

the Dalai Lama, head of the Lamaist religion. The population was formerly 70,000, but many Tibetans have fled and more Chinese have moved in since 1965. **Lu-ta** (formerly Lushun-Talien), China, comprises the old naval port of Port Arthur and the old commercial port of Dairen. The city is situated in the south of Laiotung province on Korea Bay. Population: 4,500,000.

M **Macao** is a Portuguese possession on the Chinese mainland. It lies about 65 km west of Hong

Kong. Apart from its 2 small offshore islands, it is almost entirely urban and has the

Cathedral ruin, Macao

Right: Chinese food is much favoured internationally and has many regional varieties. The Cantonese meal shown includes tea, bean curd, rice, sweet and sour pork, and spring rolls. Cantonese food forms the main cuisine of Hong Kong.

Below: Korean food, like Korean culture generally, has been heavily influenced by both China and Japan. The Korean meal shown includes tea, vegetables, rice, and rice sweetmeats.

tres were set up under management committees formed by commune members.

The Mongolian way

In Mongolia, communist since 1924, livestock farming forms the basis of the economy with over 20 million animals. The Mongolians are traditionally nomadic, but since the mid-1950s they have been organized mainly into ranch cooperatives. Some settled agriculture has been introduced and mining and manufacturing is developing. The ranch cooperatives have shops, schools, clubs and medical and veterinary facilities.

Right: The Chinese girl (*left*) wears the padded trouser suit and hairstyle of Canton. The Japanese girl (*right*) is dressed in the *kimono,* still worn by Japanese of both sexes in their own homes. The Korean girl (*centre*) comes from a country heavily influenced by both China and Japan.

cooperatives, which could afford better fertilizers, tools and machinery, developed into collective farms in which the private ownership of farms by individual families disappeared. In 1958, with China fully committed to the ideals of Chairman Mao Tsetung, rural affairs took another turn. The collective farms began to amalgamate into even larger units. Spurred on by Maoist leaders, the farmers set up people's communes in which the work and daily life of the people was closely integrated and the collective good of the commune was supposed to be put above family ties. Communal workshops, living quarters, eating places, nurseries and even communal shopping, washing and sewing cen-

Right: The Japanese meal includes tea, rice, and vegetables like the Chinese. Uniquely Japanese is *sushi* (rice balls with seaweed, filled with egg), and *tempura* (sea-food fried in batter).

world's highest population density — 18,500 people to the sq km. Over 60% of the people live in Macao City. Once the most important European port in the Far East, Macao is now a convenient outlet for the trade of China, which strongly influences the territory's government. The languages spoken are Chinese, Portuguese and English. Area: 16 sq km; Population: 295,000; capital: Macao City.
Mongolia is a remote communist republic in east central Asia and has the lowest population density of any

country — 1 person to 1 sq km. It is a bleak, landlocked area of high plateaux and mountains, with the GOBI in the south-east. About 700 years ago, the Mongolians dominated most of Asia and eastern Europe, but their empire disintegrated leaving their homeland isolated. They are a nation of stock-raisers whose communist government has settled most of them in vast ranches since the 1950s. The only large city is ULAN BATOR. Mongolians are traditionally Shamanist and Buddhist, but religion now has little

influence in the country. The main language is Khalkha Mongolian, but Turkic is also

Mongolian tribesman

spoken. Area: 1,565,000 sq km; Population: 1,675,000; capital: Ulan Bator.

N Nagasaki is an important port and industrial centre on KYUSHU, Japan. At one time it was the only port open to foreigners. The city was badly damaged by the second atomic bomb in 1945. Population: 470,000.
Nagoya, on HONSHU, is one of Japan's biggest industrial cities. Population: 2,252,000.
Nanking 'Southern Capital' has been the capital of CHINA on several occasions, the last being in 1946-49. The

city is situated on the YANGTZE KIANG, about 260 km from its mouth near Shanghai. The port handles much of the river traffic and important industries include textiles and fertilizers. Population: 2,000,000.
Nara, a town east of Osaka, was the capital of Japan in 710-784. It still preserves buildings of the period. Population: 165,000.
North Korea is a communist republic in north-east Asia. It separated from the southern part of Korea in 1945, following 35 years of Japanese occupation. The

Traditionally Japanese houses are delicately structured with sliding doors and the minimum of furniture. Beds and tables are close to the floor, which is never walked on without first taking ones shoes off. Even modern apartments keep much of the traditional style, although the charcoal-burning earthenware heating pots have mostly been replaced by gas or electric heaters. Although western dress is usually worn on the streets, the *kimono*, a loosely-tied robe of cotton or silk, is worn at home. Almost all Japanese combine to some extent the national religions of Shinto and Buddhism in their everyday lives.

The Koreans and Taiwanese

Korea, under Chinese influence for hundreds of years, was occupied by Japan between 1895 and 1945. Socially, the country reflects both Chinese and Japanese influences. Economically, the communist north has similarities with both China and the USSR, while the non-communist south has points of contact with an earlier stage of Japanese development. The Taiwanese traditional way of life was not destroyed by communism, but rather eroded by the effort to achieve a Western-style economy.

Economy

Farming occupies 65 per cent of all the workforce in China and Mongolia, 50 per cent in North Korea, 35 per cent in South Korea and Taiwan

The Japanese

In the 100 years 1868–1968 Japan changed from a feudal, medieval country to the world's third richest nation. Seventy-five per cent of all Japanese now live in towns and cities. Although in many ways the Japanese have Westernized even more than some European peoples, old values and traditions still survive, ensuring the continuation of Japan's most ancient culture. Elders and people in superior positions are respected more than in the West; bowing and ultra-polite forms of address, for example, have been retained. Feelings and emotions are kept private rather than being displayed.

Rice remains the basic food but is now part of a richer diet that includes fish (usually raw), and a variety of dishes prepared from soya bean and seaweed. Like most people in Eastern Asia, the Japanese eat from a bowl with chopsticks.

Above: Towering modern office blocks on busy Hong Kong island contrast strangely with the colony's few remaining rickshaws— now fast-disapearing oddities often bought up by wealthy trophy-seekers.

Right: The 'world's ricebowl' lies in monsoon Asia, extending from India through South-east Asia to Japan. (China and Japan are often called 'monsoon lands' although they lie north of the tropics.) The monsoon climate favours the growth of rice, which flourishes especially in Bangladesh, along the great river valleys of China, and in the fertile volcanic island of Java. Each dot represents about 250,000 tonnes of rice.

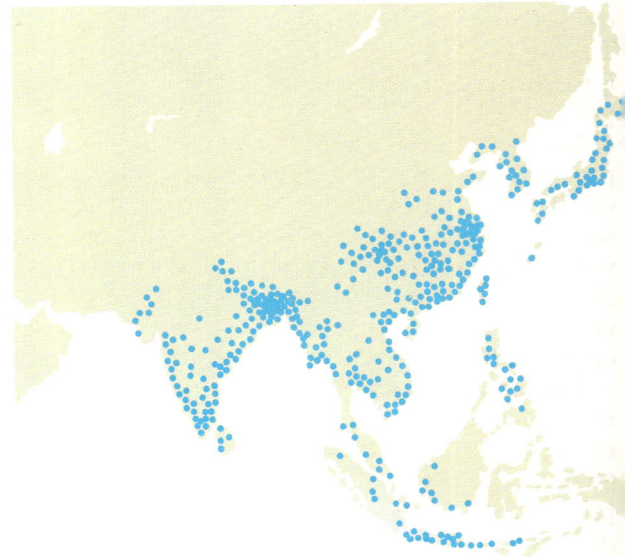

economy is heavily dependent on mining and industry. Almost all the population is Korean and speaks Korean. Over 30% live in towns, the only large city being Pyongyang. The country has a mixed religious tradition including Confucianism, Buddhism, Shamanism (belief in spirits and the powers of medicine men or shamans), Shinto and Chondokyo (a Buddhist-Christian cult). However, religion is not now dominant. Area: 120,538 sq km; population: 18,002,000; capital: PYONGYANG.

O **Osaka** is the second city of Japan. It is noted for its many waterways crossed by 800 bridges. Population: 2,950,000.

P **Pamir Knot** is a high plateau in Central Asia where the HINDU KUSH, TIEN SHAN, KUN LUN and Himalaya ranges meet to form a 'knot'. Called 'the roof of the world', the plateau straddles parts of Afghanistan, USSR, China, India and Pakistan. It rises in places to 4,600 metres and covers some 93,000 sq km.

Peking is the capital of CHINA

and one of the world's 6 most populous cities. Historically, there were 4 cities in

Imperial Palace, Peking

Peking before 1912. The Outer City was Chinese while the Inner City was reserved for the Manchu conquerors of China. Within this the Imperial City and the Forbidden City were accessible only to members of the Manchu dynasty and their retinue. Peking is now a single city, but its historic buildings still stand. Population (including surrounding rural area): 9,000,000.

Pusan is the chief port of SOUTH KOREA. It lies on its south-east coast opposite Japan. Population: 2,125,000.

Pyongyang is the capital of NORTH KOREA. Founded about 3,000 years ago, it was once the capital of all Korea. Population: 2,200,000.

R **Ryukyu Islands** are a group of about 100 Japanese islands lying between Japan and Taiwan. They include Okinawa, scene of one of the bloodiest battles in World War II. Population: 2,200,000.

S **Sapporo** is Japan's northernmost large city. It was planned in Western style. Population: 1,150,000.

Left: Japanese technology, non-existent in 1868, now challenges that of Western countries for supremacy in a world of shrinking markets. The picture shows a ship under construction at Yokohama.

But the electricity consumed reached only five per cent of that used in the USA. China's small manufacturing industries were developing fast but foreign trade remained negligible.

Japan — economic superpower

In 1976, Japan, with a gross domestic product equalling $562 billion, moved near to overtaking the USSR and becoming the world's second richest country, with imports totalling $70 billion and exports topping $80 billion. Japan was surpassed as a trading nation only by the United States and West Germany and excelled in the manufacture of cars and electronic devices.

but only 20 per cent in Japan. Trade and industry predominate in Hong Kong. The per capita income (i.e. the average income per person) in the region is only ten per cent of that in USA, but great variations exist between countries. For example, the per capita income of a Japanese is about 65 per cent of that of an American, while, at the other extreme, per capita income in China is little more than 3 per cent of that in the United States. However, the cost of living is low in China because of subsidized necessities such as housing. Hong Kong and Taiwan are the richest places in eastern Asia after Japan.

China – rousing the sleeping giant

In 1949, when the Communist Party took control of the economy, China was a 'sleeping giant'. The new leaders hoped to transform the country into an economic superpower within a short period, but their 'Great Leap Forward' failed in 1958–60. Even so, by 1977 China led in the world production of rice, millet, sweet potatoes, tobacco and jute. It came second in maize, barley, soya beans, groundnuts and tea; and third in wheat, cotton fibres, potatoes and tomatoes. Rice, grown mainly in the south, and wheat, grown in the north, accounted for over 50 per cent of all the food produced.

China, the world's third largest coal producer, mined in 1977 the equivalent of 75 per cent of the coal output of the United States. With Bolivia, China also led in antimony. Its crude oil production equalled 20 per cent of Saudi Arabia's and crude steel output was nearly 25 per cent of that of the United States or Japan.

Below: Japanese companies provide housing, holidays, medical facilities and pensions. The 'father-figure' employer even arranges marriages between employees and provides facilities to care for their children—who may become the next generation of employees. Promotion often depends on age, service and loyalty rather than ability.

Seoul (Kyongsong) is the capital of SOUTH KOREA and a leading commercial, cultural and industrial centre. The city was occupied by North Korean forces in 1950 and again in 1953. It underwent considerable reconstruction when the war ended in the same year. Population: 6,500,000.

Shanghai lies on the Whangpoo River, on the central coast of China. It grew from a small fishing port to become the world's largest city in only 130 years. This was developed as an international outlet for Chin-

ese trade, mainly by the British, French and Americans, who occupied and ran it until World War II. Despite its being the world's most populous city, its importance has declined under communist rule. Population

Street scene, Seoul

(including nearby rural areas): 12,000,000.

Shenyang (formerly Mukden) is the capital of China's Liaoning province. It was the leading city of the region once called Manchuria. Population: 5,000,000.

Shikoku is the smallest and only non-volcanic island of Japan's 4 main islands. It has only 4% of the country's population. Area: 18,257 sq km; population: 5,035,000.

Sian, as Chang-an, was an ancient capital of China. Population: 2,000,000.

Sinkiang-Uighur is CHINA'S

north-westernmost Autonomous Region. It has fewer than 10,000,000 people living in its 1,646,800 sq km owing to the barrenness of the land.

South Korea is a republic in north-east Asia. It was separated from NORTH KOREA in 1945 after 35 years of Japanese occupation. South Korea has twice as many people as North Korea crowded into less territory. It also has only 30% of the mineral resources of the North but its people are richer. Ethnically, the population is almost 100% Korean and Korean is

the main language. South Korea has the same religious traditions as the North, but religion plays a more important role. It also has a 5% Christian minority which is mainly Protestant. Cities include SEOUL, PUSAN, Taegu, Inchon and Kwaniu. Area: 98,484 sq km; Population: 38,512,000; capital: Seoul.

T Taipeh is the capital of TAIWAN. It contains in its museum many of the cultural treasures of China taken there by the retreating Nationalist armies in 1949. Population: 2,250,000.

In contrast to China — the agricultural giant — it is the industrial colossus of the east. By 1977 it had become the world's second or third largest producer of crude steel, pig iron, copper, aluminium, cadmium, zinc, magnesium and synthetic rubber. Despite this impressive record, Japan has few mineral resources and is self-sufficient only in lead, sulphur and zinc. Nearly all minerals and 98 per cent of petroleum have to be imported. Japan's barren islands, on which only 15 per cent of the land can be cultivated, have to support a population density of 320 to the square kilometre (3.5 times that of China). It is densely forested, and half the farmland is allotted to rice. Most farmers own their own land.

The smaller economies

During the 1950s and 1960s, Hong Kong became a 'pocket-sized trading giant', marketing a vast range of products manufactured either in Hong Kong or in China. These were eagerly bought throughout the world because of their cheapness. During the 1970s, prosperity brought the end of cheap labour and saw a rise in prices. First Taiwan, then South Korea, set out to undercut Hong Kong. By 1977, both countries had a flourishing foreign trade greater in value than China's. North Korea, which in the 1960s had a higher per capita income than South Korea's fell behind by the late 1970s. South Korea had by this time manufactured its own make of car, the *Pony*. The two Koreas and Taiwan have valuable mineral deposits and are heavily forested.

Above: Pharmaceutical stores set up in Maoist China became efficient but highly utilitarian. Cosmetics were considered unnecessary. Beauty treatment became part of the trend towards femininity only after Mao's death.

Below: Mao's 'Little Red Book', revered like a sacred work by China's soldiers and workers, was downgraded after his death.

Agriculture remains highly important despite industrialization. Much of Macao's income comes from tourism, with gambling casinos especially important.

History and culture

CHINA has the world's longest continuous civilization (still unbroken for 3,500 years), which is to some extent the parent of the Japanese and Korean cultures. For a century or so, around the AD 1200s to 1300s, MONGOLIA held the world's largest empire. Although art and culture generally continued to flourish in Eastern Asia, by the 1800s the region materially had fallen into decline when compared to Europe and the United States. From the mid-1800s, the West used its superior technology to dominate Eastern Asia. The Japanese quickly saw that the only way to repel Western domination was to outdo the westerners in the technology that gave them their advantage.

The transformation of Japan

In 1868, in a 'palace revolution' led by the god-emperor, JAPAN threw off feudalism and strove to become a modern state in the quickest possible time. The Japanese leaders studied Western countries carefully and took the best points from each. For example, after Germany defeated

Taiwan (also known as Formosa) is a breakaway island province of CHINA. Occupied by Japan in 1895-1945, it became the final retreat of the defeated armies of Nationalist China when China fell to the communists in 1949. The Nationalist soldiers, once a threat to mainland China, are now all well past military age. The Taiwan government still claims to represent all China and the Peking government claims Taiwan. However, for practical purposes Taiwan is now an independent republic shunned by most of the world diplomatically, but not commercially. Over 98% of the people are Chinese and the Confucianist-Taoist-Buddhist tradition is stronger than in China or HONG KONG. The island has about 180,000 aboriginal people ethnically related to Indonesians. It is a prosperous state which earns about 35% of its gross national income from industry. The main language is Mandarin, but other Chinese dialects are spoken. Area: 35,962 sq km; population: 16,800,000; capital: TAIPEH.

Tibet, at times in the past an independent or semi-independent state, became an Autonomous Region of China in 1965. It is a high, cold, bleak plateau in south central Asia containing the world's highest mountains and hundreds of lakes, many of salt. Poor soil and harsh climate render most of Tibet unfit for crop farming, but yaks, animals related to cows, provide food, clothing and transportation. Many important rivers rise in Tibet, including the YANGTZE, Mekong, Salween, Indus and Brahmaputra. Area: 1,221,600 sq km; population: 1,300,000 (1965). Since 1965, about 85,000 Tibetans are believed to have left and some 500,000 Chinese have settled there. Capital: Lhasa

Tibetan monk in India

(50,000 in 1953).

Tien Shan, a mountain system mainly in Chinese SINKIANG-UIGHUR, extends about 2,400 km north-east from the PAMIR KNOT. Pobeda Peak rises to 7,444 metres above sea level.

Tientsin, China, was once a leading centre of foreign trade, but it has now diminished in international importance. Population: 5,000,000.

Tokyo is the capital of Japan and the world's most populous city after SHANGHAI. It contains about 10% of Japan's people. It is a Wes-

France in the Franco-Prussian war of 1870–71, Japan hastily replaced its French military advisers with Germans. In less than 40 years, Japan achieved victories against both China and Russia resulting in territorial gains and 'spheres of influence' and became the most important ally of the British Empire. Rapid social and economic advance in Japan brought internal political stresses, that found release in overseas wars and conquests in Korea and China. In 1941–43, Japan finally challenged the whole of the West, seizing its empires in the Pacific area. However, the dropping of the atomic bombs on HIROSHIMA and NAGASAKI by the USA in 1945, brought the total defeat of Japan. Between 1945 and 1951 it came under American occupation. The pace of social and economic change accelerated during the following quarter century, during which Japan became one of the world's richest nations.

The Chinese revolutions

Revolution brought the end of 3,500 years of Chinese dynasties during the last days of 1911. But the republic set up in 1912 barely survived the political dissension, civil wars and Japanese invasions of the next 37 years. From 1925, the *Kuomintang* (nationalists) tried to rule China but had to fight the Japanese and the Communists led by Mao Tsetung. Mainland China finally fell to the communists in 1949, and the nationalists retreated to China's offshore island of TAIWAN. Protected by the United States, Taiwan developed into a prosperous, independent state.

China did not become fully communist for several years after 1949, but Mao was determined to implant his own form of communism — or Maoism — at almost any price. But the failure of the Great Leap Forward led to criticism of his policies by other leaders in the early 1960s. Mao's reply was to create a 'cultural revolution' in which China's youth, spearheaded by 'red guards', attacked all those who disagreed with Mao's ideas. Even the President of China was toppled, and the economy was severely disrupted. A secret power struggle continued into the 1970s. Meanwhile, China's former ally Russia became its rival, then its enemy. Gradually China moved towards friendship with its old enemy, the United States. Towards the end of his life, Mao's god-like status diminished. After his death in 1976, his policies began to be changed

Above: A Japanese priest beats the gong at a Shinto festival. Shinto involves the worship of an infinite number of *kami* (nature spirits). It has almost no foreign adherents, but nearly every Japanese practises Shinto, often alongside another religion, usually Buddhism.

rapidly. His successor as chairman was Hua Guofeng. But the man seen to be leading China away from Maoism and towards greater democracy and economic efficiency was the first vice-premier, Deng Xiaoping, a survivor of persecution during the 'cultural revolution'.

Korea, Hong Kong and Macao

The collapse of Japan in 1945 brought northern Korea under Russian occupation and southern Korea under American occupation. The Russians and Americans quit in 1948–49, leaving the country divided at the 38th parallel of latitude between a northern pro-Russian government and a southern pro-American government. Civil war followed in 1950–53 in which United Nations forces led by Americans aided the south, and Chinese forces aided the north. About a million soldiers and a million civilians died in the war. Since the armistice of 1953, North Korea and South Korea have been separate republics.

The Portuguese took Macao in about 1557 and in 1887 the Chinese recognized it as Portuguese territory. Britain took the tiny island of HONG KONG by force in 1842 and Kowloon on the mainland in 1860. It leased the larger New Territories from China for 99 years in 1898. China was content to leave the two enclaves under foreign rule.

---

ternized city much rebuilt after World War II. The city area has a density of about 16,000 people to the sq km (nearly double that of New York and over 3 times that of London). Tokyo is a leading world business centre. Jammed with vehicles, it has developed serious problems of pollution. Population: 9,250,000.
Tsingtao is one of China's chief industrial cities. Population: 1,700,000.
Turkestan is a vast area in Central Asia with no precise boundaries. It extends into China, the USSR and Af-

ghanistan. The PAMIR KNOT and the TIEN SHAN mountains divide the region into East Turkestan, which covers most of Chinese SINKIANG-UIGHUR, and West Turkestan, which belongs to the USSR except for a small area lying across the border in Afghanistan. Area: 2,600,000 sq km.
U **Ulan Bator** (Red Hero) is the capital of Mongolia and contains nearly 25% of the country's people. Population: 380,000.
V **Victoria** is the capital of HONG KONG and the col-

ony's main business centre. Population: 625,000.

W **Wuhan**, in central China, was formed

Unloading Yangtzse barges

from the former cities of Hankow, Wuchang and Hanyang. Population: 3,000,000.

Y **Yalu River** rises on the northern border of NORTH KOREA and forms its frontier with China, flowing 800 km to the Sea of Japan.
Yangtze Kiang is China's longest and most important river. It rises in the KUN LUN Mountains nearly 5 km above sea level and flows 5,000 km through Tibet and China into the Yellow Sea. More than 30% of China's population live in the

1,800,000 sq km drained by the Yangtze and its tributaries. Many people live in house boats. The river is navigable for ocean-going ships for 1,000 km inland.
Yokohama, a leading port of Japan about 30 km south of Tokyo, is connected to the capital by the industrial suburb of Kawasaki. The 3 places form the world's largest urban complex. Population: 2,600,000.

South-east Asia has been the scene of tremendous upheavals since the withdrawal of European colonial administrations. War has scarred the face of several South-east Asian countries.

South-east Asia

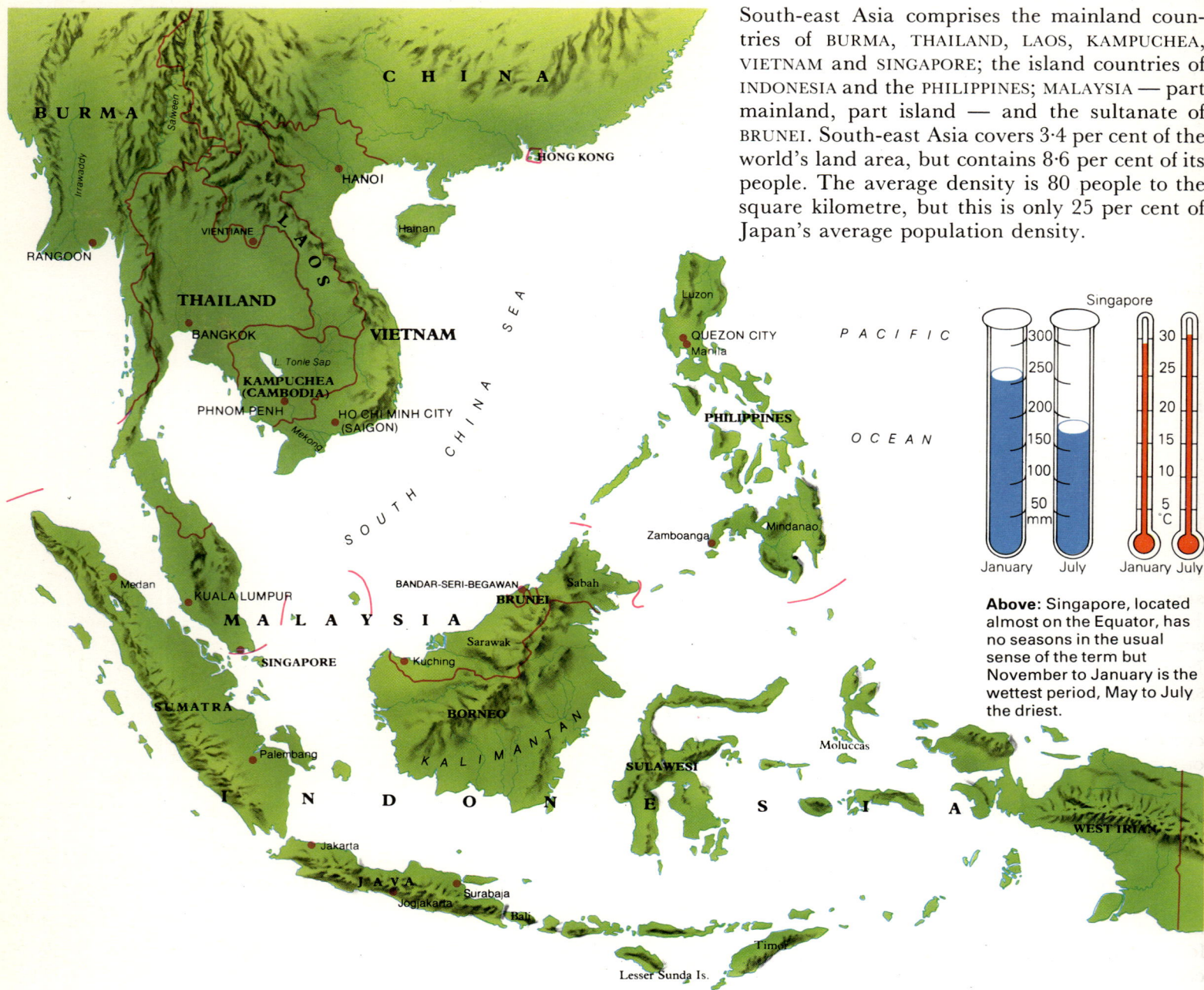

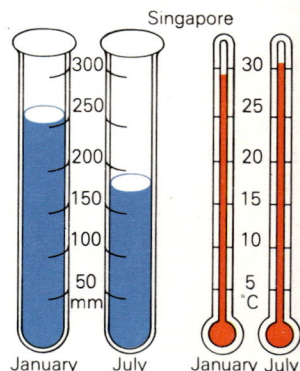

South-east Asia comprises the mainland countries of BURMA, THAILAND, LAOS, KAMPUCHEA, VIETNAM and SINGAPORE; the island countries of INDONESIA and the PHILIPPINES; MALAYSIA — part mainland, part island — and the sultanate of BRUNEI. South-east Asia covers 3·4 per cent of the world's land area, but contains 8·6 per cent of its people. The average density is 80 people to the square kilometre, but this is only 25 per cent of Japan's average population density.

Above: Singapore, located almost on the Equator, has no seasons in the usual sense of the term but November to January is the wettest period, May to July the driest.

Reference

A Angkor, in north-west KAMPUCHEA, is the site of the spectacular civilization of the Khmers.

B Bali is one of the smaller Indonesian islands. Its beauty has made it a favoured tourist spot. Population: c. 3,000,000.
Bandung, an Indonesian city in east Java, was the site of the first Afro-Asian conference in 1955. Population: 1,400,000.

Bangkok is the capital and only large city of THAILAND. It lies on the Chao Phraya River which separates it from the older city of Thonburi, now a suburb. Combined population: 4,000,000.
Borneo is the world's third largest island and is divided between BRUNEI, INDONESIA and MALAYSIA. Area: 752,000 sq km.
Borobudur is a huge Buddhist monument in east Java, dating from the late AD 700s.
Brunei is an oil-rich sultanate on the north coast of Borneo. It opted to remain a

British protected state rather than to join MALAYSIA in 1963. The small capital, Bandar Seri Begawan, has impressive Islamic architecture and the fast-growing population includes mainly Malays, Chinese and Dyaks. Area: 5,800 sq km; population: 217,000.
Burma is a socialist Buddhist republic and has undergone continuous internal unrest since independence in 1948. In 1963-75 it was almost cut off from the outside world. The country's main problems have arisen because 25% of its popula-

tion are non-Burmese. Several groups, notably the

Tribal girl, Shan, Burma

Karens, have gone to war to resist attempts to 'Burmanize' them. Under General Ne Win, the army has tried to rule the country as a socialist state, and the minority peoples, such as the Chinese, Indians, Bengalis and Karens have been encouraged to emigrate. Burma is a leading riceproducer. Its only large cities are RANGOON, Mandalay, Moulmein and Bassein. The main languages are Burmese, Chinese and Indian, but there are also local languages and dialects. Area: 676,552 sq km; population:

The mainland states

Mainland South-east Asia has several mountain ranges running north-south, with river valleys parallel between them. Two main mountain chains extend from China to separate Burma from its neighbours. The IRRAWADDY and SALWEEN rivers flow from Upper Burma southwards into the Bay of Bengal. Mountains cover northern Thailand between the Salween and the MEKONG RIVER, which forms most of the long Thai border with Laos. The high, dry Korat Plateau comprises eastern Thailand. Central Thailand is a low, flat valley formed by several rivers that flow into the Gulf of Siam. The long narrow 'tail' of tropical and mountainous southern Thailand extends 800 kilometres southwards to Malaya.

Laos lies between the Mekong River and the Annamese Mountains, one of several ranges that cross north and east Laos. The country's only good farmland lies in the lowland of the Mekong and its tributaries. Mountains separate Kampuchea from its neighbours except in the south-east, where the fertile plain extends through Vietnam to the South China Sea. In the dry season, the Tonle Sap River flows southwards from the shallow, fish-laden TONLE SAP into the Mekong at PHNOM PENH.

The island states

Indonesia consists of over 13,000 islands, the largest being KALIMANTAN (southern BORNEO), SUMATRA, WEST IRIAN (western New Guinea Island), SULAWESI, JAVA and the MOLUCCAS. The small but famous island of BALI lies east of Java. From north-east Sumatra, Indonesia extends some 5,000 kilometres to the border of Papua New Guinea. The East Malaysian states of SARAWAK and SABAH, and the sultanate of Brunei lie in Borneo, north of Kalimantan. Large rivers cut through the tropical rainforest of mountainous inner Borneo, and the coastlands are low swampy plains. Indonesia generally, is mountainous, volcanic, thickly forested and cut by many rivers with swampy banks.

More than 7,000 islands make up the Philippines, the largest of which are LUZON in the north and MINDANAO in the south. The islands are mountainous and volcanic, with thick forests and fertile plains. Forty per cent of the country's rice crop grows on its largest lowland plain, north of

Manila. Many rivers, flowing from the mountains to the sea, often flood during the rainy season. Few are navigable except by rafts or small boats.

Climate of South-east Asia

The tropical climate of South-east Asia is mainly determined by the monsoons and by closeness to the sea and the Equator. Mean temperatures at sea level average about 27°C. The annual range increases from about 2°C in Singapore to about 11°C on the high ground of northern Burma. Indonesia, which is bisected by the Equator, receives about 1,750-3,500 millimetres of rain a year. Some areas get half these amounts, but in West Irian, for example, the figures are double. Singapore receives about 2,400 millimetres, spread throughout the year. Northwards, most rain falls between May and October, averaging about 1,500 millimetres. The Philippines is subject to typhoons. Generally, the natural vegetation of South-east Asia is tropical rainforest, but palms, rattans and orchids abound.

Peoples and ways of life

South-east Asia has a greater diversity of peoples and cultures than anywhere else in the world of comparable area. Burmese are mainly akin to Tibetans. Most other peoples in mainland South-east Asia are ethnically close to Chinese, but only

Below: Rice terraces at Banaue, in Luzon island in the Philippines, have been carefully cultivated for some 2,000 years. Forty per cent of the country's rice crop is grown in the fertile plain north of Manila, which includes Banaue. The distant figures are farmers transplanting young rice shoots.

33,821,000; capital: Rangoon.

C **Cebu** is the chief city of Cebu island which lies in the south central PHILIPPINES. Its offshore island of Mactan is where the explorer Ferdinand Magellan (1480-1521) was killed. Population: 450,000.
Chiang Mai, in north THAILAND, is the country's second city. It is a leading cultural and tourist centre. Population: 117,000.

E **East Timor** is part of Timor island lying north-

west of Australia. Once a Portuguese possession, it was occupied by Indonesia in late 1975 following rebellion and civil war. Area:

Villagers of Timor

14,925 sq km; Population: 750,000.

H **Hanoi** is the capital of VIETNAM. Situated on the

Hong River (Red River) it was badly damaged during the Vietnam war. Population: 1,300,000.
Ho Chi Minh City is the largest city of VIETNAM and was formerly the capital of South Vietnam under the name of Saigon-Cholon. Population: 2,000,000.

I **Indonesia** is a republic lying between India, China and Australia. It consists of about 3,000 islands extending over 5,000 km west to east. More than 60% of the population lives crowded on the volcanic but

fertile island of JAVA, where the population density is nearly 800 to the sq km (25 times the world average). The main language is Bahasa Indonesia, a form of Malay. About 90% of Indonesians are Muslims, and some 5% Christian, especially on SUMATRA. BALI has its own form of Hinduism. Other main islands include KALIMANTAN and SULAWESI. After gaining independence from the Netherlands by war in 1949, Indonesia was ruled by President Sukarno for 18 years, during which time the economy failed to prosper.

distinctive flat straw hat with concave sides. Street and village markets are highly colourful and shortly after dawn, Buddhist monks may be seen presenting their alms bowls to traders for food.

The only large cities in the region are BANGKOK, where the main airport of South-east Asia is sited, RANGOON, HO CHI MINH CITY, HANOI and PHNOM PENH (depopulated in the late 1970s). Small cities like Mandalay (north Burma), CHIANG MAI and VIENTIANE — market and craft-manufacturing centres for the surrounding countryside — are more typical of the region.

Malaysia and Singapore

MALAYA (Western Malaysia) has many of the features of the countries to its north; 30 per cent of its people, the Chinese, are Buddhist and Taoist. Malaysia is richer than all its neighbours except Singapore, and its prosperous towns, mostly Chinese in population, are flourishing trading centres. About 45 per cent of the people of Malaysia are Malays, and nearly 50 per cent are Muslim. There are large minorities descended from immigrants from the Indian subcontinent, together with some Eurasians in Malaya. Sarawak and Sabah contain many people ethnically related to Malays. Singapore, one of the world's largest ports and business centres, has a 76 per cent Chinese population, almost entirely urban. In Brunei, more than 50

Left: These Malaysian *wayang* figures have delighted village audiences for centuries. A *dalang* (performer) manipulates the puppets behind a stretched translucent white sheet upon which falls the light of a lamp to give the shadow effect.

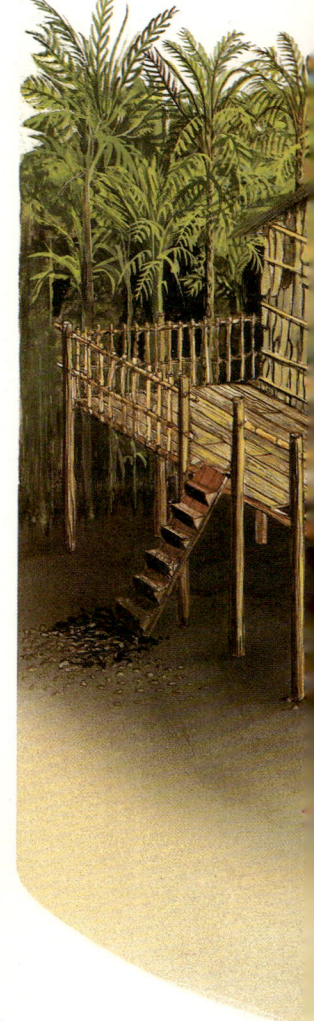

38 per cent are so in Malaysia. There, as in Indonesia and the Philippines, the dominant ethnic group is Malay. Farming is the main occupation except in Singapore. The average income per head of population (per capita income) in the region is about 4·5 per cent of that in the United States, or seven per cent of Japan's, but there are great variations. For example, Singapore has three times the per capita income of Malaysia; six times that of the Philippines and Thailand; and between ten and 20 times that of the other countries (except oil-rich Brunei).

Life in mainland South-east Asia

The predominant religion of mainland South-east Asia (except Malaysia) is Buddhism. Although religious beliefs are strong, especially in Thailand and Burma, they do not dominate daily life so much as on the Indian subcontinent. Thailand, particularly, is dotted with thousands of colourful temples, many with monasteries in which a large proportion of Thai boys spend a period as monks as part of their education. Traditional dress in the region is the *sarong*, a one-piece garment that wraps round the body. Worn by both sexes, the *sarong* takes various forms, and the Burmese version is called the *longyi*. Western dress is now more common for men, and women too, often wear trousers and blouses. The conical straw hat, a shield against sun and rain, is especially popular in Vietnam. Thai peasants and street vendors often wear a

Left: A performer dances in a temple play featuring the demon Barong in Bali, Indonesia's most popular tourist island. The Balinese practise a unique form of Hinduism which dominates all aspects of their lives. The island has some 30,000 temples, many in private homes.

Sukarno's rule resulted in economic chaos and the massacre of some 250,000 people in 1965-66, mainly Chinese charged with being communist. Indonesia's second president, Suharto, sought to improve the country's prosperity by closer relations with the West. More than 60% of Indonesia is forested and the chief occupations are forestry and agriculture. Area: 2,027,087 sq km; population: 154,712,000; capital: Jakarta.
Irrawaddy River flows about 2,100 km through

Burma to enter the Bay of Bengal near Rangoon.

J Jakarta, INDONESIA's capital, is a port and sprawling city in north-west JAVA. The number of people living there has been boosted by migrants from the countryside. Population: 6,000,000.
Java is the fourth largest but most populous of the Indonesian islands. It contains the capital, JAKARTA. Rice cropping and other farm and forest products are the mainstay of the economy. Area: 130,510 sq km; population: 100,000,000.

Jogjakarta is a Javanese city prominent in Indonesian culture. Population: 425,000.

Child drying rice, Java

K Kalimantan is Indonesia's largest island territory and forms much of BORNEO. It is almost the size of France. Area: 500,000 sq km; population: 6,500,000.
Kampuchea (formerly Cambodia and the Khmer Republic) has been a communist republic since the capital, PHNOM PENH, was captured in 1975 at the end of a civil war. From 1975 the communist government depopulated the towns to force almost all civilians into the countryside to grow food. It was an unpopular policy that killed many thousands of

people. The population is about 87% Buddhist and Khmer, with Vietnamese, Chinese and Cham minorities. Khmer is the main language but French is also spoken. Area: 181,035 sq km; population (not accounting for wartime and subsequent casualties): 9,329,000; capital Phnom Penh.
Kuala Lumpur is the capital of MALAYSIA. It is a mainly Chinese city located in a tin-mining and rubber area. Population: 600,000.
Kuching, a largely Chinese river town, is the capital of

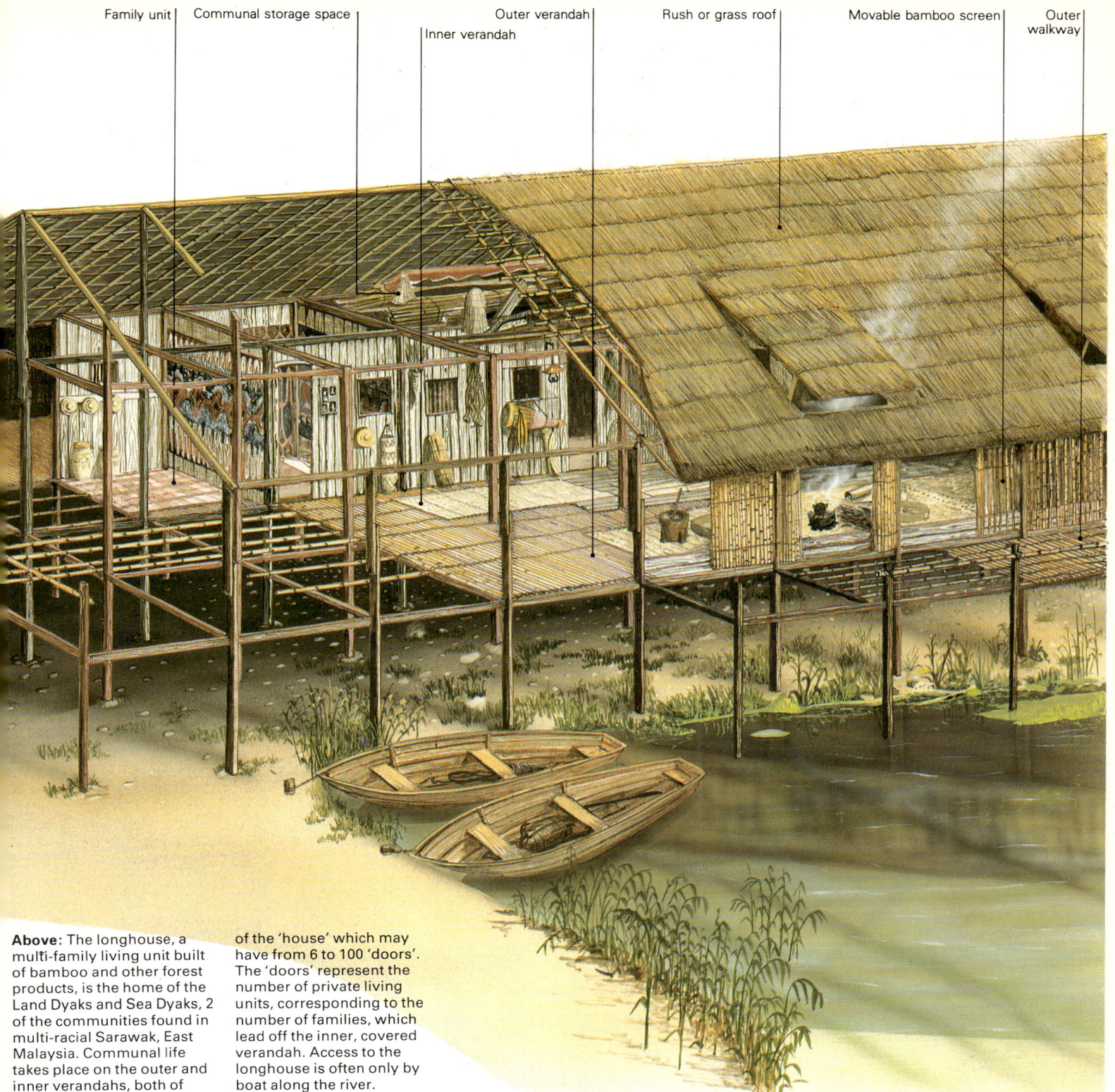

Family unit | Communal storage space | Outer verandah | Rush or grass roof | Movable bamboo screen | Outer walkway

Inner verandah

Above: The longhouse, a multi-family living unit built of bamboo and other forest products, is the home of the Land Dyaks and Sea Dyaks, 2 of the communities found in multi-racial Sarawak, East Malaysia. Communal life takes place on the outer and inner verandahs, both of which extend the full length of the 'house' which may have from 6 to 100 'doors'. The 'doors' represent the number of private living units, corresponding to the number of families, which lead off the inner, covered verandah. Access to the longhouse is often only by boat along the river.

SARAWAK, Malaysia. Population: c. 82,000.

L Labuan is a small island off Sabah and part of MALAYSIA. Area: 75 sq km; population: 20,000.
Lake Toba is a huge lake in north SUMATRA that contains Samosir Island, home of the Batak people.
Laos, once known as the 'kingdom of a million elephants', is a landlocked Buddhist country in Indo-China. It was a kingdom until 1975, when it became a communist state after many years of civil war. This was part of the larger pattern of the Indo-China wars. Only 50% of the people are Lao. The several minorities include mountain tribes who follow local religions mixed with Buddhism. Lao, French and tribal dialects are the languages spoken. Area: 236,800 sq km; population: 3,690,000; capital: Vientiane.
Luzon is the northernmost large island of the PHILIPPINES. It produces 40% of the country's rice crop north of Manila. Area: 104,688 sq km; population: 22,000,000.

M Malacca, once the greatest port in South-east Asia, is now a small town 'in Malacca state, MALAYSIA. Population: 115,000.

Laotian cart

Malaya became the western part of MALAYSIA in 1963, 6 years after its independence from Britain. It is composed of 9 sultanates (Johore, Kedah, Kalantan, Negri Sembilan, Pahang, Perak, Perlis, Selangor and Trengganu) and 2 other states (Malacca, Penang and Province Wellesley). Area: 131,587 sq km; population: 11,700,000.
Malaysia is a kingdom divided into east and west by a 1000-km stretch of the South China Sea. West Malaysia comprises Malaya while East Malaysia comprises SARAWAK and SABAH. SINGA-PORE became a member state of Malaysia in 1963 but seceded in 1965. Malays form about 45% of the population, Chinese 38%, and Indo-Pakistanis 9%. About 8% of the people descend from tribes such as the Land or Sea Dyaks of Sarawak and the Dusuns or Kadazans of Sabah. A variety of languages are spoken including Malay, English and Chinese, besides several indigenous languages and dialects. Islam, the state religion, is practised by almost all Malays. Other important religions include Buddhism,

per cent of the people are Malays; the Chinese come next, and there are Land and Sea Dyak communities.

Indonesia and the Philippines

Indonesia is 90 per cent Muslim in religion and predominantly Malay ethnically, with Papuan and Chinese minorities. The island of Bali has its own form of Hinduism and some five per cent of the population are Christian, especially in northern Sumatra. Indonesia has many of the features of other South-east Asian countries, but its way of life also resembles to some degree that of Muslim areas in the Indian subcontinent. The huge capital of JAKARTA has attracted millions of people from the surrounding countryside to form straggling settlements in and around the city. SURABAJA and BANDUNG are the only other large cities. JOGJAKARTA is a cultural centre.

The Philippines is 83 per cent Roman

Above: Bangkok, Thailand's capital and a leading city of South-east Asia, is built around a network of waterways. Vendors sell fruit and other commodities from the city's 'floating market'. Despite its popularity with tourists, the floating market is fast disappearing as a result of rapid urbanization. The straw hats of the vendors are unique to Thailand.

Catholic, reflecting its 400 years of Spanish rule. About nine per cent of the people are Protestant, a result partly of 44 years of American domination. The five to seven per cent in the extreme south, who are Muslims, have never fully accepted foreign or Christian rule. Manila is by far the largest of several cities which are mainly medium-sized. However, only 30 per cent of Filipinos live in urban areas. The Philippines combines, to some extent, the characteristics of other South-east Asian countries, but its Christian religion and the common use of the English language give it cultural links with the West.

Economy

The general diversity of South-east Asia carries over into its products. Agriculture, forestry and fishing form the basis of the economy, together with mining and small-scale manufacturing. Between 50 per cent and 75 per cent of workers in every country except Singapore work on the land as farmers.

Farm and forest products of South-east Asia

Many agricultural and forest products are found throughout this tropical region. They include the following (the countries in brackets are the main producers): rice (Indonesia, Thailand and Burma); sweet potatoes, sugar, maize, pepper (Indonesia and Malaysia); groundnuts, soya beans, tea and coffee (Indonesia); coconuts and pineapples (Philippines); copra, cinchona (Indonesia and Laos); tapioca, from cassava or manioc (Indonesia, Malaysia and Thailand); cotton (mainland states); tobacco, palm oil (Indonesia and Malaysia); rubber (Malaysia, Indonesia and Thailand); timber and bamboo.

Teak is found mainly in Burma and Thailand, and mahogany in the Philippines. The Philippines is also known for *abaca*, a tall plant from which fibres are taken for Manila hemp. Burma is noted for sesame seeds and Laos for citrus fruits, *cardamom* (a kind of ginger) and opium. Laos and Indonesia produce *benzoin* (gum benjamin) used for perfumes, incense and friar's balsam. Kapok grows in Indonesia, the Philippines and KAMPUCHEA; and jute in Thailand.

Stockraising and fishing

Water buffaloes, including carabaos in the Philippines, are reared for transport and

---

Taoism, Hinduism, and Christianity. Its wealth grew by exporting rubber and tin, although palm oil is now even more important. Malaysia's cities include KUALA LUMPUR, Georgetown (generally called PENANG), Ipoh and KUCHING. Area: 329,749 sq km; population: 13,791,000; capital: Kuala Lumpur.
Manila is the largest city and port of the PHILIPPINES. It has a spacious central area flanked by densely-populated environs. Population: 1,770,000.
Mekong River rises in east

Tibet and flows about 4,200 km through China, Burma, Laos, Thailand, Kampuchea and Vietnam.
Mindanao is the southernmost large island in the PHILIPPINES. It is mainly unexploited economically. Area: 94,628 sq km; population: 9,700,000.
Moluccas are a group of islands in eastern INDONESIA. They were controlled by the Dutch from the mid-1600s to 1949. Area: 86,286 sq km; population: 1,285,000.

P **Penang** (Pinang) is an island off north-west

MALAYSIA and one of the former 'Straits Settlements'. It is now part of Malaysia.

Igorots, Luzon, Philippines

Philippines is an island republic comprising over 7,000 islands, but only about 730 of the larger ones are inhabited. The biggest islands, LUZON and MINDANAO, comprise 70% of the country's land area and contain 65% of its people. Filipinos are of Malay descent with Mongoloid, Indonesian and Spanish admixture. Filipino, based on Tagalog, and English are the two languages spoken. Filipinos are about 80% Roman Catholic — a result of 300 years of Spanish rule (1565-1898) — and 10% Protestant. In the south,

especially around the city of ZAMBOANGA and in the Sulu Archipelago, some 7% are Muslims (or 'Moros'). The Moros have never ceased to rebel against Christian rule, whether by Spaniards, Americans (1898-1942) or Filipinos (since 1946). American rule was effectively ended by the Japanese occupation in 1942-45. Following political unrest and increasing lawlessness, President Marcos imposed martial law in 1972, which was endorsed by later referenda. About 60% of the land is forested. About 30% of the

farmwork, especially in rice paddies. Cattle are raised for transport and for meat. However, Muslims do not eat pork, which the Chinese and Vietnamese much prefer, and many Buddhists either do not eat beef or are vegetarians. The leading beef countries of the region are Indonesia and the Philippines while Vietnam and the Philippines lead in pork production. Only Indonesia produces sizable quantities of mutton — the meat preferred by most Muslims. The leading fish and sea-food countries include Indonesia, the Philippines and Vietnam.

Minerals, petroleum and manufacturing

South-east Asia is rich in a wide variety of minerals. Vietnam and Indonesia have sizable coal reserves and Malaysia and Thailand are among the world leaders in tin. Burma, and to a lesser extent Thailand, are rich in precious metals and stones. Vietnam and Kampuchea extract iron and manganese. Indonesia is the most important producer of crude oil in the region, followed by Malaysia. Brunei's wealth also derives from oil and Singapore profits from oil refining.

Singapore, lacking land, has only three per cent of its workforce employed in farming but 20 per cent in manufacturing. It specializes in ship building and repairing, electronics, textiles and food, rubber and timber processing. It is one of

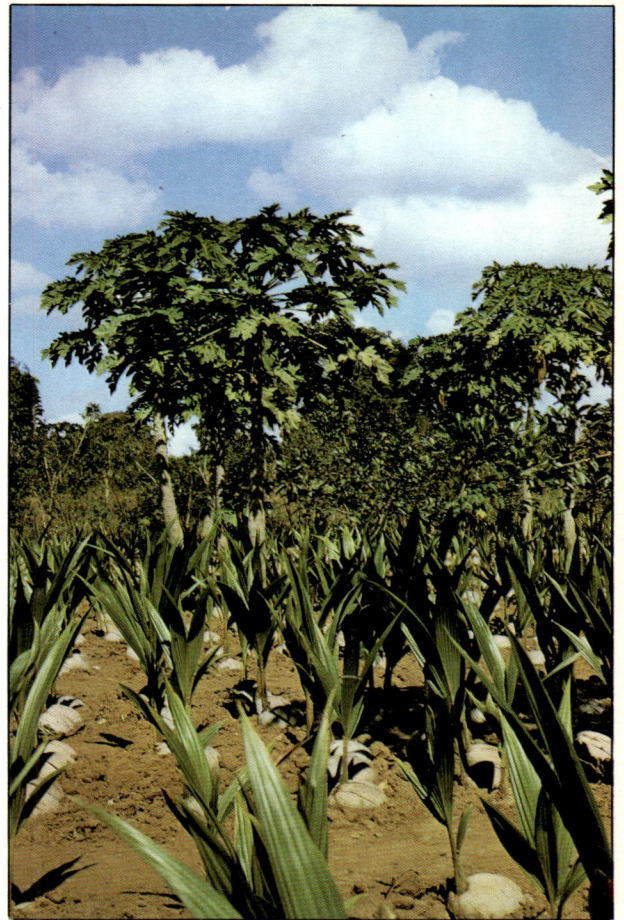

Left: Singapore has grown rapidly to become a major international financial centre. The picture catches a lively moment at the Singapore Stock Exchange.

Above: Sprouting coconut seedlings will reach 30.5 metres as mature trees. Copra, the dried kernel of the fruit, is a valuable source of oil.

the world's leading banking, trading and tourist centres. All other South-east Asian countries have less than ten per cent of their workforces employed in manufacturing, except the Philippines (11 per cent). Small crafts, such as wood and stone carving, rattan work, jewellery making, silverwork, spinning and weaving of silk and cotton, and pottery work, flourish throughout the region. These are mainly dependent upon local materials and customs.

History and culture

The countries of mainland South-east Asia were heavily influenced by Indian seaborne visitors

gross national product comes from agriculture and forestry and 17% from mining and manufacturing. Manila is the largest town. Area: 300,000 sq km; population: 49,051,000; capital: QUEZON CITY.

Phnom Penh is the capital of Kampuchea. It became a 'ghost city' following its evacuation forced by the communist government in 1975 at the end of civil war. Its population in 1974 was about 2,000,000, including refugees. The population began to return to the city in 1979.

Q **Quezon City**, the official capital of the PHILIPPINES, adjoins Manila. Population: 1,000,000.

R **Rangoon** is the capital of Burma and the site of the Shwe Dagon, a Buddhist shrine constructed over 2,400 years ago. Population: 2,250,000.

S **Sabah**, formerly British North Borneo, became part of MALAYSIA in 1963. Population: 740,000.

Saigon, see HO CHI MINH CITY.
Salween River rises in Tibet and flows 2,400 km

through China and Burma.
Sarawak, once ruled by the 'white rajahs' of the English Brooke family, became part of MALAYSIA in 1963. Area:

Village in Sabah

125,206 sq km; population: 1,280,000.
Singapore is an important city and republic at the southern tip of the Malay peninsula. Having very little territory or resources, the country has concentrated on commerce, finance, shipping and manufacturing. Singaporeans are 76% Chinese, 14% Malay, and 8% Indo-Pakistani in origins. Some Europeans and Eurasians also live in the country. Malay, English, Chinese and Tamil are the main languages spoken. The various religions are not dominant.

Singapore has a high population density of 4,000 people to the sq km. Area: 581 sq km; population: 2,427,000.
Sulawesi (formerly Celebes) is INDONESIA's third largest island. It is well forested and has a small population for its size. Area: 189,484 sq km; population: 11,000,000.
Sumatra is the second largest of INDONESIA's islands. Area: 473,607 sq km; population: 25,000,000; capital: Medan.
Surabaja is a port in northeast JAVA and INDONESIA's

over 2,000 years ago. Later, this influence was superseded by the Chinese who also immigrated to the region. Arab traders brought Islam to INDONESIA, MALAYSIA and the southern PHILIPPINES by the early 1400s. Christian Europeans arrived in South-east Asia a century later. Eventually, the whole area fell under European rule except THAILAND. By the late 1800s, Britain held BURMA, present-day Malaysia and SINGAPORE; France had taken LAOS, KAMPUCHEA and VIETNAM, the Netherlands ruled Indonesia; and Spain held the Philippines until 1898 when they were seized by the United States. Japan occupied the whole region in 1942-45, forcing Thailand into alliance, but independence came to all countries between 1946 and 1965, except that BRUNEI chose to remain a British-protected sultanate.

Post-war events in the mainland states

Since World War II, mainland South-east Asia has been in a state of turbulence. Burma, for example, a mountainous land with many rebellious tribes, has experienced an unbroken series of rumbling, rather than violent, revolts since independence in 1948. The greatest upheaval was in Vietnam where people endured 30 years of bloody warfare. A colonial war against France forced the French to leave, and the country was partitioned along the 17th parallel of latitude in 1954. In the north the communists, led by Ho Chi Minh, took control of government while the south was acknowledged as an independent entity. Civil war developed as a result of the north's attempts to unify Vietnam. The USA heavily supported the South Vietnamese while communist countries gave limited assistance to the north. Victory came to the north in 1975 after America had withdrawn its troops. But Communism was not accepted by everyone and hundreds of thousands of people, including many from the Chinese minority, quit the country.

By the end of the Vietnam war, neighbouring Laos and Kampuchea had been dragged into the fighting and were under communist governments. In Kampuchea, the Khmer Rouge (Red Khmer government forces) depopulated all the towns, forcing the population to toil in the countryside. Such unpopular policies led to further civil war and some two million people are reported to have died in the war and its

Above: The agony of Vietnam began with the Japanese occupation in 1940, and fighting continued even after the communist triumph of 1975. The picture shows a Vietnamese refugee group during the war in the early 1970s, before American troops pulled out.

Below: U Thant was Secretary-General of the United Nations during 1962-72. Although he proved a popular choice in this most international of jobs, his own country, Burma, remained isolated from the rest of the world.

aftermath. However, in 1979, anti-Khmer Rouge communists, heavily supported by Vietnamese forces, ousted the Khmer Rouge government. In contrast to all these disturbances Thailand has remained relatively peaceful.

Malaysia and the island states

In Malaya, the British fought a gruelling war against guerillas before independence came in 1957. In 1963, it joined with Singapore, Sarawak and Sabah to form Malaysia, but Singapore dropped out to become an independent country in 1965. The existence of Malaysia was challenged by Indonesia, which pursued a policy of 'confrontation' (limited war) against it until 1967. Indonesia achieved its independence from the Netherlands only by war between 1945 and 1949. It annexed West Irian in 1962-63 and EAST TIMOR in 1975.

The Philippines gained independence from the United States peacefully in 1946, but a Huk (communist group) rebellion ensued until the mid-1950s. Increasing lawlessness in the country, which won Manila the nickname of 'Dodge City East', led President Marcos to declare martial law in 1972. This was retained, following approval by national referenda. The situation was complicated by the continued revolt against the Manila government by the Muslim minority in the south of the country.

---

main naval base. Population: 2,000,000.

T **Thailand** (formerly Siam) is the largest country of mainland Southeast Asia. It is also the only South-east Asian country never to have been under European rule, so it has kept its culture vigorous and independent. Over 90% of the population is Buddhist and distinctive temples dominate the landscape. Most of the people are Thai, but 10% are Chinese and 2% Malay. About 1% belong to the northern hill tribes which

include Meo, Lisu, Lahu, Yao, E-Kaw, Shan and Karen. Thai is the main language but Chinese, Malay and

Elephant in Thailand

tribal dialects are also spoken. Area: 514,000 sq km; population: 47,978,000; capital: Bangkok.

Tonle Sap is a lake in KAMPUCHEA fed by the MEKONG RIVER. It varies between 2,500 and 25,000 sq km in area, according to season, and is rich in fish.

V **Vientiane** is the capital of LAOS. Population: about 185,000.
Vietnam, a war torn country in South-east Asia was finally united in 1976 after more than 30 years of wars. It then became a single communist

republic and many Vietnamese fled abroad. Over 85% of the people are Vietnamese who follow Confucianist-Taoist-Buddhist cults. Some 5% are Catholic. Vietnamese is the main language, but Chinese, Khmer, French and English are also spoken. Rice farming is the dominant occupation. Area: 329,556 sq km; population (not allowing for migration); 52,159,000; capital: Hanoi.

W **West Irian** (Irian Barat), the western part of the island of New Guinea, was transferred from Dutch

to Indonesian rule by 1963 Population: 1,200,000.

Z **Zamboanga** is the chief market town of the southern PHILIPPINES in southwest MINDANAO and a main centre of the Moro people Population: 250,000.

Africa, formerly called the 'Dark Continent,' has emerged into the light of independence in the last 30 years. However, political independence has left many complex problems in its wake.

Africa

Africa is a continent in transition. By 1945 only four African countries, EGYPT, ETHIOPIA, LIBERIA, and SOUTH AFRICA, were independent. The rest were ruled by either Belgium, Britain, France, Italy, Portugal or Spain. But since then, a 'wind of change' has blown throughout Africa. By the end of 1978, African nations occupied over 30 per cent of the seats in the United Nations General Assembly. This large representation gives Africa a powerful voice in world affairs.

The emergent nations of Africa have faced many economic, political and social problems since they achieved independence. Some problems have been caused by poverty and some by the fact that nearly three out of every four Africans are illiterate. Disunity and rivalries have arisen in many countries because of ethnic, language and religious differences, and these factors have led to military coups and the adoption of autocratic, rather than democratic,

Below: Dar es Salaam is the capital and chief port of Tanzania. As the centre of communications, education and industry, it has grown rapidly, attracting talented people from all over the country. In the 1980s, the capital will be relocated at Dodoma, which is closer to the geographical centre of the country.

systems of government. Some problems arise from Africa's size. Africa is the world's second largest continent, with an area of 30,319,000 square kilometres. This is nearly three times as large as Europe (including European Russia).

The estimated population of Africa in 1980 was 458 millions. In terms of population, Africa comes third among the continents, after Asia and Europe, which are both much more densely-populated than Africa, where the average population density is only 15 people to every square kilometre. This low population density results from the fact that vast tracts of burning-hot desert and dense tropical forests are virtually uninhabited. However, Africa's population is increasing rapidly, by about 2.7 per cent per year. At this rate, the population increases make it difficult for African countries to achieve real advances in the standards of living of their people.

Land Features

Most of Africa consists of vast plateaux. About 60 per cent of the continent is more than 370 metres above sea level. These plateaux are especially pronounced in the African countries south of the equator, where 50 per cent of the land is over 900 metres above sea level. Coastal plains are mostly narrow and Africa generally lacks deep inlets. The high plateaux near the coasts once made inland travel difficult. This factor was important in discouraging Europeans from exploring the interior until the 1800s.

The highest mountains, MOUNT KILIMANJARO and MOUNT KENYA, are extinct volcanoes. Other igneous (cooled molten rock) massifs are the Ahaggar, Darfur and Tibesti mountains in the north and the Cameroon mountains in west-central Africa. The lofty Ruwenzori range in east-central Africa, however, is an uplifted block bordering the massive East African rift valley,

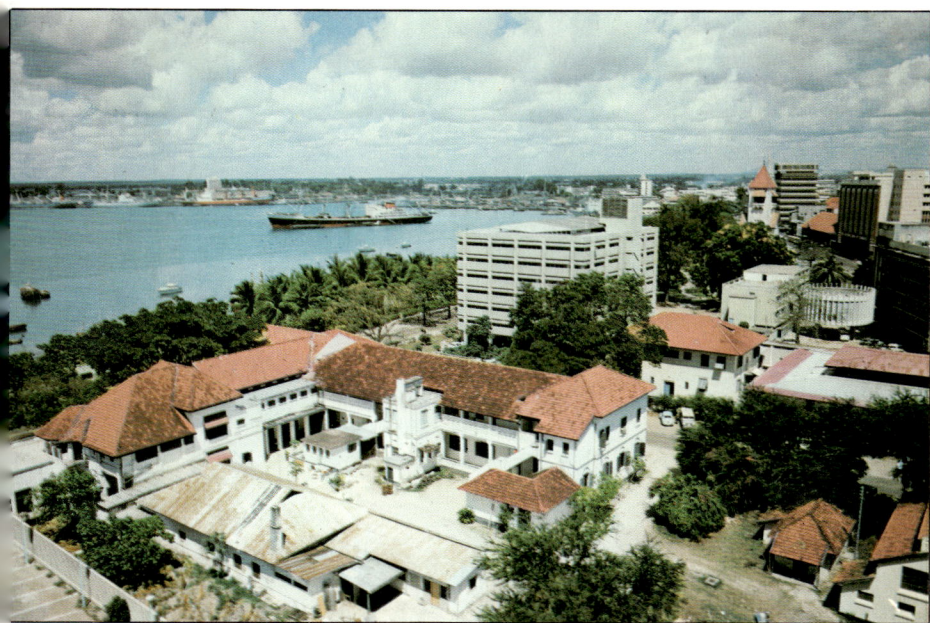

Reference

A

Abidjan, capital of IVORY COAST, is a trading and administrative centre. Its outport is Port-Bouet. Population: 850,000.

Accra, capital of GHANA, grew up around British forts of the 1600s. Population: 636,000.

Addis Ababa, capital of Ethiopia, contains the headquarters of the United Nations Economic Commission for Africa. Population: 1,083,000.

Alexandria is the chief seaport of EGYPT. It was founded in 332 BC and was a brilliant cultural centre about 2,000 years ago. Population: 2,259,000.

Algeria, formerly a French territory, became an independent republic in 1962. Most of the million or so French settlers left the country. Today most people are Muslim Arabs, and Arabic is the official language. But 19% are Berbers, including the Kabyles and the nomadic Tuaregs of the Sahara. The majority of the population farm in the Atlas mountains and Mediterranean coastal regions in the

Veiled Tuareg

north. The almost empty Sahara, covering about 85% of Algeria, contains oil and natural gas deposits. Algeria's per capita gross domestic product is above the African average. Area: 2,381,741 sq km; population: 19,627,000; capital: ALGIERS.

Algiers is the capital and chief seaport of ALGERIA. It was founded in the AD 900s. Population: 1,504,000.

Angola, formerly a Portuguese overseas province, became an independent republic in 1975, following a guerilla war. A civil war was

then fought between the main groups of Bantu-speaking people, namely the Kongo in the north; the Mbundu and mesticos (people of mixed origin) in central Angola; and the Ovimbundu, Angola's largest ethnic group, in the south. The MPLA, the Mbundu-mesticos party, with help from the USSR and Cuba, triumphed in early 1976. Farming is the chief occupation and coffee is the main crop. Area: 1,246,700 sq km; population: 5,646,000; capital: LUANDA.

Above right: The lofty Drakensberg range in southern Africa is the uplifted rim of the African plateau. In Lesotho, it reaches its maximum height of 3,482 metres above sea-level. The Drakensberg, also called Quathlamba, extends for about 1,600 km.

Above left: This bleak desert region lies in the Sahara, in southern Tunisia. The world's largest desert, the Sahara covers more than 25% of Africa, and is nearly as big as the United States. Other large tracts of southern Africa are deserts or semi-deserts.

Left: The Kerio River flows through the Chebloc Gorge in Kenya. During the rainy season, African rivers may become raging torrents, sweeping away large amounts of silt and sand. However, in the dry season, many rivers are reduced to a trickle or dry up completely.

while the DRAKENSBERG range in southern Africa is an uptilted plateau rim. Africa is mostly an ancient landmass. The only fold mountains are the ATLAS MOUNTAINS in the north-west and the Cape ranges of South Africa.

Much of Africa's scenery is spectacular. This is particularly true of the East African rift valley. This deep gash in the Earth's crust, which runs from Mozambique to the Red Sea, was caused by continental drift (two landmasses drifting together, apart, or past each other). It extends through the Red Sea into Syria, in south-west Asia. Parts of the rift valley are bounded by steep walls and it contains many great lakes, including TANGANYIKA and NYASA. But Africa's largest lake, VICTORIA, is not in the rift valley. It occupies a shallow depression in the plateaux between two arms of the rift valley in KENYA, UGANDA and TANZANIA. Three of the world's longest rivers, the NILE, ZAIRE (formerly the Congo) and NIGER, are in Africa. Their courses are interrupted by rapids and waterfalls as they descend from the plateaux.

Climate

Africa is divided almost equally from north to south by the equator and over 60 per cent of the continent is in the tropics. It is the hottest continent and the world's highest air tempera-

Antananarivo, formerly Tananarive, is the capital of MADAGASCAR. Population: 400,000.

Aswan High Dam, on the NILE in EGYPT, controls flood-water, and its turbines generate electricity. It was inaugurated in 1968.

Atlas Mountains are in north-west Africa. The highest peak is 4,165 metres above sea-level, in MOROCCO.

B Bamako, capital of MALI, stands on the River NIGER. Population: 400,000.

Bangui is the capital of the CENTRAL AFRICAN EMPIRE. This river port has a population of 302,000.

Banjul (formerly Bathurst) is the capital of GAMBIA. Population: 43,000.

Bantustans (or homelands) are areas in SOUTH AFRICA designated for the black African population. The 10 Bantustans cover a combined area which represents 13% of South Africa. One Bantustan, Transkei, became independent in 1976 and another, Bophuthatswana, in 1977. But only South Africa recognizes them.

Benin (formerly Dahomey) became independent from France in 1960. This republic has 50 ethnic groups, the Fon being the largest. Because so many languages are spoken, French remains the official one. Farming is the chief industry and palm products are the main exports of this poor nation. Area: 112,622 sq km; population: 3,557,000; capital: PORTO NOVO.

Bissau is the capital and chief port of GUINEA-BISSAU. Population: 65,000.

Bophuthatswana, see BANTUSTANS.

Botswana, formerly British Bechuanaland, became an independent republic in 1966. Most people belong to

Herero people, Botswana

one of the branches of the Tswana group, although about 30,000 Bushmen live in the dry KALAHARI desert. The Tswana are mostly cattle-herders in the east. The recent discovery of minerals, notably diamonds, is changing the economy. Area: 600,372 sq km; population: 804,000; capital GABORONE.

Brazzaville, on the River ZAIRE, is the capital of CONGO. Population: 290,000.

Bujumbura, on Lake TANGANYIKA, is the capital of BURUNDI. Population 100,000.

Map labels

Tangier · ALGIERS · TUNIS · MEDITERRANEAN SEA
RABAT · Casablanca · TUNISIA · TRIPOLI · Benghazi · Alexandria · Suez Canal · CAIRO
MOROCCO · ATLAS MOUNTAINS
Canary Is. · L Nasser
Nouakchott · MAURITANIA · S A H A R A · ALGERIA · LIBYA · EGYPT · RED SEA
Senegal · SENEGAL · NIGER · CHAD · KHARTOUM
DAKAR · GAMBIA · BAMAKO · M A L I · NIAMEY · L Chad · N'DJAMENA · SUDAN · DJIBOUTI · DJIBOUTI
GUINEA-BISSAU · OUAGADOUGOU · Kano
CONAKRY · GUINEA · UPPER VOLTA · NIGERIA
SIERRA LEONE · FREETOWN · Niger · BENIN · Ibadan · ADDIS ABABA · ETHIOPIA
MONROVIA · IVORY COAST · GHANA · TOGO · LAGOS · CENTRAL AFRICAN REP.
LIBERIA · ABIDJAN · Volta · ACCRA · LOME · PORTO NOVO · White Nile · Blue Nile
CAMEROON · YAOUNDE · BANGUI · SOMALIA · MOGADISHU
MALABO · EQUATORIAL GUINEA · UGANDA · KAMPALA · KENYA
LIBREVILLE · GABON · CONGO · Zaire · Kisangani · RWANDA · L Victoria · NAIROBI · MOMBASA
BRAZZAVILLE · Kasai · ZAIRE · KIGALI · BURUNDI · INDIAN OCEAN
CABINDA (ANGOLA) · KINSHASA · BUJUMBURA · L Tanganyika · TANZANIA
LUANDA · Shaba · DAR ES SALAAM
ANGOLA · L Malawi · MORONI · Comoro
ZAMBIA · LUSAKA · LILONGWE
SALISBURY · MADAGASCAR · ANTANANARIVO
NAMIBIA · Kalahari Desert · ZIMBABWE RHODESIA · MOZAMBIQUE · Mozambique Channel · Port-Louis MAURITIUS
WINDHOEK · BOTSWANA · KALAHARI · GABORONE
PRETORIA · MAPUTO · SWAZILAND
Johannesburg · MASERU · LESOTHO · Durban
Orange · SOUTH AFRICA
CAPE TOWN · Port Elizabeth
CAPE OF GOOD HOPE

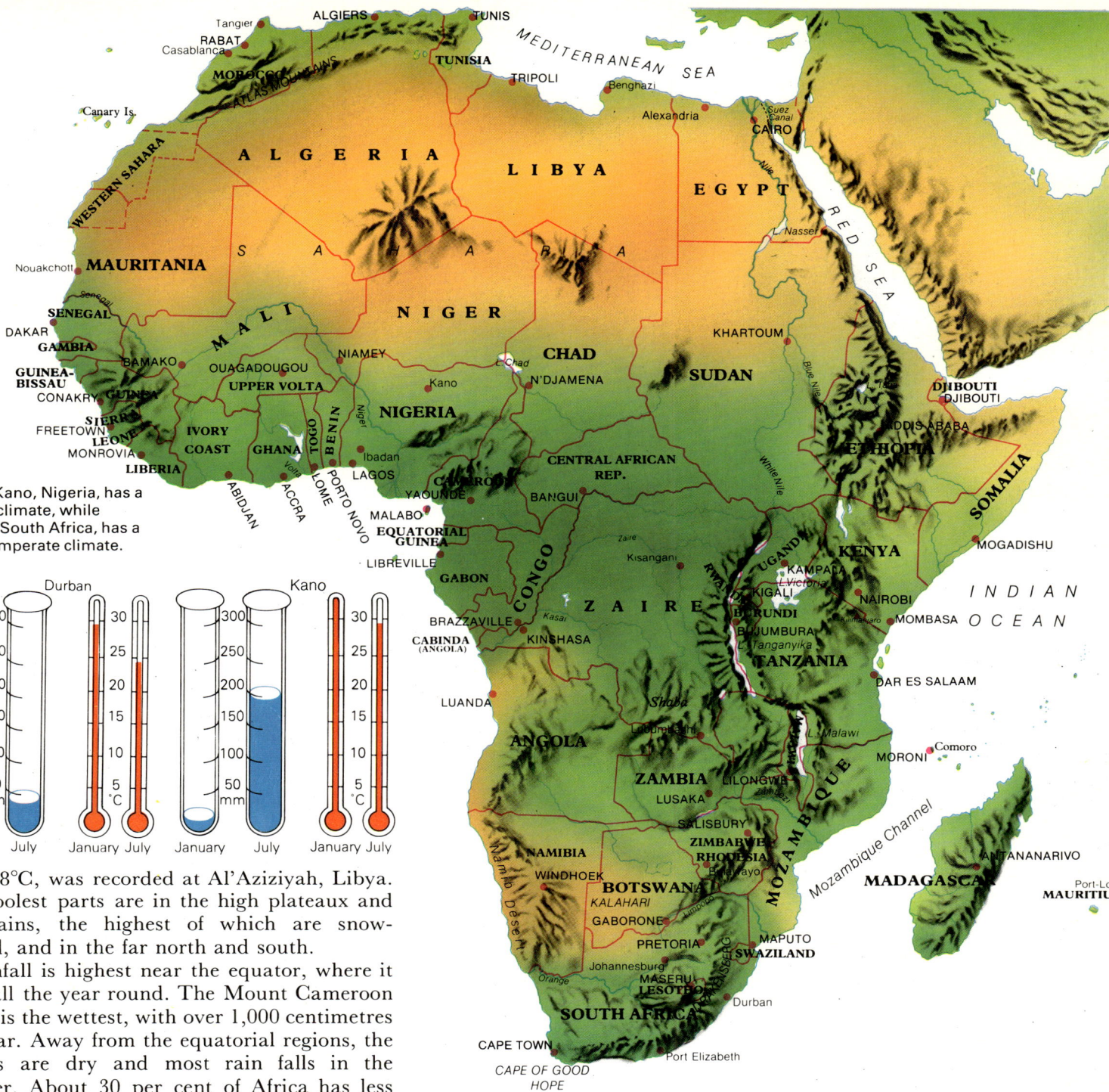

Below: Kano, Nigeria, has a tropical climate, while Durban, South Africa, has a warm temperate climate.

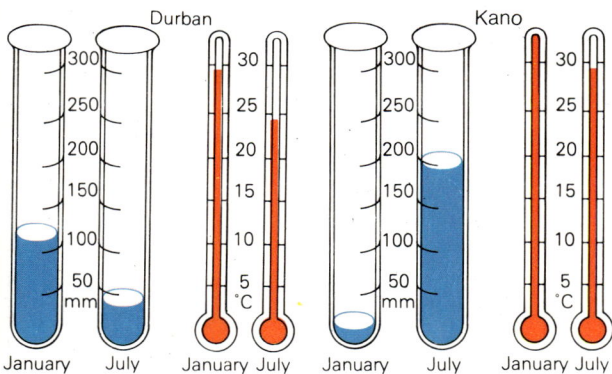

Durban — January / July — January July °C
Kano — January / July — January July °C

(rainfall and temperature charts: 300, 250, 200, 150, 100, 50 mm; 30, 25, 20, 15, 10, 5 °C)

ture, 58°C, was recorded at Al'Aziziyah, Libya. The coolest parts are in the high plateaux and mountains, the highest of which are snow-capped, and in the far north and south.

Rainfall is highest near the equator, where it rains all the year round. The Mount Cameroon region is the wettest, with over 1,000 centimetres per year. Away from the equatorial regions, the winters are dry and most rain falls in the summer. About 30 per cent of Africa has less than 25 centimetres of rain per year. Low rainfall combined with a high rate of evaporation have caused large deserts to form. In the north is the SAHARA, the world's largest desert. In the south,

---

Burundi, an overpopulated, remote republic, was part of the Belgian Ruanda-Urundi until 1962. The tall Tutsi people (Hamites), who form 15% of the population, ruled Burundi as a monarchy, but the mwami (king) was deposed in 1966. The Hutu, a Bantu-speaking group, form 85% of the population. They are mostly subsistence farmers. Coffee is the chief export. Area: 27,834 sq km; population: 3,864,000; capital: BUJUMBURA.

C Cairo, Africa's largest city and capital of EGYPT,

is on the NILE. This historic city was founded in AD 969. Population: 5,715,000.

Cameroon is a republic, consisting of former French

Mohammed Mosque, Cairo

Cameroon and part of British Cameroon. French and English are both official languages. The population is extremely diverse. Sudanese Negroes, Hamitic Fulani and Arab Choa live in the grassy north, and many Bantu-speaking groups live in the forested south. Most people are poor farmers. Coffee and cocoa are exported. Area: 475,442 sq km; population: 7,042,000; capital: YAOUNDE.

Canary Islands form two Spanish provinces in the Atlantic Ocean. Area: 7,273 sq km; population: 1,170,000.

Cape Town is the legislative capital of SOUTH AFRICA. This major port has a population of 1,097,000.

Cape Verde Islands, formerly Portuguese, became an independent republic in 1975. These volcanic islands are in the Atlantic, west of Senegal. Area: 4,033 sq km; population: 329,000; capital PRAIA.

Casablanca, a major seaport in MOROCCO, has a population of 1,506,000.

Central African Empire is a poor, inland nation. The largest ethnic groups are the Banda and Baya, who are

farmers in the wet south. Coffee and cotton are exported. Formerly French, the country became an independent republic in 1960. It was made an empire in 1976. Area: 622,984 sq km; population: 1,637,000; capital: BANGUI.

Chad, formerly a French territory, became an independent republic in 1960. The arid north contains Sudanese Negroes and Berber Tuaregs. The poor Negroid peoples of the south are mostly farmers, but some are fishermen in LAKE CHAD. Cotton is the main export.

the Namib is a total desert, while the large KALAHARI is a semi-desert. Mediterranean zones, with mild, moist winters and hot, dry summers, occur in the north and along the south-west Cape coast. South Africa also contains the temperate, fairly arid, high veld and a warm temperate zone in the east. This coastal zone, which extends into Mozambique, gets about 1,000 millimetres of rain per year.

Vegetation zones

The main vegetation regions in tropical Africa are the rain forests, the savanna, the deserts and the uplands. The dense rain forests flourish in the wet equatorial lowlands, which cover about 10 per cent of Africa. These forests, including coastal mangrove swamps, extend through most of West Africa from GUINEA-BISSAU to GABON. The largest rain forest is in the ZAIRE RIVER basin. Another zone is in MADAGASCAR. Savanna (tropical grassland with trees) borders onto the rain forests and is most luxuriant where the summer rains are the heaviest. As the rainfall decreases to the north and south, the savanna merges into dry scrub and desert.

The uplands of tropical Africa contain a series of sub-zones determined by altitude. A typical sequence is savanna at the base of a mountain, merging into mountain rain forest, upland grassland, moorland then tundra and, on the highest peaks, permanent snow and ice.

Above: Cheetahs, one of the animals which roam the African savanna, are shown here in Nairobi National Park, which is a short drive from the capital of Kenya.

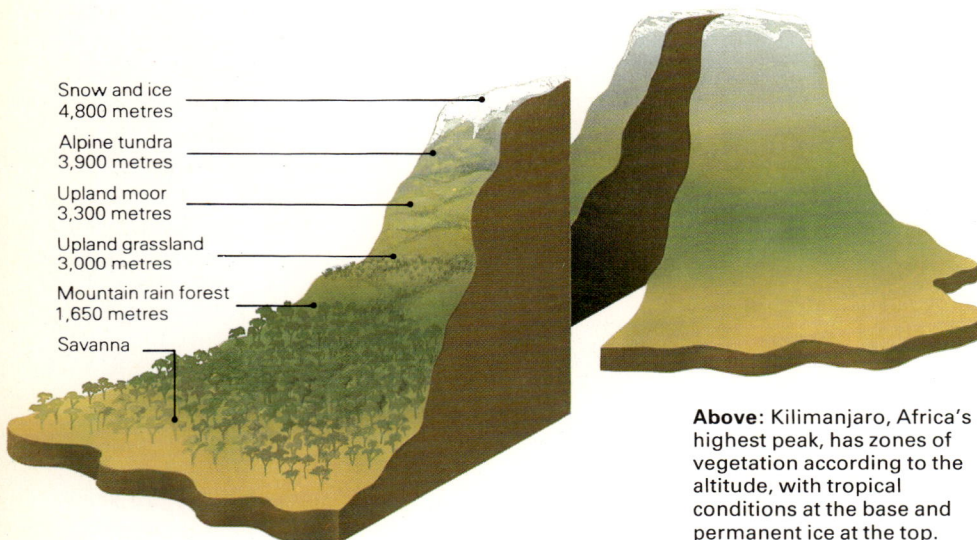

Snow and ice
4,800 metres

Alpine tundra
3,900 metres

Upland moor
3,300 metres

Upland grassland
3,000 metres

Mountain rain forest
1,650 metres

Savanna

Above: Kilimanjaro, Africa's highest peak, has zones of vegetation according to the altitude, with tropical conditions at the base and permanent ice at the top.

In the Mediterranean climate regions of northern and south-western Africa, the plants are adapted to the summer drought. The characteristic vegetation is maquis, consisting of shrubs and low trees, such as myrtle and olive, which are drought-resistant. Two other distinctive regions occur in southern Africa. The high veld is a grassland region with few trees. The warm temperate zone in south-eastern Africa, however, is largely forested.

Wildlife

The wildlife of Africa is extremely varied, although some species are threatened by poaching and, especially, by the spread of people into areas which were once the sole preserve of animals. The main animal regions, each with its own abundant and characteristic fauna, are the forests, the savanna and the uplands. National parks and reserves in these zones attract an increasing number of tourists, who bring much-needed revenue to many African countries.

The population of Africa

Africa has the highest birth rate of any continent,

Area: 1,284,000 sq km; population: 4,473,000; capital: N'DJAMENA.
Chad, Lake, is a shallow lake in an inland drainage basin, mostly in CHAD. The maximum area is 25,600 sq km.
Comoro Islands are an independent island republic in the northern Mozambique Channel. Area: 2,171 sq km; population: 347,000; capital: MORONI.
Conakry is the capital and main seaport of GUINEA. Population: 526,000.
Congo is a republic which became independent from

France in 1960. The main peoples are the Bakongo, Teke, Bobangi and Gabonais – all Bantu-speaking groups. Most are subsistence farmers, but timber and timber products are the main exports. Congo's government describes itself as Marxist. Area: 342,000 sq km; population: 1,540,000; capital: BRAZZAVILLE.

D Dakar, capital, chief seaport and industrial centre of SENEGAL, has a population of 581,000.
Dar es Salaam is the capital and chief seaport of TAN-

ZANIA. Population: 522,000.
Djebel Toubkal, in MOROCCO, is the highest peak in the ATLAS MOUNTAINS. It is 4,165 metres above sea level.

Market in Dakar, Senegal

Djibouti, formerly French Somaliland and, later, the Territory of the Afars and Issas, became an independent republic in 1977. This hot, dry country exports cattle and hides from its capital, Djibouti (pop. 62,000). The main peoples, the Issas (a Somali clan) and the Afars (Danakils), are Muslims. Area: 22,000 sq km; population: 118,000.
Dodoma, a town in central TANZANIA, will become the nation's capital in the 1980s. Population: 24,000.
Drakensberg, a mountain range bordering the central

plateau in SOUTH AFRICA and LESOTHO, reaches 3,482 metres above sea level.
Durban is a major seaport in Natal, SOUTH AFRICA. Population: 843,000.

E Egypt has been called the 'gift of the Nile.' The NILE valley covers only 4% of the land, but 99% of the people live there. A few live in the hot deserts east and west of the Nile, mainly at oases. The Nile valley was the home of the brilliant Ancient Egyptian civilization. Egypt was conquered by the Arabs in AD 640. Most people

with about 47 live births per every 1,000 people per year. But the death rate is also high, at about 21 per 1,000 per year. The high death rate is caused by several factors, including poverty, poor sanitation, inadequate health services to combat the various diseases, and poor diets. Africa's population is youthful by comparison with developed continents. In 1976 about 44 per cent of Africa's people were under 15 and only 2.9 per cent were over 65.

The average life expectation varies from region to region. The Europeans of SOUTH AFRICA and ZIMBABWE-RHODESIA live almost as long, on average, as people in Europe and North America, while Africans in tropical regions have shorter lives. For example, the average life expectation in MALI (1970-5) was 36.5 years for men and 39.6 years for women. In North Africa, people live longer. For example, in ALGERIA (1970-5), the average life expectation for men was 51.7 years and for women it was 54.8 years.

Peoples and languages

More than 1,000 languages are spoken in Africa. In some Black African countries, many languages and dialects are spoken and a European language and/or a local lingua franca must be used as an official language. For example, TANZANIA has more than 120 languages. The official languages are English and Swahili. Swahili is an East African coastal language

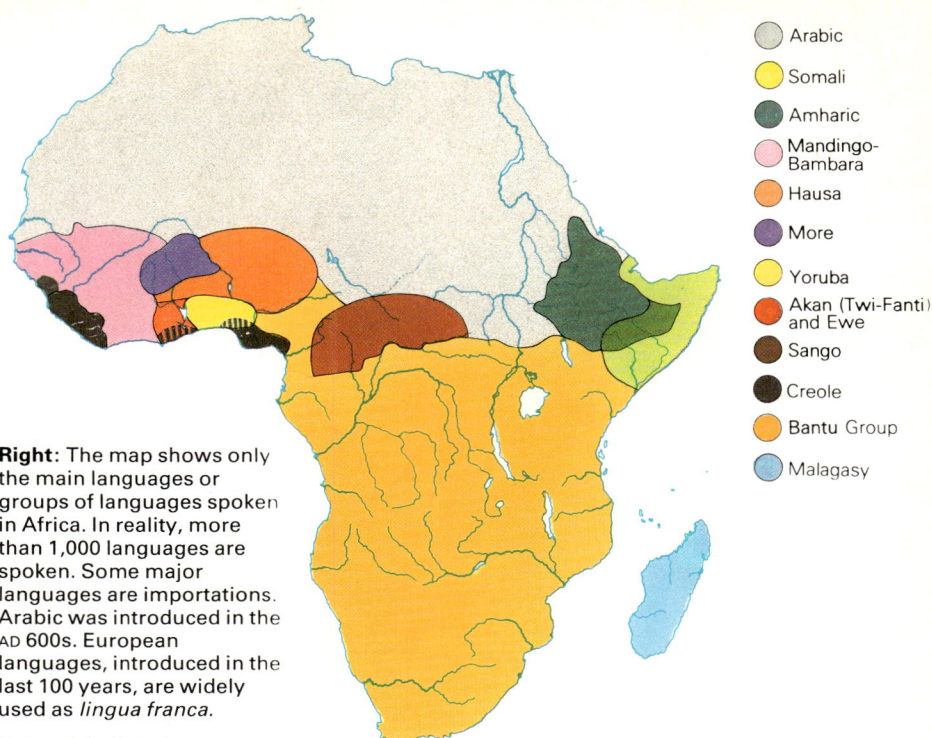

Right: The map shows only the main languages or groups of languages spoken in Africa. In reality, more than 1,000 languages are spoken. Some major languages are importations. Arabic was introduced in the AD 600s. European languages, introduced in the last 100 years, are widely used as lingua franca.

Below left: This Dogon village in Mali is built from baked mud. The walls are protected by thatched roofs. The Dogon have an elaborate philosophy based on myths and symbols. Villages are often arranged in the shape of an egg, a symbol of fertility.

Below: The diagram shows that Ghana, like many African countries, has a youthful population. More than 80% of the people are under 15, and the average life expectancy is only about 48 years.

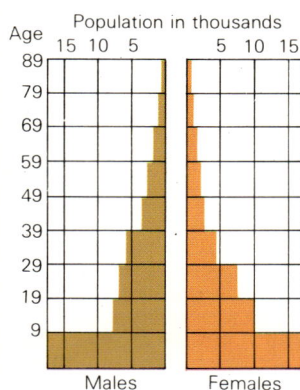

Legend:
- Arabic
- Somali
- Amharic
- Mandingo-Bambara
- Hausa
- More
- Yoruba
- Akan (Twi-Fanti) and Ewe
- Sango
- Creole
- Bantu Group
- Malagasy

which is comparatively easy to learn and has become a lingua franca throughout East Africa and eastern Zaire.

Ethnically, the people of Africa belong to two main groups: Caucasoids and Negroids. The Caucasoids of North Africa include the Hamitic Berbers and the Arabs, who conquered North Africa in the AD 600s, introducing a brilliant Islamic culture. The chief language in North Africa is Arabic, although some Berber tongues are also used. Many Arabs and Berbers are farmers or stock-rearers, but several cities, including ALEXANDRIA, ALGIERS, CAIRO and CASABLANCA, have populations of over a million. The Nubians of SUDAN, the Somalis and various Ethiopian groups are also basically Caucasoid, although some have Negroid features. Negroids occupy most of Africa south of the Sahara. The two largest language families are traditionally classed as the West Atlantic group in West Africa and the Bantu of central and South Africa.

The West Africans
Most of the people of West Africa, who live between the Gulf of Guinea coast and the SAHARA, speak one of the West Atlantic lan-

are now of Arab or Coptic (ancient Egyptian) origin. Most are Muslims, but there are some Coptic Christians. Egypt, a republic since 1952, is Africa's second most industrialized nation. Although cheap power supplies come from the ASWAN HIGH DAM, most people remain poor farmers. Cotton is the chief crop and export. Wars with Israel have hampered progress since 1948, but in 1979 Egypt signed a peace treaty with Israel. Area: 1,001,449 sq km; population: 42,118,000; capital: CAIRO.

Equatorial Guinea, a republic, independent from Spain in 1968, contains mainland Rio Muni and the island Macias Nguema Biyoga (Fernando Poo). The largest ethnic group is the Fang and farming is the chief industry. Area: 28,051 sq km; population: 338,000; capital: MALABO.
Eritrea has been part of ETHIOPIA since 1952. It was the scene of a secessionist war in the 1970s.
Ethiopia was the home of an ancient empire until an army group deposed Emperor Haile Selassie and set

up a socialist republic in 1974. This largely highland

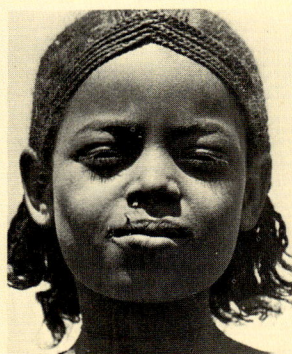

Ethiopian girl, Galla tribe

nation depends on farming, and coffee is the main product. The ruling people, the Amharas, speak a Semitic language. Other groups include the Galla and Somalis, with Negroid peoples in the south-west. Christianity was introduced in the AD 300s and about half of the people are now Coptic Christians. But Muslims live in the south and east. Area: 1,221,900 sq km; population: 31,779,000; capital: ADDIS ABABA.

F **Freetown**, capital of SIERRA LEONE, was founded in 1787 as a home for

freed slaves. Population: 274,000.

G **Gabon**, a former French territory, became an independent republic in 1960. It is fairly wealthy, by African standards, because of its mineral resources, particularly oil. Forestry and farming are also important industries. The people are divided into 40 Bantu-speaking groups, the largest of which is the Fang. Area: 267,667 sq km; population: 567,000; capital: LIBREVILLE.
Gaborone is the capital of BOTSWANA. It is on the South

guages. These peoples include the Ashanti (GHANA), the ubiquitous Fula, or Fulani (spread out through SENEGAL to northern CAMEROON), the Hausa, Igbo and Yoruba (NIGERIA) and the Wolof (SENEGAL).

In the forest regions, most people are cultivators. Inland, however, the people of the savanna have a mixed arable and pastoral economy, while some are exclusively pastoralists. Traditionally, many people have lived in large villages. Some of these have developed into major cities and West Africa has a substantial educated middle class. West Africa also has great artistic traditions, especially terracotta, wood, stone and bronze sculpture.

The Bantu-speaking Africans

South of a line from Cameroon to northern KENYA lies the southern 30 per cent of Africa. Most people in this region speak one of the many Bantu languages. They include the Ganda (UGANDA), the Kikuyu (Kenya), the Kongo and Luba (ZAIRE), the Ndebele and Shona (ZIMBABWE-RHODESIA), the Tsonga (MOZAMBIQUE), the Tswana (BOTSWANA) and the Zulu and Xhosas (SOUTH AFRICA). Most Bantu-speaking people are farmers, who grow crops and rear livestock. Like the West Africans, they have artistic traditions. For example, wood sculpture is important among forest peoples and, the oral tradition of story-telling, especially in verse, has reached great heights.

Other peoples

Smaller groups in east-central Africa are the

Left: Africa has its own distinctive styles of music and musical instruments. These bowharps probably originated in Egypt 5,000 years ago. The sound box is hollowed out of wood and covered with skin.

Right: The Fulani are a widespread, essentially nomadic, cattle-keeping people. They have spread across the West African savanna from Senegal to northern Cameroon. They are a major group in northern Nigeria, where they seized power from the Hausa in the late 1800s.

Right: This Yoruba family lives in south-western Nigeria. Most Yoruba are farmers. They have important artistic traditions. The Yoruba city of Ife was a great centre for sculpture between the 1100s and 1300s.

Above: A Hausa drummer. Most Hausa are Muslim farmers, who live in northern Nigeria. Their language, which has incorporated much Arabic and English, is one of Africa's richest. The Hausa founded powerful city-states between the 800s and 1800s.

Right: These Igbo (or Ibo) are playing *ayo,* a game which is popular throughout Africa. Between 1967 and 1970, many Igbo supported a secessionist movement, which tried, unsuccessfully, to establish a separate state, called Biafra.

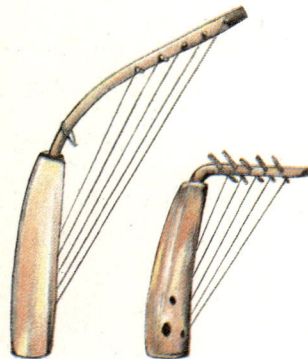

Africa-Zimbabwe railway. Population: 37,000.
Gambia, Africa's smallest mainland nation, is a republic. It became independent from Britain in 1965. There are 5 main ethnic groups, the largest being the Mandingo. Groundnuts account for 95% of the country's exports. Area: 11,295 sq km; population: 596,000; capital: BANJUL.
Ghana, formerly the Gold Coast, is a West African republic which became independent from Britain in 1957. The people are divided into about 50 groups, the

Cleaning a shark, Gambia

largest of which is the Akan (including Ashanti, Fante and Twi). Most people are farmers and cocoa is the main export. Economic problems have dogged Ghana's progress. Area: 238,537 sq km; population: 11,603,000; capital: ACCRA.
Guinea, a republic, became independent from France in 1958. It turned for help to communist nations, but it now also enjoys good relations with the non-communist world. The main peoples are the Fulani (Peul) and Malinke. The majority are Muslims. Farming is the main industry, but bauxite and aluminium dominate the exports. Area: 245,957 sq km; population: 4,980,000; capital: CONAKRY.

Guinea-Bissau, formerly Portuguese Guinea, became independent in 1974, following a guerilla war. Farming is the main activity and groundnuts, groundnut products, palm products and copra are exported. There are about 30 ethnic groups. Area: 36,125 sq km; population: 567,000; capital: BISSAU.

▎**Ibadan,** capital of Oyo state, NIGERIA, is a manufacturing and university city. Population: 847,000.
Ivory Coast, formerly a French territory, became an independent republic in 1960. By African standards, it is stable and affluent, and the average gross domestic product per person (1976) was US $610. Coffee, cocoa and timber are the main exports and manufacturing is important, especially in Abidjan. There are about 60 groups of people. The largest are the Anji and Baule, of the Akan group. Area: 322,463 sq km; population: 5,559,000; capital: ABIDJAN.

J **Johannesburg,** SOUTH AFRICA'S largest city, is a major financial and indust-

Below: The Hausa, Fulani and Kanuri are leading peoples of northern Nigeria, while the Yoruba are based in the south-west and the Igbo in the south-east. With over 70 million people, Nigeria has a larger population than any other African nation and its population is increasing quickly by about 2.7% per year. At this rate, the population could double in 25 years. The population of Nigeria is extremely diverse. The country has about 250 language groups in all. But the 5 groups shown here, together with 5 others (the Edo, Ibibio, Ijaw, Nupe and

Tiv), make up about 80% of the population. Islam is the chief religion in the north and nearly 50% of all Nigerians are Muslims. However, Christianity and traditional religions are practised in the south. Because of its human diversity, Nigeria has suffered in the past from communal tensions. It now has a federal constitution, with a central federal government and local governments in each of the 19 states. Life is now changing rapidly in Nigeria as revenue from oil production is being used to develop the economy.

Left: The Nigerian head-dress and mask are typical of the elaborate decorations used in ceremonies and celebrations. Many of the patterns and shapes used in such objects have a religious or symbolic meaning.

Nilotes, a mixed Hamitic and Negroid group, who are mostly cattle-owners, hunters or fishermen. They include the Dinka and Nuer (Sudan) and the Luo (Kenya). The Nilo-Hamitic group includes the Masai of Kenya and Tanzania.

Pygmies are hunters and gatherers in the equatorial rain forests, especially in Cameroon and Zaire. These short people number less than 200,000. In southern Africa, the first inhabitants, before Bantu groups arrived, were the Khoi-San. The Khoi (Hottentots) include the Nama, who are pastoralists and hunters in NAMIBIA, while the San (Bushmen) are hunters in the KALAHARI. In Madagascar, the people are mostly descendants of Black Africans from the mainland and Indonesians who settled on the island in the early Middle Ages. The official Malagasy language is related to Indonesian tongues.

Non-indigenous peoples include about five million of European origin, most of whom live in southern Africa, and about 850,000 Asians living

Above: A Kanuri leather-worker produces goods employing traditional designs. Leather goods were one of the items in medieval trans-Saharan trade.

Left: Modern Nigerian bead work often uses forms associated with traditional African art. The abstract nature of most black African art was condemned by early European visitors as crude. But it later had great influence on such European painters as Picasso and Modigliani.

rial centre in a mainly gold-mining region. Population: 1,433,000.

Kalahari, a region of semi-desert, is mainly in BOTSWANA and NAMIBIA. Some Bushmen live there.
Kampala is capital and chief commercial centre of UGANDA. Population: 331,000.
Kenya, formerly a British colony, became independent in 1963, and a republic one year later. Since then, it has enjoyed stable government. Kenya has superb national parks. Tourism is increasing rapidly. The largest

of the 40 ethnic groups are the Kikuyu and Luo, but Swahili (the lingua franca) and English are the official languages. Farming is the main industry, but only 15% of this upland nation has enough rainfall for cereal cultivation. Coffee and tea are the main exports. Area: 582,646 sq km; population: 15,951,000; capital: NAIROBI.
Khartoum, capital of SUDAN, was founded near the junction of the White and Blue NILE rivers in 1822. Population: 334,000.
Kigali is capital of RWANDA. Population: 54,000.

Kinshasa, formerly Léopoldville, is capital of

Wood carver, Lagos

ZAIRE. A major industrial city, it has 1,991,000 people.

Lagos is the capital and one of the major seaports of NIGERIA. Population: 1,061,000.
Lesotho, a mountainous kingdom, formerly called Basutoland, became independent from Britain in 1966. This poor farming nation largely depends on SOUTH AFRICA, which encircles it. Many Basothos work in South Africa. Area: 30,355 sq km; population: 931,000; capital: MASERU.
Liberia became an indepen-

dent republic in 1847, after having been established as a home for freed slaves by an American anti-slavery organization. Iron ore is the chief export, but income also comes from rubber and Liberia's merchant navy. Liberia has 16 ethnic groups, but the Americo-Liberian minority remains influential and English is the official language. Area: 111,369 sq km; population: 1,880,000; capital: MONROVIA.
Libreville, capital of GABON, was founded in 1849 as a home for freed slaves. Population: 251,000.

in eastern, central and southern Africa. Over two million Coloureds also live in South Africa. The Coloureds are the result of intermarriage between the early European settlers, Asian labourers and the indigenous peoples.

Substantial European populations once lived in other African countries, such as ALGERIA, ANGOLA, MOZAMBIQUE and in the cool, high plateau regions of tropical Africa. Only a few lived in the hot, tropical lowlands. Throughout Africa, Europeans had a profound effect. They introduced new ideas, encouraged economic development, set up schools and health services, created large cities and opened up isolated areas with new roads and railways. Some effects, however, were less beneficial. For example, many Africans were attracted by the cities. But, without skills, they often became almost permanently unemployed, living in poverty in sprawling shanty towns on the outskirts of the cities. Many also lost their beliefs in the values of their traditional societies. In SOUTH AFRICA, an extremely complex racial situation has arisen, in which the Europeans are trying to maintain their own culture and their control of the economy and government, despite the fact that they constitute only 17.5 per cent of the total population.

Religions
Two of the world's great religions, Christianity

Right: Christian missions provide much of the education in Black Africa and overseas missionary societies raise finance and train teachers for many schools. Christianity has had a great impact in Black Africa and the number of Christians is still increasing.

Below: Mosques in Mali are often built from mud which is plastered on to a wooden framework. Poles protruding from the walls make it easy for people to effect repairs. About 65% of the people of Mali are Muslims. Islam is the chief religion of northern Africa.

and Islam, have many followers in Africa. Christianity was introduced into ETHIOPIA in the AD 300s by Byzantine missionaries. It survived in the highlands despite the rise of Islam from the AD 600s. From the early 1800s, European missionaries converted many people in sub-Saharan Africa to Christianity and the number of Christians is still increasing.

Islam spread throughout North Africa, from Arabia, in the AD 600s. Later, many peoples of the savanna lands, south of the Sahara, became Muslims and many groups in the coastal regions of East Africa were also converted by the Arabs.

Many Black Africans, however, still follow traditional, or ethnic, religions. These religions are very varied, but all believe in a creator God or Spirit who, while remote from men, is finally responsible for all that happens to them. Between men and this Spirit are other powers, such as ancestors' ghosts and water or nature spirits that inhabit such things as stone or trees. For example, wood carvers may ask the forgiveness of a tree before cutting off a branch. Sculpture in Africa is often associated with religion and many pieces are carved for use in religious ceremonies rather than as works of art.

Economy
Most people in Africa are poor and the United Nations classifies all African countries, apart from SOUTH AFRICA, as developing nations. This distinguishes them from developed nations, such as those of Western Europe. The gross domestic product (GDP) of a country, which is the total value of all products and services, is an indicator of a nation's wealth. The countries with the

Libya was ruled by Italy from 1912 to 1943 and then by Britain and France until it became an independent monarchy in 1951. It became a republic in 1969. This Muslim nation is mostly desert and the mainly Arab people live on the north-west and north-east coasts. Berbers form about 5% of the population. The chief resource is oil and Libya has Africa's highest per capita gross domestic product. Area: 1,759,540 sq km; population: 2,257,000; capital: TRIPOLI.
Lilongwe has been capital

of MALAWI since 1975. Population: 103,000.
Limpopo, River, rises in SOUTH AFRICA and flows 1,440

Col. Khadafy, Libya

km to its outlet in MOZAMBIQUE.
Lomé is the capital and main seaport of TOGO. Population: 214,000.
Luanda is a major port and capital of ANGOLA. Population: 481,000.
Lusaka, capital of ZAMBIA, is a major commercial centre, being the focus for an important farming region. Population: 401,000.

M Madagascar, formerly the Malagasy Republic, is an island nation, which is about 400 km from the African mainland. The people of

this republic (a French territory until 1960) are mostly of African and Indonesian origin. The largest of the 18 ethnic groups is the Merina. Coffee is the main export of this chiefly agricultural nation. Area: 587,041 sq km; population: 9,303,000; capital: ANTANANARIVO.
Madeira Islands, situated off north-west Africa, form a province of Portugal. Farming and fishing are important. Area: 796 sq km; population: 251,000; capital: Funchal.
Malabo, formerly Santa Isabel, is capital of EQUATO-

RIAL GUINEA. Population: 20,000.
Malawi, formerly the British protectorate of Nyasaland, became independent in 1964, and a republic in 1966. Water covers 20% of this poor but scenic nation. The chief Bantu-speaking peoples include the Tumbuka, Nyanja-Chewa, Yao and Lomwe. Tobacco and tea are the main exports. Area: 118,484 sq km; population: 5,735,000; capital: LILONGWE.
Mali, formerly French Sudan, became an independent republic in 1960. Tuareg nomads live in the

highest GDPs are South Africa, an industrialized country, NIGERIA, a major oil-producer, and EGYPT, a partly industrialized nation.

The average *per capita* GDP is the GDP divided by the population. In Africa, in 1976, the per capita GDP averaged about US$430. This was very low compared with France ($6,550), West Germany ($7,380), and the United States ($7,890). LIBYA, with its small population and valuable oil production, had the highest per capita GDP in 1976, at $6,310. But Libya is not a developed country and most of its people are still farmers. The developed nation of South Africa had a per capita GDP of $1,340. Nigeria, whose

Left: The date palm, the most characteristic plant of North Africa, thrives in hot, dry climates. It has many uses which are shown in the diagram. On the left, the leaves are woven into baskets and also mats, while the stalks are used to make fences and roofs. The flowers are made into brooms and brushes. In the centre, the trunk is a source of timber. It may be used to make furniture, such as stools. Logs are burned as fuel or made into ropes and sacking. The date, a valuable food, hangs from the tree in rich golden clusters, each of which may contain 200 dates. A commercial date palm (*right*) produces about 90 kilos of dates per season. The stones have various uses. They can be ground down to make cattle feed or roasted and used to make date coffee. Some dates are compressed and others are sun-dried. Packed in attractive case, they are exported and sold throughout the world. Some dates are dried and turned into date flour but many, of course, are eaten fresh.

Trunk Fuel Rope Sacking

Fruit

Stems Fences and roofs

Leaves Baskets and mats

Flowers Brushes and brooms

Ground stones (cattle food)

Dateflour

Stones roasted (date coffee)

Fresh

Compressed

Sun-dried

total GDP was second only to that of South Africa, had a much lower per capita GDP of $380, because it is Africa's most populous nation. However, Nigeria's GDP has recently been growing faster than that of other African countries, owing to its oil exports. With its enormous resources and its large population, Nigeria is the potential economic giant of Africa.

By contrast, some nations have extremely low per capita GDPs. For example, RWANDA and UPPER VOLTA had per capita GDPs of only $110, and BURUNDI, CHAD and SOMALIA each had per capita GDPs of about $120 in 1976. One important reason for the poverty of much of Africa is that 74 per cent of the people are farmers, a higher proportion than in any other continent. In some countries, including Burundi, MALAWI, NIGER, Rwanda and TANZANIA, over 90 per cent of the people live by farming. Many farmers live at subsistence level – that is, they

Right: Farmers in southern Ethiopia use primitive wooden instruments to till the soil. Many people in tropical Africa are subsistence farmers. When the rains fail or pests destroy the crops in savanna regions, famines occur which may cause great suffering.

desert north. But most people are Black farmers in the southern, NIGER RIVER region. The largest ethnic group is the Bambara. This poor, land-locked nation exports livestock, but many animals were lost during droughts in the 1970s. Area: ,240,000 sq km; population: 6,451,000; capital: AMAKO.

Maputo, formerly Lourenço Marques, is the capital and a major port of MOZAMBIQUE. Population: 600,000.

Maseru, capital of LESOTHO, has a population of 30,000.

Mauritania, formerly a French territory, became an independent Islamic republic in 1960. 80 per cent of the people are of Arab or Berber descent, while the rest are Black Africans. Iron ore is the main export, but farming and fishing are the chief occupations, although much of the land is desert. In 1976 Mauritania took part of WESTERN SAHARA. But Saharan guerillas have since fought against Mauritania. Area (not including Western Sahara): 1,030,700 sq km; population: 1,481,000; capital: NOUAKCHOTT.

Mauritius, an island monar-

chy east of MADAGASCAR, became independent from Britain in 1968. Indians make up over 60% of the people. Sugar is the main export of this farming nation. Area: 2,045 sq km; population: 942,000; capital: PORT-LOUIS.

Mbabane, capital of SWAZILAND, was founded in 1909. Population: 22,000.

Mogadishu is the capital and a major port of SOMALIA. Population: 350,000.

Mombasa is the main seaport of KENYA. Population: 340,000.

Monrovia, capital of LIBERIA,

was founded as a settlement for freed slaves in 1822. Population: 172,000.

Morocco, a kingdom in

Marrakesh, Morocco

north-west Africa, became independent in 1956. Most people are Muslim Arabs, but 30% are Berbers, who live mainly in the mountains, notably the rugged ATLAS range. Farming is the main occupation, but about 40% of the people live in cities. Phosphates are the chief export. In 1976 Morocco took part of WESTERN SAHARA. Saharan guerillas, supported by Algeria, have fought Moroccan troops. Area (not including Western Sahara): 446,550 sq km; population: 17,828,000; capital: RABAT.

produce only about enough food for their families and so contribute little to the GDP. Africa's chief exports are, in order of value, oil, copper, cotton, coffee, cocoa, iron ore, timber and phosphates. Although minerals are important, farming still accounts for about 60 per cent of Africa's export earnings. Africa's share in world trade is low – in 1976 it accounted for 4.6 per cent of the world's total exports and imports.

Agriculture and forestry

Although farming is the leading sector of Africa's economy, cropland covers only about 7.5 per cent of the continent. About 60 per cent of the land is too arid for any kind of agriculture and most of the rest is dry savanna, which is fit only for grazing.

In many farming areas, the rainfall is erratic and severe droughts often cause crop failure, which leads to famine. In the Sahel (dry savanna) region, south of the Sahara, several devastating years of drought in the late 1960s and early 1970s caused the deaths of millions of livestock. Water supplies dried up, plants died and the pastoralists starved. Pastoralism is a major activity throughout the savanna regions, but African livestock are generally of poor quality and pests and diseases, such as nagana, which is spread by tsetse flies, limit the grazing land. Many Africans assess their wealth by the number, rather than the quality, of the livestock they own. This leads to over-stocking, over-grazing and consequent soil erosion. In the temperate regions in the north and south of the continent, especially on European farms in South Africa, livestock-rearing is generally more scientific and more productive.

The chief food crops in Africa are: wheat in Mediterranean regions; sorghum and millet in the drier parts of the north-west; rice, cassava, sweet potatoes and yams in the rain forests; plantains (cooking bananas) in parts of East Africa; and maize in the south-eastern savanna. By world standards, yields are low and farming methods are often primitive. Many farmers are equipped only with digging sticks, hoes and

Below: Many African farmers are extremely poor and their farming methods have changed little since ancient times. To raise their standards of living, African farmers must learn new methods. Some modern techniques are shown in the picture.

1 Irrigation is necessary in much of Africa, where the rainfall is barely adequate for growing crops and is often unreliable.
2 Fertilizers renew the richness of the soil. In this way, the old method of shifting cultivation can be replaced by modern farming.

3 Storage facilities must be built so that food can be stored in good years to guard against other bad years when the crops fail.

4 Tractors and other modern farm machinery make farming more efficient and the yield per farm-worker can be greatly increased.

5 Weed killers and pesticides are essential items for combating the many problems faced by farmers in tropical Africa.

Moroni is the capital of the COMORO ISLANDS. Population: 12,000.
Mount Kenya, an extinct volcano in KENYA, is Africa's second highest mountain, at 5,199 metres above sea level.
Mount Kilimanjaro, an extinct volcano in TANZANIA, is Africa's highest mountain, at 5,895 metres above sea level.
Mozambique, formerly an overseas province of Portugal, became an independent republic in 1975, after a long guerilla war. The people of this tropical country are mostly Bantu-speaking Black Africans, as most of the Europeans left in 1975. Farming is the main industry and exports include cashew nuts, cotton, sugar, tea and copra. Area: 783,030 sq km; population: 10,343,000; capital: MAPUTO.

N **Nairobi**, capital of KENYA, was founded in 1899 on the Mombasa-Uganda railway line. Population: 700,000.
Namibia (SOUTH-WEST AFRICA) is an arid nation whose main resources are minerals, including diamonds, lead, tin, uranium and zinc. Most people are Black Africans, but about 80,000 Europeans also live there. Germany ruled the area from 1884,

Bushman, Namibia

until SOUTH AFRICA conquered it in 1915. In 1919 the League of Nations mandated South Africa to rule the country. But, in 1946, South Africa refused the trusteeship which replaced the original mandate. Since then, South Africa and the UN have disputed Namibia's government and future. Area: 824,292 sq km; population: 762,000; capital: WINDHOEK.
N'Djamena, formerly Fort Lamy, is capital of CHAD. Population: 193,000.
Niamey, capital of NIGER, has 102,000 people.
Niger, formerly a French territory, became an independent republic in 1960. Groundnuts are the main export of this extremely poor nation. Tuareg nomads live in the desert north. The Hausa, Djerma-Songhai and Fulani are the main groups in the savanna lands in the south. Area: 1,267,000 sq km; population: 5,259,000 capital: NIAMEY.
Niger, River, Africa's third longest river, rises in GUINEA and flows about 4,180 km to its outlet on the Gulf of Guinea, in NIGERIA.
Nigeria is Africa's most populous nation. It ha

When world prices of such crops fall, these countries face severe economic problems.

Africa is a major timber producer, accounting annually for about 14 per cent of the world's roundwood (untreated tree trunks). However, exploitation of valuable hardwoods in the tropical forests is difficult, because the trees are scattered and transport facilities are often poor. Forestry is practised mainly near rivers and logs are floated down to the sea.

Fishing

Sea-fishing is an important industry in several countries, including ANGOLA, NAMIBIA, Senegal and South Africa, and South Africa is a major fish exporter. The production of fish from inland lakes and rivers is less than that from the sea, but it is an extremely important source of protein for the people who live around inland waters.

Mining

Mining is Africa's second most important industry. The most valuable export is crude oil and, in 1977, Africa accounted for 9.9 per cent of world production. The leading oil producers were NIGERIA (35 per cent of Africa's output), LIBYA (33 per cent) and ALGERIA (16 per cent). Algeria and Libya are also important sources of natural gas. The other oil producers are Egypt, GABON, Angola, TUNISIA, CONGO and ZAIRE. The oil-exporting nations received boosts to their economies in the 1970s, when oil prices rose sharply. Much of the revenue derived from oil sales was used to develop and diversify the economies of the fortunate few. However, oil price rises caused severe economic problems for those countries which imported oil.

Above: The Argungu fishing festival is held once a year on a tributary of the River Niger, near Sokoto, in Nigeria. The river contains few fish for most of the year but, on a given date, the 'keeper of the river' says that fish will arrive. As many as 5,000 fishermen catch the Nile perch, which appear in great numbers.

Right: Gold is refined and moulded into ingots in South Africa. South Africa is the world's main gold producer and it is also fortunate in having reserves of many other minerals. Its great resources have helped South Africa to become Africa's leading economic power.

wooden ploughs. The staple foods are also low in proteins which are essential for a healthy diet.

European influence has greatly affected farming techniques in many areas. From the late 1800s, Europeans introduced a cash economy into Africa and developed plantation agriculture to produce cash crops for export. Major cash crops in tropical forest regions include palm products and cocoa. Africa leads in cocoa production, yielding about 70 per cent of the world's total output. Africa also accounts for about 30 per cent of the world's coffee, which is grown on plantations in upland areas. Tea is becoming increasingly important in similar regions. The wetter parts of the savanna are ideal for groundnut and tobacco-growing and cotton flourishes on irrigated land, notably in EGYPT and SUDAN. South Africa, with European technology, produces a wide variety of tropical, Mediterranean and temperate crops. It is particularly famous for its canned fruit exports.

One major problem arises from the over-dependence of certain countries on one or two cash crops for export and, therefore, for foreign earnings. For example, cocoa accounts for over half of GHANA'S exports and SENEGAL relies on groundnuts for 75 per cent of its foreign earnings.

---

bout 250 ethnic groups, including the Hausa and ulani in the savanna lands f the north, and the Igbo bo) and Yoruba in the hot, rested south. Nearly half f the people are Muslims. he rest practise Christianity r traditional religions. Be-ause of its cultural diversi-y, Nigeria is governed as a ederal republic, containing 9 states. Nigeria is noted or its early cultures and art, specially that of Nok, Ife nd Benin. Nigeria became a nited country, under Bri-ain, in 1914. Independence as achieved in 1960.

Nigeria is now Africa's leading oil producer and is developing. But most people still depend on farming. The chief farm exports are cocoa,

Groundnut pyramid, Nigeria

groundnuts, palm oil and kernels, and rubber. Area: 923,768 sq km; population: 72,031,000; capital: LAGOS.

Nile, River, the world's longest river, flows from the East African plateau to the Mediterranean Sea.

Nouakchott is capital of MAURITANIA. Population: 70,000.

Nyasa, Lake, is called Lake Malawi in MALAWI. It is 570 km long and has a maximum width of 80 km.

O Orange, River, in South Africa, rises in the DRAKENSBERG range and flows about 2,180 km to the Atlantic Ocean.

Ouagadougou is the capital of UPPER VOLTA. Population: 169,000.

P Port-Louis is capital and chief port of MAURITIUS. Population: 141,000.

Porto Novo is capital of BENIN. Population: 104,000.

Praia, capital of the CAPE VERDE ISLANDS., has a total population of 6,000.

Pretoria is the administrative capital of SOUTH AFRICA. Population: 562,000.

R Rabat, capital of MOROCCO, was founded on the Atlantic coast in 1160. Population: 368,000.

Réunion is a French island east of MADAGASCAR. Sugar is

Copper is the second most valuable mining commodity. ZAMBIA, Zaire and South Africa are the leading producers. Zambia is especially dependent on copper, which accounts for 90 per cent of its foreign earnings. Fluctuations in world prices for copper have caused economic problems in Zambia in recent times. Zambia and Zaire also lead the world in cobalt production.

Iron ore is mined in LIBERIA, MAURITANIA and South Africa and in smaller amounts in other countries. The development of iron-mining, except in South Africa and Egypt, has been hampered by the lack of resources to process the ore. Phosphates are mined in north-western Africa. The leading producer, MOROCCO, acquired one of the world's largest deposits in 1976 when WESTERN SAHARA was partitioned between Morocco and Mauritania. Morocco took about 60 per cent of Western Sahara to the north, which included massive deposits of phosphates at Bou Craa. GUINEA is Africa's leading bauxite producer and Nigeria and Zaire lead in tin.

South Africa has already been mentioned as a producer of copper and iron ore. But it also possesses Africa's most varied mining industry. It produces over 60 per cent of the world's gold and is a leading producer of gem-quality diamonds, although Zaire has a far greater output of mainly industrial diamonds. South Africa also has most of the continent's coal, and other important minerals include antimony, asbestos, chrome ore, manganese, nickel, platinum, thorium, uranium and vanadium.

Mining still offers great potential for Africa's future. This is because large areas have not yet been fully prospected and some known deposits are in places which are, as yet, inaccessible.

Energy

Apart from the few oil, natural gas and coal producers, Africa is generally short of fossil fuels. Much of the electrical energy is generated at hydro-electric stations at dams and along rivers. It is estimated that Africa has about 40 per cent of the world's hydro-electric potential. Major dams already supplying electrical energy include the Cabora Bassa Dam on the ZAMBEZI in MOZAMBIQUE: the ASWAN HIGH DAM on the NILE in Egypt: the Inga complex on the ZAIRE RIVER: the Kariba Dam on the Zambezi between Zambia and ZIMBABWE-RHODESIA: and the Volta Dam on

Legend (map):
- ▽ Diamonds
- ● Phosphates
- ■ Coal
- ● Uranium
- ▲ Petroleum
- ● Cobalt
- ● Gold
- ● Chrome
- ● Copper
- ✴ Manganese
- ● Tin
- ● Iron Ore
- ● Lead
- ● Nickel
- ○ Bauxite

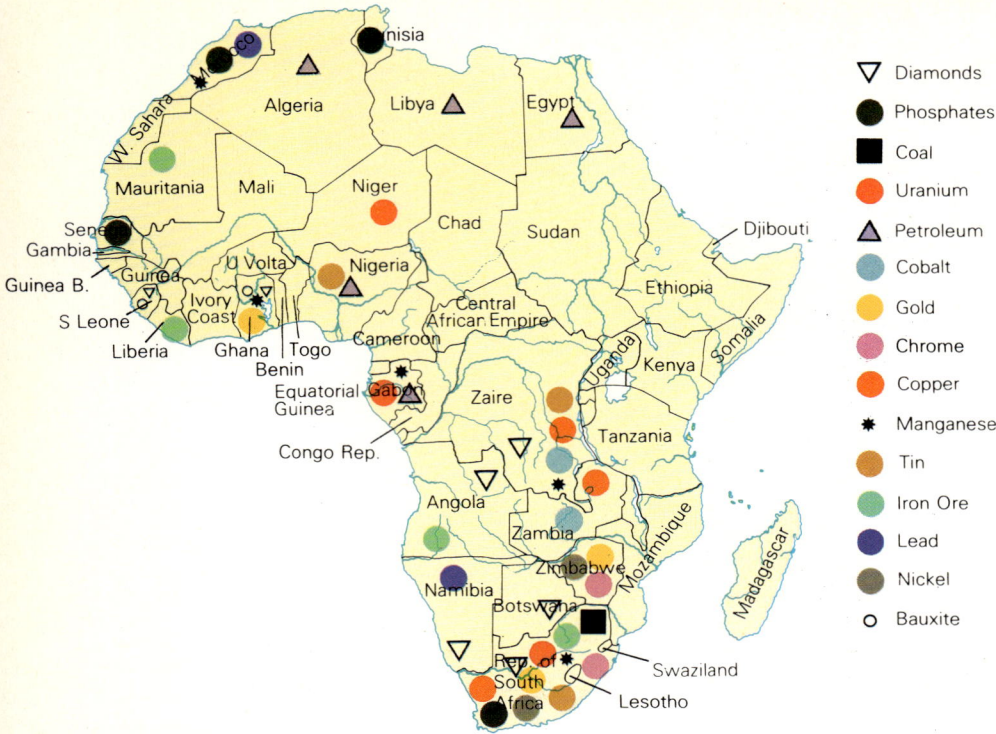

Above: The map shows that Africa is a major source of minerals. Most countries export the bulk of their mineral production, because they lack the industries to process them and use them to make manufactured goods. Problems arise when the prices paid for minerals fall. Price fluctuations can cause economic crises.

Below: The Kariba Dam was built between 1955 and 1960 across the Zambezi, which divides Zambia from Zimbabwe-Rhodesia. The 128-metre-high dam holds back a vast lake. Hydro-electricity produced at Kariba is supplied to both countries. This source of energy is vital in countries which lack fossil fuels.

the chief product and rum is also exported. Area: 2,510 sq km; population: 559,000; capital: St-Denis.

Rhodesia, see ZIMBABWE-RHODESIA.

Rwanda, a remote and densely-populated republic, was part of Belgian Ruanda-Urundi until 1962. Most people are Bantu-speaking Hutus, but about 9% are Hamitic Tutsi pastoralists. Many Tutsi were killed during communal clashes in the 1960s. Rwanda's chief export is coffee. Area: 26,338 sq km; population: 4,753,000; capital: KIGALI.

S Sahara, the world's largest desert, covers about 8.4 million sq km.

Saint Helena is a volcanic British island in the South Atlantic Ocean. Area: 122 sq km; population: 5,000; capital: Jamestown.

Salisbury is capital and commercial centre of ZIMBABWE-RHODESIA. Population: 566,000.

São Tomé is a port and capital of SAO TOME & PRINCIPE. Population: 3,000.

São Tomé and Principe, formerly a Portuguese province, became an independent republic in 1975. The main export of this island nation in the Gulf of Guinea is cocoa. Area: 964 sq km; population: 86,000; capital: SAO TOME.

Senegal, formerly a French territory, became an independent republic in 1960. The largest ethnic group is the Wolof, and Islam is the chief religion. Most people are farmers, and groundnuts and groundnut products dominate the exports. Area: 196,192 sq km; population: 5,115,000; capital: DAKAR.

Seychelles, formerly a British colony, became an independent republic in 1976. It includes about 90 islands in the Indian Ocean, east of

Cotton tree, Freetown, S. Leone

Kenya. The people are of African, Chinese, Creole, French and Indian descent. The chief export is copra. Area: 280 sq km; population: 64,000; capital: VICTORIA (pop. 23,000), Mahé island.

Sierra Leone, formerly a British territory, became independent in 1961. The country became a base for freed slaves in 1787 and the 42,000 Creoles are their descendants. But there are also 18 groups of indigenous Africans, including the Mende and Temne. Most people are farmers or pastoralists. But diamonds, iron ore, bauxite

the Volta River in GHANA. But Africa has the lowest energy consumption per capita of any continent, about 20 per cent of the world's average. And North America consumes more than 30 times as much energy as Africa per head of the population.

Manufacturing

The development of manufacturing, which generally marks the evolution of a developing nation into a developed one, has been hampered by several factors. First, there is a widespread lack of cheap energy resources. Next, most countries lack the capital required to invest in factories and machinery. Third, there is a lack of skilled workers. In most African countries, manufacturing is confined to small-scale processing of local raw materials and the production of consumer goods, such as clothes, beer and soft drinks, shoes, and so on. The development of consumer industries is restricted by the generally small home markets.

SOUTH AFRICA accounts for about 40 per cent of Africa's industrial output, and manufactures most of the continent's steel. In South Africa, manufacturing is now the leading sector of the economy, providing nearly 25 per cent of its GDP. Manufacturing accounts for more than 10 per cent of the GDP in only 14 other African nations. Of these, EGYPT is, at present, the most important. However, some nations, notably NIGERIA, ALGERIA, LIBYA and MOROCCO, have fast-developing manufacturing industries.

Transport and communications

Until the 1900s, shipping provided all coastal transport, while interior travel was arduous. Explorers and traders moved mostly on foot, with pack animals and porters to carry baggage and commodities. Sometimes, they sailed on inland waterways, but many African rivers are interrupted by rapids and waterfalls.

In the late 1800s, the railway age began. The first railways were built in the far north and south and, from the early 1900s, they were constructed in the tropics. The railways encouraged European settlement, because they enabled settlers to get their produce to the coasts. Towns on the railways became major trading centres.

Today, Africa has about 72,000 kilometres of railways. The railways of South Africa and Zimbabwe-Rhodesia, totalling about 16,000 kilometres, handle the most freight. Inland waterways, however, have mostly declined in importance. Air transport is now used to carry passengers and high-value commodities quickly over long distances. Light aircraft provide medical and other services to isolated areas.

From the 1920s, a massive road network was developed throughout Africa. Road haulage is now the chief form of transport in many areas. Most main roads remain open in all weathers, but many local dirt roads dissolve into mud after heavy rains.

The isolation of remote peoples has also been reduced by the expansion of communications, including telephones, telegraph services, and so

Below: The *Uhuru* (freedom), or Tanzam, railway, linking Tanzania and Zambia, was opened in 1975. It enabled Zambia to export goods through a friendly nation.

Left: Human porterage was the chief form of transport in Africa until recently, and it remains important in rural areas where foods and other goods, such as pots, are carried long distances to local markets. However, Africa's economy now depends on faster means of transport.

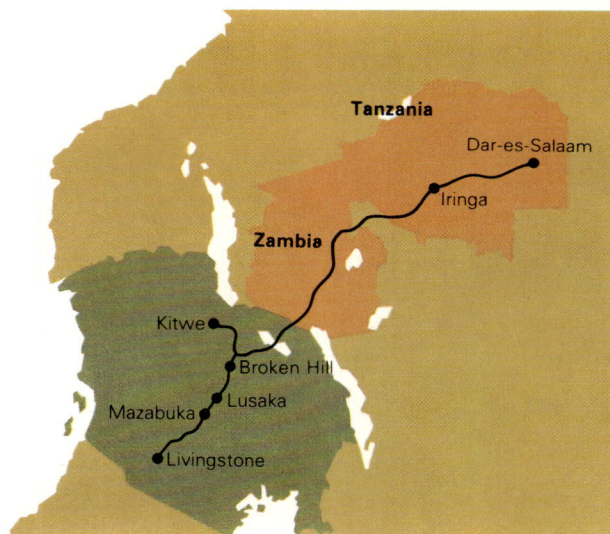

Right: The map shows that the *Uhuru* railway from Dar es Salaam to the Zambian copper belt, will open up formerly remote regions in both nations.

---

and rutile dominate the exports. Area: 71,740 sq km; population: 3,556,000; capital: FREETOWN.

Somali people

Somalia, officially the Somali Democratic Republic, became independent in 1960 when the former British Somaliland united with Italian Somaliland. The land is largely arid and most people are nomadic pastoralists. Livestock and animal products form about 65% of the exports. The Muslim Somalis would like to unite with other Somalis who live in ETHIOPIA, DJIBOUTI and KENYA. Area: 637,657 sq km; population: 3,614,000; capital: MOGADISHU.

South Africa is Africa's most developed nation. Its population is mixed. Europeans, who speak either Afrikaans or English, form 17.5% of the population.

They control South Africa's government and economy. Black Africans form 70.2%. They include the Zulus and Xhosas. Coloureds (of mixed origin) form 9.4% and Asians, 2.9%. Government policy is aimed at developing the cultures of each group separately. BANTUSTANS have been set up for the Black Africans, although over 50% of them live and work in European areas. The most valuable part of the economy is manufacturing, especially in the Witwatersrand (including JOHANNESBURG) and in CAPE TOWN,

DURBAN and Port Elizabeth. South Africa's mines produce gold, diamonds, coal, copper, iron ore, uranium and many other minerals. European farming is highly efficient, but most Black African farmers live at subsistence level. The Union of South Africa was formed in 1910. South Africa became a republic in 1961. Area: 1,221,037 sq km; population: 28,870,000; capitals: CAPE TOWN; PRETORIA.

South-West Africa was renamed NAMIBIA by the UN in 1968.

Sudan, Africa's largest

on. Radio has had, perhaps, the greatest social impact. In most parts of Africa, people can hear news, educational and entertainment broadcasts. For example, Nigeria had a listening audience of 30 millions in 1969. Television is enjoyed by comparatively few at present, but is proving useful in education.

Modern Africa

In 1945 thousands of African troops who had served in European armies returned home. Many of these ex-servicemen were no longer content to live and work as second-class citizens in foreign-ruled colonies. News from Asia, particularly the independence of British India in 1947, further encouraged nationalist movements to grow throughout the continent.

In the early 1950s, several important events occurred. First, in 1951, LIBYA became the fifth independent nation in Africa and, in 1952, Colonel Gamal Abdel Nasser (1918-70) came to power in EGYPT. He made Cairo a centre of anti-colonialism. In the same year, an armed rebellion, organized by a secret society named

Right: The 10 homelands, or Bantustans, of South Africa, shown on the map, are regions for Black African settlement. Their combined area represents 13% of the total area of South Africa. The homelands are fragmented and most people are poor farmers. Transkei and Bophuthatswana were made independent in 1976 and 1977 respectively and, eventually, South Africa plans to make the others independent. Only South Africa recognizes their independence. The UN believes that they rely too much on South Africa and cannot be considered truly independent.

Below: The University of Nairobi in Kenya was once a college within the University of East Africa, but it became an independent university in 1970. African universities now provide the higher education that was available only overseas.

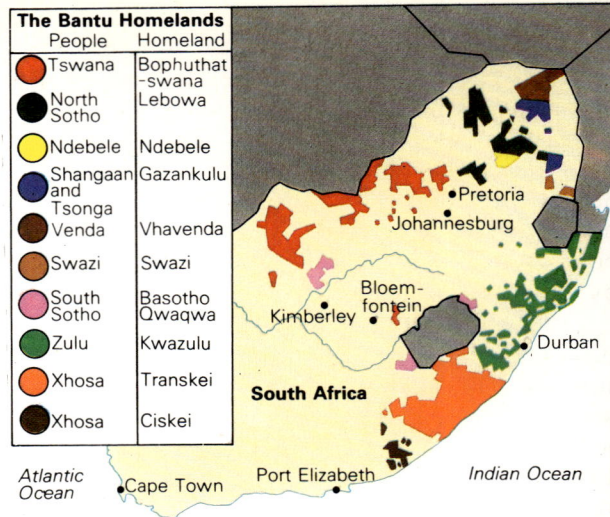

The Bantu Homelands

People	Homeland
Tswana	Bophuthat-swana
North Sotho	Lebowa
Ndebele	Ndebele
Shangaan and Tsonga	Gazankulu
Venda	Vhavenda
Swazi	Swazi
South Sotho	Basotho Qwaqwa
Zulu	Kwazulu
Xhosa	Transkei
Xhosa	Ciskei

South Africa

Atlantic Ocean · Cape Town · Port Elizabeth · Indian Ocean

Mau Mau, broke out in KENYA. Mounting nationalism, together with the possibility of facing long and costly colonial wars, changed the attitudes of many people in Europe, especially as Europeans had their own problems of post-war reconstruction.

In 1956 three North African countries, SUDAN, MOROCCO and TUNISIA, became independent and, in 1957, GHANA became the first Black African country to achieve independence. Between 1957 and 1978, nearly all African nations won their independence, some by peaceful means and others after long guerilla wars. Independence, however, was only a beginning and many countries faced profound problems.

Problems of independent Africa

In 1960 the Belgian Congo (now ZAIRE) became independent. Almost immediately, law and order broke down as the army mutinied for more pay and as a protest against the fact that Belgian officers were still in command. At the same time, the people of the mineral-rich Katanga (now Shaba) province attempted to secede and establish their own country. The United Nations sent in a force to restore order, and this was finally achieved in 1964, although further revolts occurred in 1966, 1967 and 1977. Zaire is about 60 per cent of the size of Western Europe. It contains about 200 ethnic and language groups and exemplifies the problems of many African nations. In an attempt to establish national unity, Zaire became a one-party state in 1970.

---

country, became an independent republic in 1956. Desert covers the north and centre, but the south is wetter. The Arab and other peoples of the north and centre are Muslims, but the mainly Negroid peoples of the south practise Christianity or traditional religions. Cultural differences led to a civil war (1964-72). Cotton is the chief product. Area: 2,505,813 sq km; population: 16,126,000; capital: KHARTOUM.

Suez Canal, in EGYPT, links the Red and Mediterranean seas. It is 162 km long.

Swaziland, formerly a British protectorate, became an independent kingdom in 1968. The economy of this scenic, land-locked nation is based on farming, but there is also some mining. Area: 17,363 sq km; population: 568,000; capital: MBABANE.

Tanganyika, Lake, between BURUNDI, TANZANIA, ZAIRE and ZAMBIA, is the world's longest freshwater lake. It has an area of 32,890 sq km.

Tanzania consists of the former British territories of Tanganyika and Zanzibar.

Tanganyika became independent in 1961 and Zanzibar in 1963. They formed the United Republic of Tan-

zania in 1964. This farming nation produces coffee, cotton, sisal and other crops. There are 125 Bantu-

Eland farm, Tanzania

speaking groups, and Arab, Asian and European minorities. Area: 945,087 sq km; population: 17,362,000; capital: DAR ES SALAAM.

Togo, formerly a French territory, became an independent republic in 1960. The people of this poor nation are divided into about 30 ethnic groups, including the Ewe and Cabrais. Most people are farmers and cocoa and coffee make up half of the exports. Phosphates are also important. Area: 56,000 sq km; population: 2,530,000; capital: LOME.

Various other countries, including TANZANIA and ZAMBIA, have also become one-party states, because their governments believed that multi- or two-party systems of democratic government, along European lines, were not appropriate for these countries with their diverse populations. Several countries have been taken over by military groups, some of which have been fairly benevolent, while others have maintained power by brutal and dictatorial means.

Civil wars, caused by ethnic, language, cultural and religious differences, have caused much suffering and loss of life in some places. In NIGERIA, the Igbos of the south-east tried to secede and establish their own country, Biafra, in 1967, but they were finally defeated in 1970. In SUDAN, the Nilotic, Nilo-Hamitic and Sudanic peoples of the south fought against the Muslim northerners, a mixture of Arabs, Hamitic and Negroid peoples, between 1964 and 1972. A similar cultural division between northerners and southerners bedevilled the development of CHAD in the 1970s.

Some African nations have been in conflict because of boundary problems. Many frontiers drawn by Europeans divided ethnic groups between two or more countries. For example, the lands occupied by the Somalis in the Horn of Africa were divided between Italy, Britain, France, Ethiopia and Kenya. Italian Somaliland and British Somaliland were united as SOMALIA in 1960. But Somalia has long desired to reunify its people and, in 1977–8, it supported an unsuccessful uprising of Ethiopian Somalis against the Ethiopian government.

Southern Africa

Problems of a different kind have disturbed southern Africa. In 1965 Rhodesia (now ZIMBABWE-RHODESIA), a British colony, declared itself independent. But its government was controlled by Europeans, who formed only four per cent of the population. Britain refused to accept the independence of this country until it had a government which was representative of the majority. International economic sanctions were applied against Rhodesia, but its defiance was, initially, successful. However, with the independence in 1975 of two formerly friendly nations, the Portuguese territories of Angola and Mozambique, Rhodesia's position was

Above: The Parliament buildings in Gaborone were built when it was decided to make this formerly small market town in Botswana the country's capital. Gaborone officially became the capital in 1965.

Below: The struggle for independence in Angola, as in the other Portuguese territories of Mozambique and Portuguese Guinea (now Guinea-Bissau) was preceded by a guerrilla war. These costly wars became unpopular in Portugal and were a major factor in causing a coup to take place in Portugal in 1974. One of the first aims of the new government was to arrange a rapid hand-over of power in Africa.

---

ranskei, see BANTUSTANS.

ripoli, capital of LIBYA, is lso the chief port. Population: 735,000.

unis, capital and main port f TUNISIA, stands near the uins of the ancient city of arthage. Population: 44,000.

unisia, formerly a French rritory, became an independent republic in 1956. lost people are Muslim rabs but Berbers live in the uth. The northern ATLAS gion has the most rainfall d the south is largely esert. Farming is the main ccupation, but the chief ex-ports are minerals, particularly oil and phosphates. Tourism is an important source of revenue. Area: 163,610 sq km; population: 5,737,000; capital: TUNIS.

Coffee nursery, Uganda

U Uganda, a former British territory, became independent in 1962 and a republic in 1967. An army group, under Gen. Idi Amin, ruled from 1971 to 1979. This land-locked nation depends on farming, and coffee and cotton are the main exports. Water covers about 15% of Uganda. There are 40 ethnic groups, the largest being the Baganda. Area: 236,036 sq km; population: 13,599,000; capital: KAMPALA.

United Republic of Tanzania, see TANZANIA.

Upper Volta, formerly a French territory, became an independent republic in 1960. The largest of the various Black African groups is the Mossi. Most people in this poor, land-locked nation are subsistence farmers. Livestock and meat are exported. Area: 274,200 sq km; population: 6,762,000; capital: OUAGADOUGOU.

V Victoria Falls, on the ZAMBEZI RIVER, are 108 metres high and are divided into 3 main sections.

Victoria, Lake, is Africa's largest lake. It has an area of 69,485 sq km, in parts of KENYA, TANZANIA and UGANDA.

W Walvis Bay is the chief seaport of NAMIBIA. It is in a small enclave which, historically, belongs to Cape Province, SOUTH AFRICA.

Western Sahara was known as Spanish Sahara until 1976, when Spain withdrew and it was partitioned between MOROCCO (taking the northern part) and MAURITANIA (the southern part). The chief resource of this desert area is the phosphate deposit at Bou Craa in the north. However, nationalists, supported by Algeria, attacked Moroccan and Mauritanian troops.

weakened. The government then sought an internal, majority-rule settlement.

SOUTH AFRICA, which helped the break-away Rhodesian regime, has special problems of its own. There, the Europeans, who first settled in South Africa in 1652, account for 17.5 per cent of the population. The others are Black Africans (70.2 per cent), Asians (2.9 per cent) and Coloureds, of mixed racial origin (9.4 per cent). The Europeans are divided into two main groups. Afrikaners form 60 per cent of the total. They are the descendants of the original Dutch settlers and they have their own language, Afrikaans. Most of the other Europeans are descendants of English-speaking British settlers. These two groups, once in conflict with each other, are now trying to maintain their own culture and to retain their control of the government and the economy. The South African government has applied a policy, called

Below: The map shows the political changes in Africa since 1951. At the start of 1951, only 4 African countries were independent, while the rest were ruled by European powers. By 1979, African countries occupied 33% of the seats in the UN General Assembly.

Above: Somalis celebrated their independence in 1960 when the former Italian and British Somalilands united to form the Somali Republic.

separate development, or apartheid, by which the Black African population has been allocated homelands which, together, form about 13 per cent of the country. In these homelands, or BANTUSTANS, the Black Africans are supposed to preserve and develop their own culture. However, more than 50 per cent of the Black Africans live and work in European areas, where they have no rights. Also the homelands have much poor land and are therefore financially dependent on South Africa. This policy has caused internal unrest and been condemned by the UN.

The way ahead

While some countries have suffered great upheavals since independence, there are others where steady progress has been made. Some countries, such as IVORY COAST and KENYA, have remained stable despite their ethnic and language diversity by following free enterprise policies. Others, such as GUINEA and TANZANIA, have favoured socialism. Whatever their ideologies, African governments have all had to shape their policies to make them relevant to African realities and traditions, which differ from those in other parts of the world. By seeking African solutions to African problems, new ideas have been thrown up and Africa has been evolving a distinctive voice which is increasingly heard in world councils.

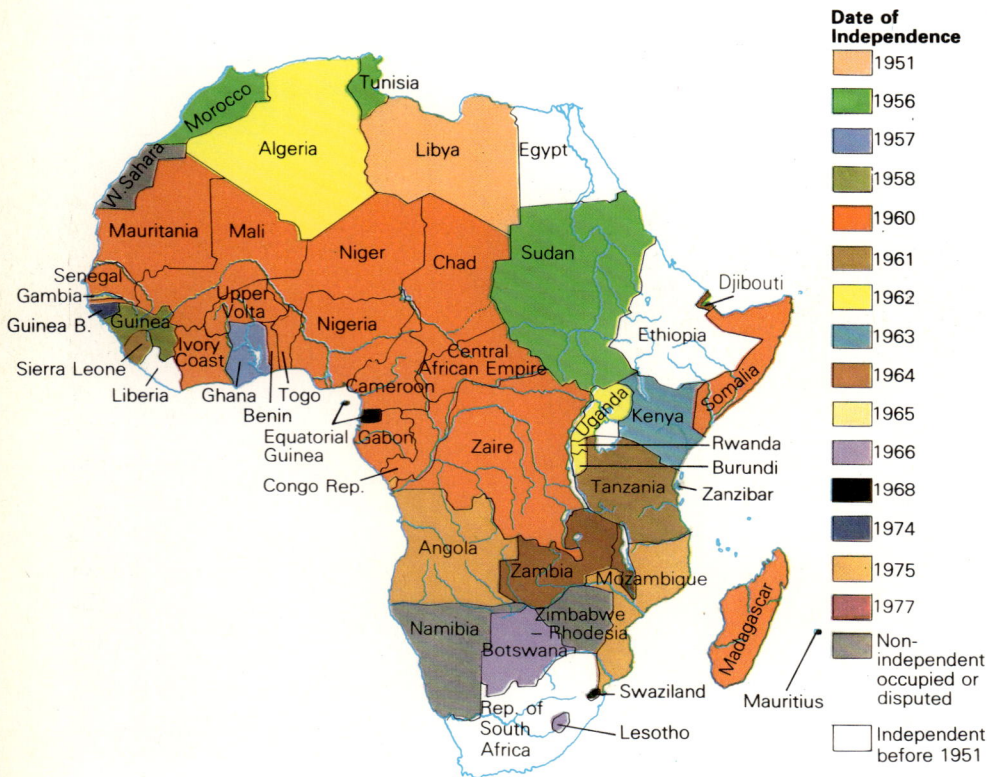

Date of Independence

	1951
	1956
	1957
	1958
	1960
	1961
	1962
	1963
	1964
	1965
	1966
	1968
	1974
	1975
	1977
	Non-independent occupied or disputed
	Independent before 1951

Area: 266,000 sq km; population: 180,000.
Windhoek, the capital of NAMIBIA, was founded in 1890. Population: 61,000.

Y Yaoundé is a commercial centre and capital of CAMEROON. Population: 274,000.

Z Zaire, formerly the Belgian Congo, became an independent republic in 1960. Army mutinies, communal strife and the attempted secession of the mineral-rich Katanga (now Shaba) province caused a breakdown of order which was restored by the UN by 1964. Zaire, Africa's second largest nation, contains about 200 ethnic groups. Most people are subsistence farmers, but copper is the main export. Area: 2,345,409 sq km; population: 28,622,000; capital: KINSHASA.
Zaire, River, formerly the Congo and Africa's second longest river, is 4,670 km.
Zambezi, River, Africa's fourth longest river, rises in north-west ZAMBIA and flows 2,620 km eastwards to its outlet in MOZAMBIQUE.

Zambia, formerly British Northern Rhodesia, became an independent republic in 1964. It contains over 70 groups of people, most of whom speak Bantu languages or dialects. Farming is the chief occupation, but copper dominates the exports. Area: 752,614 sq km; population: 5,896,000; capital: LUSAKA.
Zanzibar was a British island protectorate until 1963. In 1964 it united with Tanganyika to form TANZANIA.
Zimbabwe-Rhodesia is the name Rhodesia has adopted following independence. About 95% of the people are Bantu-speaking Africans. Europeans make up 4%. From 1923 the country was

Radio factory, Zimbabwe

the self-governing British colony of Southern Rhodesia. In 1965 the European government made a unilateral declaration of independence (UDI). This was denounced by Britain as an illegal act. Guerilla warfare began in the 1970s and the principle of majority rule was conceded by the government in 1977. In 1979 some African parties joined the government, but fighting continued. Area: 390,580 sq km; population: 7,493,000; capital: SALISBURY.

Oceania, the smallest continent, contains two young nations, Australia and New Zealand. Both are lands of opportunity, which contrast with the beautiful but far less developed Pacific islands to the north and west.

Oceania

Oceania contains some of the world's most varied cultures and landscapes. Here, in the vast Pacific Ocean, is the huge island continent of Australia, which in 200 years has become one of the world's major suppliers of food and raw materials. It contains PAPUA NEW GUINEA, part of New Guinea, the world's second largest island, where some Stone Age tribes have never been visited but glimpsed from the air. Here also are some 10,000 coral islands, many of whose people

Below: Sandstone outcrops known as the Olgas look across the desert interior of Australia to one of the continent's major Aboriginal shrines—Ayers Rock. Jutting from the vast and arid plain, the rock glows vivid orange at sunrise and sunset. There are many very old Aboriginal rock paintings here. Today, Ayers Rock is a major tourist attraction.

have customs, languages and art forms quite different from their neighbours. Oceania had probably not been visited by man earlier than 30,000 years ago. The first settlers possibly came by boat from Asia, travelling south through the islands, and eventually reached Australia and NEW ZEALAND, where their descendants, the Aboriginals and Maoris, still live. Europeans began to explore the region in the 1600s and 1700s. While earlier peoples had accepted the vastness of Oceania and adapted themselves to live in harmony with its nature, the Europeans set about changing the environment, mining its minerals and introducing Western farming methods.

One result was to make Oceania the most ethnically mixed region of the world: more Indians live in FIJI than native Fijians; Greek language papers are published in Melbourne; and American-style policemen of Chinese origins work in HAWAII. While the Maoris of New Zealand retain some of their own farms, many

Above: Society Islanders make ready for an outrigger canoe race. Remote in their huge ocean, Polynesian islands such as these are only now beginning to become tourist playgrounds.

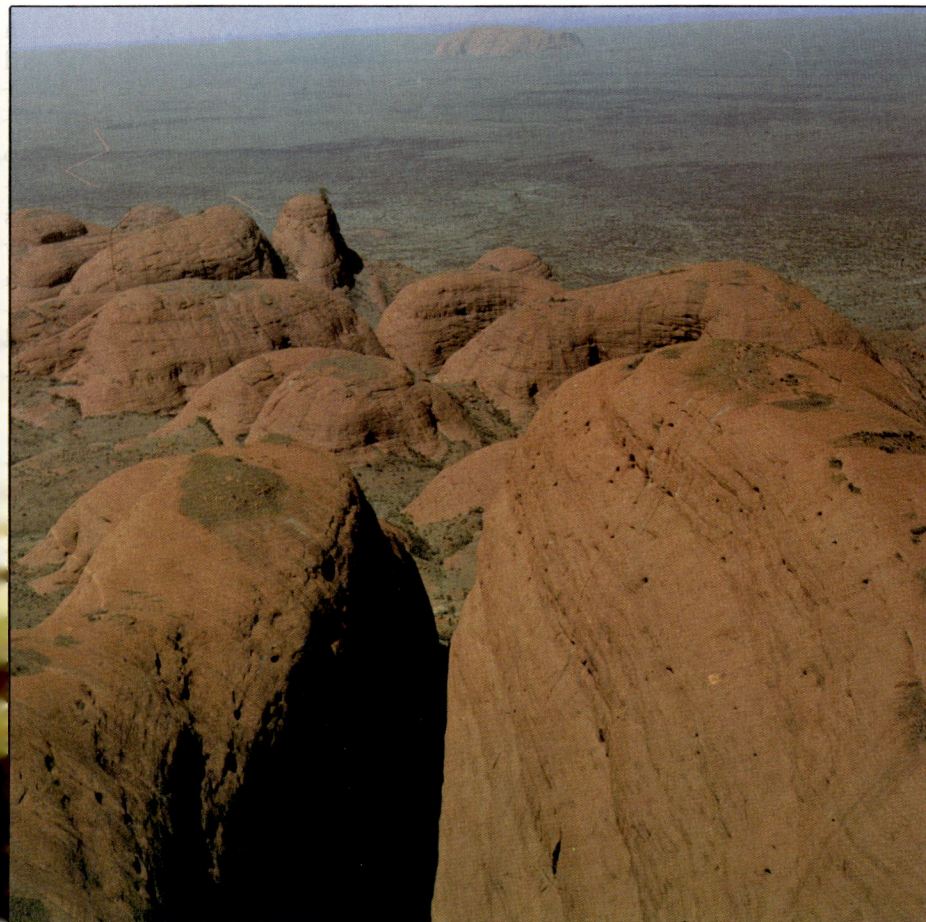

Reference

A **Aboriginal** is a name given to peoples who came to Australia some 30,000 years ago from the north. Skilled hunters with boomerang, spear and noose, they spread across the land in small clans. Their stories, songs, dances and paintings on rock and bark tell of the Dreamtime of their ancestors. The first white settlers hunted them for sport and killed all in Tasmania. Today, Aboriginals

Painted Aboriginal

have full rights as citizens and few live as nomads. But their rights to own mineral resources on lands reserved for them are still argued.

Adelaide, capital of South Australia is a fast-growing industrial centre and port. It

is a lively, international city whose suburbs spread 64 km across the Adelaide Plains. Skyscrapers of the inner city stand on the grid of broad streets laid down by Colonel William Light in 1836. The population is 809,000. A world famous Festival is held every two years.

Alice Springs is a remote township in the centre of Australia. Made famous by Nevil Shute's novel *A Town Like Alice* it is now a popular tourist destination. Population: 11,000.

Arnhem Land is a major

Aboriginal reserve in the Northern Territory where many sacred sites and paintings survive. The dense jungle mangrove swamps and rugged tableland remain little explored.

Auckland is NEW ZEALAND's largest port, second largest city and a focus for road, rail and air links. Sited on Waitemata harbour in NORTH ISLAND, Auckland has national museums and is home to New Zealand's largest Maori community.

Australian Alps in southeast Australia are the watershed between the Murray

and Snowy rivers and include Australia's largest national park, Kosciusko, 5,376 sq km.

Australian Capital Territory is 2,332 sq km of New South Wales set aside in 1909 as the region in which CANBERRA, the national capital would be built. 50% of the region is forested. It was agreed that the capital should not stand on the land of any existing state lest that state had undue advantage in national affairs as a result.

Ayers Rock is a sandstone outcrop 333 metres high in a vast plain in Australia's

Aboriginal people have been displaced. This has frequently been by force of arms. British settlers in TASMANIA deliberately wiped out the existing Aboriginal population, hunting them with dogs for sport. During World War II, the peaceful palm-fringed coral atolls were the scene of bitter fighting between the United States and Japanese armies. It seems likely that future developments in the area will bring an increasing sense of identity to its many lands. The nations of the West are giving up their claims to the islands of Oceania, and several have begun life as independent communities. Australia and New Zealand are loosening ties with Britain, creating their own life-styles and position in world affairs.

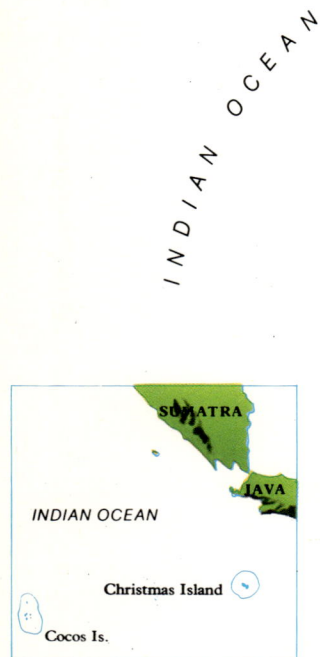

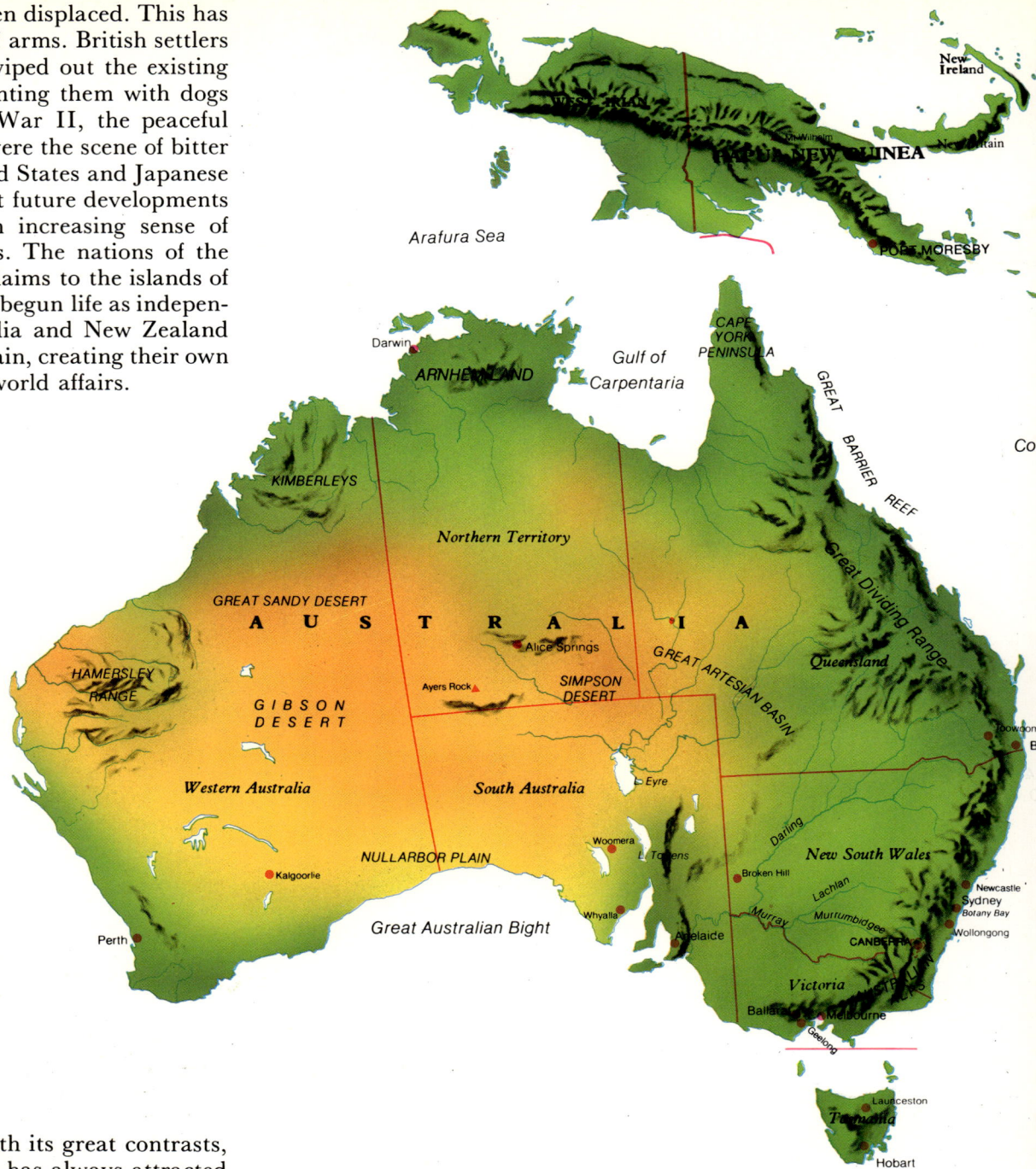

The area as a whole, with its great contrasts, beauties and opportunities has always attracted those in search of a new life. From the days of the first castaways and beachcombers, through the hectic times of the gold rushes to the present day, people from other countries all over the world have emigrated to settle anew in Australia or New Zealand.

Northern Territory. Cave dwelling Aboriginals painted mythical figures on the walls of their homes. At dawn and dusk the rock glows bright orange.

B Ballarat is the most important inland city of Victoria, a market for a fertile farming region and a sale-yard for cattle. An 1851 gold rush brought some 40,000 prospectors here – Chinese, British and Americans among them. One nugget found weighed 63 kg. In 1854 miners rebelled against licence laws, in the Eureka Stockade incident. Government troops quelled them but they won reforms. Population: 38,910.

Barossa Valley, in South Australia, is the country's

Ballarat, Eureka monument

most famous wine growing region. German settlers put the first vines here in 1847 and German family names still survive.

Blue Mountains cover 1,400 sq km of New South Wales. They are named from the blue haze which often forms, a result of droplets of eucalyptus tree oil in the air. The City of the Blue Mountains, formed in 1947, is one of the world's largest urban areas. It is made up of 24 towns, spread through the mountains.

Botany Bay was where Europeans first landed on Australia's east coast, on 29 April 1770. A naturalist in Captain Cook's party gave it the name because of the many wild flowers on shore. Now it is a developing commercial area 11 km north of Sydney.

Brisbane, capital of Queensland, is Australia's largest river port, 32 km from the coast on both sides of the Brisbane River. It handles some 70% of Queensland's trade. Brightly coloured shrubs in 4,000 sq km of parkland grace the city, whose commercial centre is dominated by

tower blocks and City Hall Brisbane began as a convict settlement called Moreton Bay. It was named then after Sir Thomas Brisbane (1773–1860), a governor of New South Wales. Badly flooded in 1973, the city thrived again. Population: 986,000.

British Solomon Islands are an island chain covering 28,446 sq km in the South West Pacific. Melanesian peoples live here on low coral atolls and rugged volcanic isles. The capital is Honiara. The population is 191,000.

Broken Hill is the world's

Ocean Is.

Kiribati (Gilbert Is.)

Howland Is.

Mariana Is.

Wake Is.

Guam

Marshall Is.

Solomon Is.

Caroline Is.

Phoenix Is.

MICRONESIA

Tuvalu (Ellice Is.)

MELANESIA

New Hebrides

Tokelau Is.

Western Samoa

FIJI   SUVA

New Caledonia

Noumea

TONGA

PACIFIC OCEAN

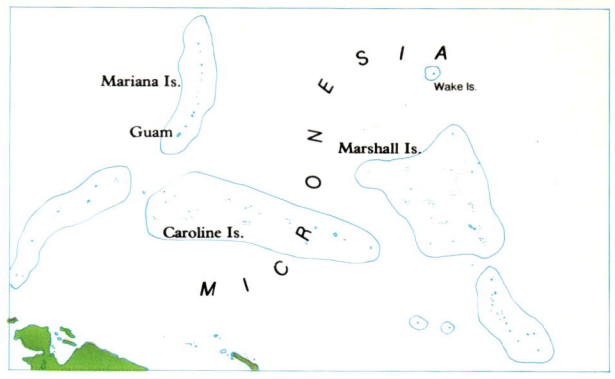

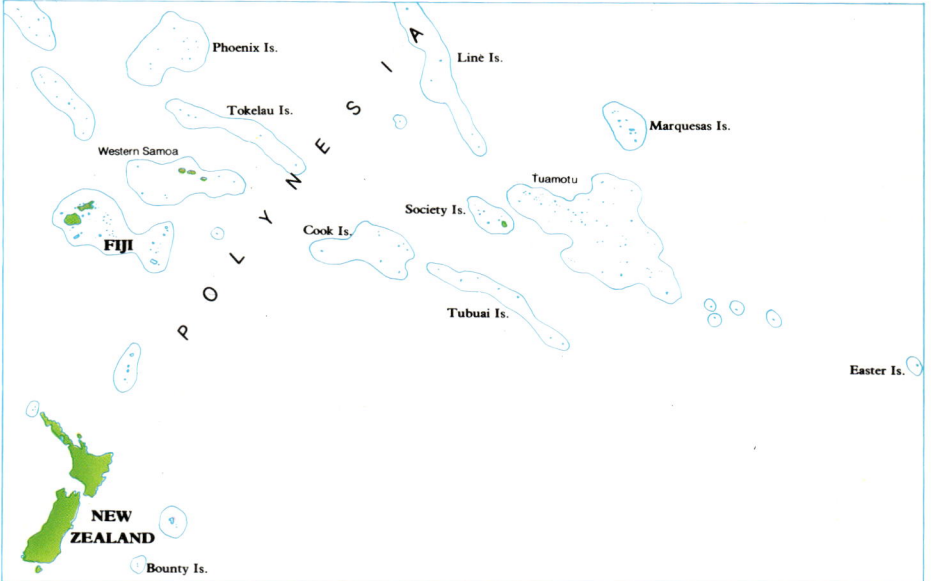

Below: Alice Springs in Central Australia has a desert climate with very little rainfall, while Sydney on the coast, although still hot in January, has more rain.

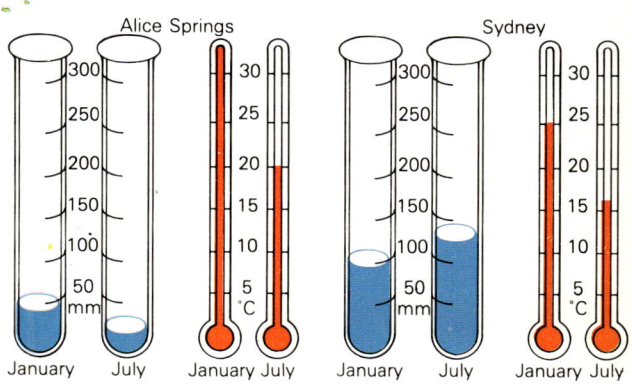

Alice Springs

Sydney

300		30		300		30
250		25		250		25
200		20		200		20
150		15		150		15
100		10		100		10
50 mm		5 °C		50 mm		5 °C

January July   January July   January July   January July

NEW ZEALAND

Auckland

NORTH ISLAND

Hamilton

Rotorua

WELLINGTON

SOUTH ISLAND

Christchurch

SOUTHERN ALPS

Dunedin

Stewart Is.

Invercargill

Chatham Is.

Bounty Is.

Auckland Is.

Phoenix Is.

Line Is.

Tokelau Is.

POLYNESIA

Marquesas Is.

Western Samoa

Tuamotu

Society Is.

FIJI

Cook Is.

Tubuai Is.

Easter Is.

NEW ZEALAND

Bounty Is.

---

richest store of silver, lead and zinc. Prospectors in this part of New South Wales gave colourful names to towns they founded in the 1880s, among them, 'Terrible Dick' and 'Maggie's Secret'. Broken Hill, still known as 'the Silver City', is a base for Australia's largest business organization, Broken Hill Proprietary.

C Canberra is Australia's federal capital, a city of wide parades and avenues designed by American architect Walter Burley Griffin (1876–1937) and built this century in the AUSTRALIAN CAPITAL TERRITORY. Triangular in its design, Canberra is the setting for national occasions. More than 50% of the working population is based in government offices. The National University, Parliament House, and the broad dome of the Academy of Science are among the many fine buildings. Diplomats from the world's embassies enjoy free trout fishing in a huge artificial lake; over 50% of the city area is open space or parkland. The population is 160,000.
Caroline Islands in the

West Pacific cover 1,050 sq km and are part of the UN Trust Territory of the Pacific Islands. Many nations have fought to own these islands, especially the Japanese in World War II. The capital is Saipan. The population is 60,000.
Christchurch, New Zealand, is New Zealand's largest administrative city and second most important industrial centre. Sited on the east of South Island's Canterbury Plains, it is known as the 'Garden City of the Plains'. Rail and road tunnels link it to its port at

Lyttelton, 11 km to the south-east. The population is 320,530.
Cocos Islands are a group of coral islands in the Indian Ocean covering 1,359 km and forming an Australian external territory. From 1827, the Clunies Ross family dominated the islands and the copra plantations worked by Malays.
Coober Pedy, an opal mining community in South Australia, has attracted adventurers since 1915. Its church and many homes are carved underground, to avoid fierce surface heat.

D Darling River is Australia's longest, flowing 2,720 km from the Great Dividing Range to the Murray River. But much of the year it exists only as isolated water holes.
Darwin is the capital of Australia's Northern Territory.

Cocos Islands

Land, climate and vegetation

Australia is the world's flattest, most low lying and (except for Antarctica) least forested continent, with some of the world's oldest rocks. Long separated from other land masses, its flora and fauna include many found nowhere else – among them the best known are the marsupials, or pouched animals.

Ranging from the tropical swamps and forests of the far north, to the apple orchards far south in Tasmania, Australia spans many climatic zones. Its interior is a vast brown desert of scrub or pebble-strewn waste which may flower dramatically after rare but torrential rains. Over 60 per cent of Australia is too dry for farming and only two per cent of it can raise crops. Even so, Australia, with some 150 million sheep, 30 million cattle and huge wheatlands, has in 200 years become one of the world's greatest food suppliers. Some four in ten of Australia's cattle roam huge 'properties' of the far north during the 'Wet' or the months of November to March. At the beginning of the 'Dry' they are mustered, most being destined for hamburger stalls in the United States or Japanese dinner tables.

Further south, sugar cane, bananas, and pineapples flourish in Queensland's long, tropical, rainy season. South of Queensland the

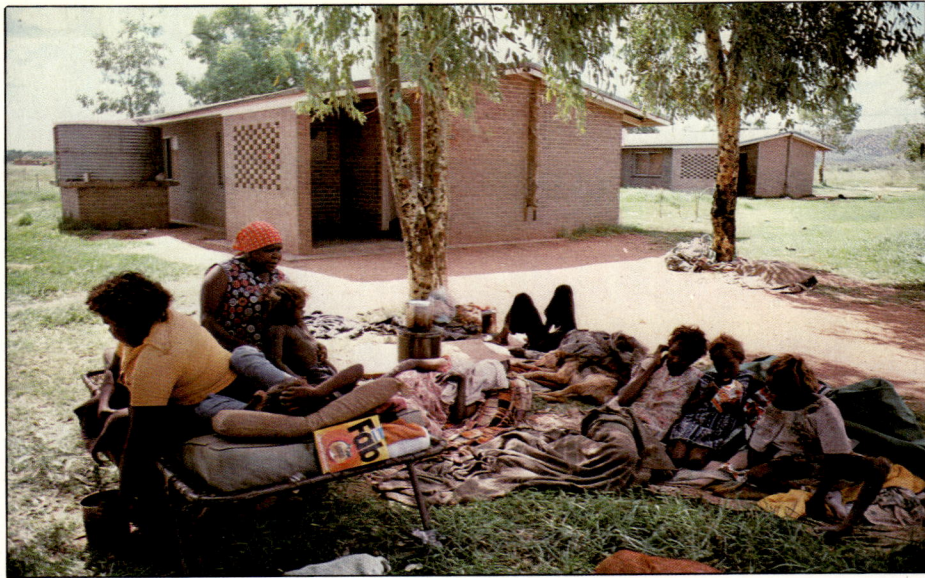

Above: State education and modern settlement are available to today's Aboriginals. But for many the jump to Western lifestyles is not an easy one.
Below: Aboriginals perform a spear dance in an ancient ritual. Dance, body painting and story-telling are key art forms.

climate is more temperate, so that sheep and wheat are raised in plains that stretch to the south-east and west. 50% of Australia's cropland is devoted to wheat, while the sheep are mainly the silky haired Merinos, first bred in Spain and yielding 75 per cent of Australia's wool. On the eastern hills of the south, beef cattle thrive better than sheep. The temperate south also raises traditional European crops: fine wines are made in the BAROSSA VALLEY, and the best hops for Australian beer are grown in TASMANIA.

NEW ZEALAND is composed of NORTH ISLAND and SOUTH ISLAND and some smaller islands. It lies 1,600 kilometres from Australia, far south in the Pacific Ocean. High mountains form the backbone of both islands. In the South Island mountains rise well above the snow line. Mount Cook, the highest peak, reaches over 4,000 metres. This glaciated landscape of snowfields, lakes and fiords in the west leads down to alluvial plains in the east. The North Island landscape includes fold mountains, volcanoes, hot springs and geysers, while the coastal and valley lowlands contain most of New Zealand's rich agricultural land. The climate is temperate, with prevailing west winds. About 15 per cent of New Zealand is forested and owing to the country's isolation, certain plant species have developed in a way not found elsewhere. Tree-ferns for example, grow up to 16 metres high in the dense evergreen forest.

Built on a fine harbour, 3,200 km from other centres, Darwin is known as Australia's 'front door'. Only one road, called 'the Bitumen' links it southwards. On Christmas Day 1974, Cyclone Tracy devastated Darwin, where many homes were built on stilts. The population is 41,000.
Dunedin, far south on the east coast of New Zealand's South Island, is the nation's fourth largest city and a deep water port.

E Easter Island is dominated by some 600 huge

stone figures raised about 1,500 years ago. Set in the Pacific 3,860 km from South America, the population is 1,000 and the capital is Hangaroa.

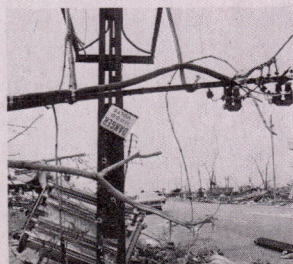
Cyclone damage, Darwin

F Fiji is an independent dominion in the Commonwealth of Nations and consists of some 840 islands extending to 18,274 sq km in all. The capital, Suva, is on the largest island, Viti Levu. Sugar is the main export of the humid, tropical islands. The native Fijians, mostly Melanesians, lived in villages of single roomed, thatched houses. But European influence and tourism have brought changes. The Indian population, descendants of immigrants from the 1800s, outnumbers the native Fijians. Fiji became

independent in 1970. The population is 572,000.
French Polynesia is a group of many widely scattered Pacific islands, including TAHITI and TONGA. In all, the group covers 4,000 sq km. The capital is Papeete. The population is 128,000.

G Geelong is a major port and industrial centre in Victoria. Its huge wheat terminal handles much of the state's export trade. Geelong Grammar School and Geelong College are among Australia's best known schools. The population is 116,000.

Gibson Desert is an arid region of rock and stone in Western Australia. It is bounded by Lake Macdonald and Lake Disappointment.
Gilbert Islands (now Kiribati) are some 40 coral atolls in the south-west Pacific. With Tuvalu (the former Ellice Islands) they cover 744 sq km. The capital is Tarawa. Most islanders live in hut villages. Tuvalu became independent in 1978 and the Gilbert Islands in 1979. The population of the Gilbert Islands is 48,000.
Great Artesian Basin is Australia's largest source of

Some 10,000 islands lie in the vast Pacific Ocean, which covers over 30 per cent of the world's surface. New Guinea, of which PAPUA NEW GUINEA is part, is the world's largest island after Greenland. It is dominated by a high chain of mountains, with tropical rain-forest as its predominant natural vegetation. The climate is equatorial with high temperatures and abundant rainfall. Most of the Pacific islands are small – either the tips of volcanoes that have risen from the sea floor or dazzling white coral atolls. Most of the islands lie in the tropics where the climate is warm with little variation in the seasons. Heavy rainfall on Hawaii contrasts with arid conditions on some of the coral atolls, such as those in Micronesia.

Peoples and ways of life

Australia has been called a desert surrounded by people. It is the most urbanized nation in the world: 82 per cent of Australians are city dwellers with 55 per cent living in the four great state capitals of the south-east, ADELAIDE, BRISBANE, MELBOURNE and SYDNEY.

In these thriving cities one can hear the languages and sample the foods of most European nations, for one in five Australians was born

Above: Cricketer Jeff Thomson bowls another entry into the record books to add to Australia's fame as a nation of sportsmen.

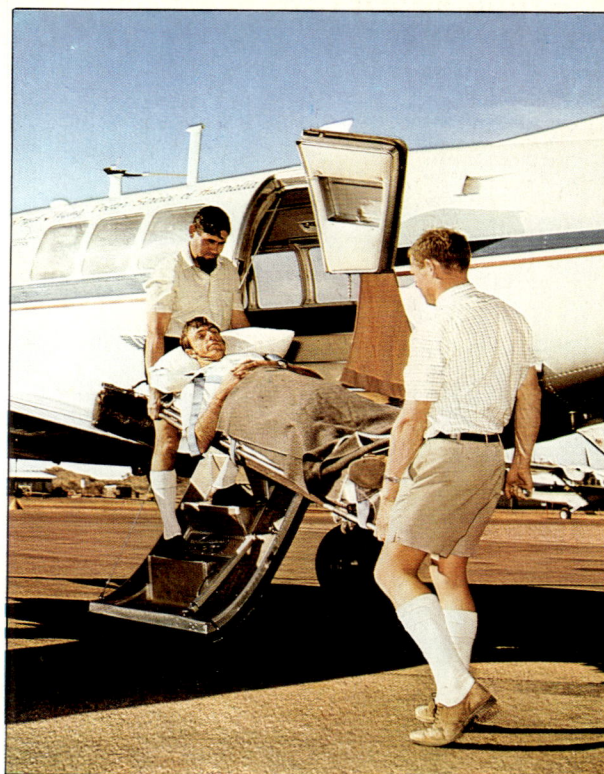

Left: Alice Springs, a remote township in central Australia, won fame from Nevil Shute's novel *A Town Like Alice.* Now it is a tourist centre. A 'regatta', run on wheels down a dry watercourse, is an annual festivity that emphasizes the blistering heat of the town's location.

Above: For patients in the Australian interior, the 'flying doctor' service remains the fastest way to medical aid. But much help is given by 2-way radio and telephone to assist emergency care on the spot. Many schoolchildren, too, receive much of their education from radio programmes.

in Europe. In the past, nearly all new Australians were British, but after World War II the nation opened its doors to refugees and settlers from Italy, Greece, Yugoslavia, Poland and other countries. Though anxious to expand its population, Australia must still limit the rate of immigration; there must be sufficient manpower to raise the homes and maintain the essential services the newcomers will need. Once settled in, most think of themselves as Australians, rather than Greek or Italian, though many live in communities where their native language is spoken, and keep ties with the 'old' country.

underground water. Trapped deep in porous rock it gushes to the surface through bore holes, providing vital water supplies to farmers. The basin extends over 1,536,000 sq km, including over 60% of Queensland.
Great Barrier Reef is a spectacular reef formed from the skeletons of more than 300 different types of coral. The reef runs 2,000 km from Gladstone in Queensland to the Gulf of Papua, covers 204,800 sq km and includes some 700 islands. Hundreds of species of tropical fish abound. In recent

years the Crown of Thorns starfish has caused immense destruction by feeding on living coral polyps. Great efforts to destroy the starfish continue.
Guam is the largest of the Mariana Islands in the west Pacific and covers 549 sq km. It was a major US air and naval base but is now self-governing. The capital is Agana. The population is 98,000.

Hawaii is a beautiful island group in the central Pacific. A 'crossroads' for the whole ocean, Hawaii

is a busy, tourist-conscious place. Since 1959 it has been the 50th state of the US. On 7 December 1941, its Pearl Harbor was the scene of the Japanese attack that brought the US into the war. Its capital is Honolulu. The population is 769,000.
Hobart is the capital of Tasmania and Australia's second oldest city. Splendidly sited between Mount Wellington and the River Derwent, it is 19 km from the sea but has an excellent deep water harbour. Much of the state's produce is exported through Hobart. A major

bridge, the Tasman Bridge, spans the Derwent River and was spectacularly damaged in 1975 when an ore carrier brought down three spans. One of the year's great events in Hobart is the finish of the Sydney to Hobart

Hobart, Tasman Bridge

yacht race. The population is 130,000.

Kalgoorlie is at the centre of Australia's most important goldfield, in Western Australia. Its wide streets were laid out for the wagons of the first settlers here in the 1890s. The region is still a major gold producer. Water comes to the town in a 553-km-long pipeline from a reservoir near Perth. Its population is 21,000.
Kimberleys are a rugged region of Western Australia where rivers have carved

Australia is a very young country – over fifty per cent of its citizens are under thirty and it is fast developing its own identity and place in world affairs. Though few now live the traditional 'outback' life, where drovers still run big 'mobs' of cattle hundreds of kilometres from huge cattle stations to remote railheads, the 'Great Outdoors' is still Australia's best loved asset. Golden beaches with fine sports facilities in an ideal climate and spacious parks are the setting for Australian leisure. Australians are enthusiastic travellers: a weekend camping trip may mean driving hundreds of kilometres and air travel, more than anything, has opened Australia to the world and to itself. Some 130,000 kilometres of internal air services carry about eight million passengers cheaply round the continent each year. Railways, mainly busy with freight, also run air-conditioned expresses between Sydney and Perth and a network of national highways rings the country.

As a result, Australians are no longer isolated and although the continent's population, at just over 13 million, is only equal to that of the Netherlands (in a country 200 times larger), it commands some of the world's most valuable natural resources.

Above: Though not high in the world's table of populations, New Zealand has won world status in sport. Good food and a fine year-round climate has produced first-class performers. New Zealand's All Black rugby football team, seen in action against the British Lions, is one of the world's strongest sides.

Right: This elaborately carved building is a Maori meeting house in Rotorua, North Island, New Zealand. Although the Maoris are well integrated into New Zealand society, these traditional meeting houses are still an important focal point of local community life.

gorges deep in the sandstone. There are also huge ranges where over 60% of the state's cattle graze.
Kiribati, see GILBERT ISLANDS.

Lake Eyre is Australia's largest lake. Set in South Australia, it extends 7,680 sq km after torrential rains. But usually it is a dry expanse of salt crusted mud.

Maoris were the first settlers in New Zealand, arriving from Polynesia in the 1300s. Tall, brown-skinned and courageous warriors, they settled their families and clans in villages whose wooden houses were often finely decorated with carvings. After clashing with early white settlers they agreed, under the Treaty of Waitangi of 1839, to become British subjects. But bitter

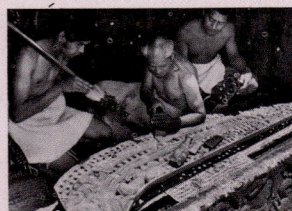

Maoris carving, Rotorua

wars about land ownership continued from 1845-70, reducing their numbers to some 42,000 by the early 1900s.
Marble Bar is a small township in Western Australia and known as the hottest place on the continent in summer. Temperatures of 49°C have been recorded. The population is 621.
Mariana, Caroline and Marshall Islands are in the west Pacific. The capital is Saipan. The population is 101,590.
Melanesians live in the islands north and north-east of Australia, including FIJI,

NEW CALEDONIA, NEW HEBRIDES, BRITISH SOLOMON ISLANDS and the eastern part of New Guinea, now independent as PAPUA NEW GUINEA. Melanesia means 'black islands', so called because of the people's dark skins.
Melbourne is the capital of VICTORIA and is Australia's second largest port after Sydney. Over 30% of Australian manufactured goods are created in the Melbourne region, which is now one of the world's largest cities. Many parks and wide, tree-lined streets also make it one of Australia's most beautiful

cities. Melbourne has a thriving cultural and leisure life, climaxing in the annual Moomba Festival (*moomba* is an Aboriginal word for 'joyful get together'). The city's Chinatown and strongly Italian suburb of Brunswick are centres for two of the many national groups that have created their own distinctive shops and restaurants. Sport plays a special part in Melbourne life. The Melbourne Cricket Ground is the site of Test matches, and, in winter, the Grand Final Match of the Australian Rules Football

Two in three New Zealanders live on North Island, where the nation's capital, WELLINGTON and the second largest city, AUCKLAND, are sited. Most MAORIS live on North Island. Fully integrated into society now, their first relations with New Zealand's white settlers were stormy.

Immigration from Britain began slowly in the mid-1800s. No convicts were sent, as they were to Australia. New Zealand became a separate colony in 1841, and an independent dominion in 1907. A short-lived gold rush in the 1860s boosted immigration, and many stayed on to farm when the gold ran out. Links of trade and affection between New Zealand and Britain remained strong and New Zealand is still a main supplier of meat and dairy produce to Britain. However, dissatisfaction with the quality and delivery of finished goods from Britain to New Zealand has grown.

New Zealanders have a prosperous life style, most people's homes being detached bungalows. Air travel has ended New Zealand's isolation and her citizens are able to afford a certain amount of foreign travel. Outdoor sports are a main leisure activity, particularly water sports, skiing and Rugby Football. The formidable All Blacks rugby team is one of the world's greatest.

Many races have moved through the Pacific islands, which are now grouped by the names given to their first inhabitants, the MELANESIANS, MICRONESIANS and POLYNESIANS. For most islanders, fishing and the growing of such crops as bananas, breadfruit and copra have been the traditional way of life. But air travel and tourism have brought many changes. Some twenty shipping lines and airlines work in the area, though a journey to the West from a remote island may take weeks. Radio and radio-telephone services bring news of the world beyond, broadcasting in the region's many languages. These include English, French and Pidgin (now the official language of independent Papua New Guinea, where hundreds of local languages, each unlike another, are spoken). A South Pacific Commission advises governments on technical and scientific affairs.

In their arts and customs, the islands are as different as the peoples that inhabit them, and are much influenced by the Western countries who long dominated different areas. The American sphere of influence covered the island region north of the equator, including HAWAII, Eastern SAMOA and GUAM. The French came to FRENCH POLYNESIA and NEW CALEDONIA. The British recently gave independence to FIJI and TONGA and Australia handed control to the citizens of Papua New Guinea. In general, the countries of the West are 'moving out' of a region to which they came as traders, missionaries and colonial powers in the 1700s and 1800s. Artists and poets

Right: Samoa has long been studied by anthropologists intrigued by its relaxed and happy family life. In the traditional wood and thatch homes of its village communities, young and old live in harmony. In the foreground beach pebbles are for sale in woven palm-frond baskets.

Below: Headhunters of Papua dance a ritual that Western visitors are only now beginning to see as a major form of art. Such peoples living in the remote highlands developed a complex society which included inter-tribal head-hunting raids. These dancers were performing to welcome Queen Elizabeth II.

season. For the Melbourne Cup, the nation's greatest horse race, there is a public holiday. Melbourne became a city in 1847. Its population is 2,503,000.

Micronesians dwell on the islands of Micronesia, meaning 'small islands'. Spread over 7,770,000 sq km of the central Pacific, the islands include the CAROLINE and GILBERT ISLANDS, GUAM and the Marshall Islands. Most Micronesians are fishermen and also raise crops such as bananas, breadfruit, coconuts and yams.

Mount Isa is a major mining centre in Queensland, producing 65% of the nation's copper.

Mount Kosciusko is Australia's highest peak, rising 2,230 metres in the Australian Alps of New South Wales. It is snow-covered between June and October and is a skiing centre. Australia's largest park, the Kosciusko National Park, surrounds it.

Murray River is Australia's second longest, but the largest in water volume. From its source in the Snowy Mountains of New South Wales it runs 2,560 km to the sea in South Australia. For much of its length it forms the boundary between New South Wales and Victoria. The three states share out the river's waters. The Hume dam checks the river near Albury-Wodonga.

N **New Caledonia** is the name of a French territory and its largest island, set in the south Pacific. The island is 19,058 sq km and surrounded by the world's second longest coral reef. Nickel ore is the main export. The capital is Noumea. The population is 100,600.

Newcastle is NEW SOUTH WALES' second largest city and lies 160 km north of Sydney at the mouth of the Hunter River. Steelworks, fuelled by huge coal deposits nearby, produce 40% of the nation's steel. Other industries include heavy engineering and chemical production. The wheat, wool and produce of most of northern New South Wales is exported here.

New Hebrides are twelve islands in the south-west Pacific, covering 14,763 sq km. Long administered by France and Britain, the islands have been settled by many peoples, including Vietnamese. In 1979 the New Hebrides offered sanctuary to Vietnamese refugees. The capital of the islands is Vila. The population is 93,000.

New South Wales is the richest and most populated state in Australia. 50% live in

Parramatta, NSW, 1825

low by cloud en route to Perth, noticed a rust-coloured gorge that looked as if it was made of iron. It was. He became a multi-millionaire. 'New' minerals – such as bauxite, source of aluminium and nickel, vital ingredient in stainless steel – have also made (and lost) Australian fortunes. Uranium, discovered by chance in the NORTHERN TERRITORY in 1954, may prove most valuable of all, as fuel for nuclear reactors. Meanwhile, coal, natural gas and hydro-electric power are Australia's main energy sources: the world's largest brown coalfield is at Latrobe Valley, Victoria. Measuring 15 kilometres by 65 kilometres, its reserves may last 750 years.

Australian governments have made great efforts to encourage industry – so that raw materials can be turned to finished goods in Australia, rather than all exported. One in four Australians now works in industry – one in ten in the motor industry. Shipbuilding is important in a land with a 19,300-kilometre coastline and few overland routes for transporting goods, while the chemical industry is the fastest expanding, comprising more than forty large petrochemical plants. Much of industry is owned by foreign companies; American companies for example control all three car manufacturers. Foreign markets still prefer to see Australia as the world's larder and quarry, rather than supplier of finished goods, so agriculture is still the main export business of the nation. 'Living off the sheep's back' may no longer be a way of life for many, but it is still, as in the 1800s, one of the ways to wealth.

Legend (map)

- ● Iron
- ● Lead
- ■ Coal
- ● Tin
- ● Gold
- ○ Silver
- ● Opals
- ● Copper
- ● Uranium
- ● Zinc
- ● Aluminium
- ★ Manganese
- △ Oil and Gas

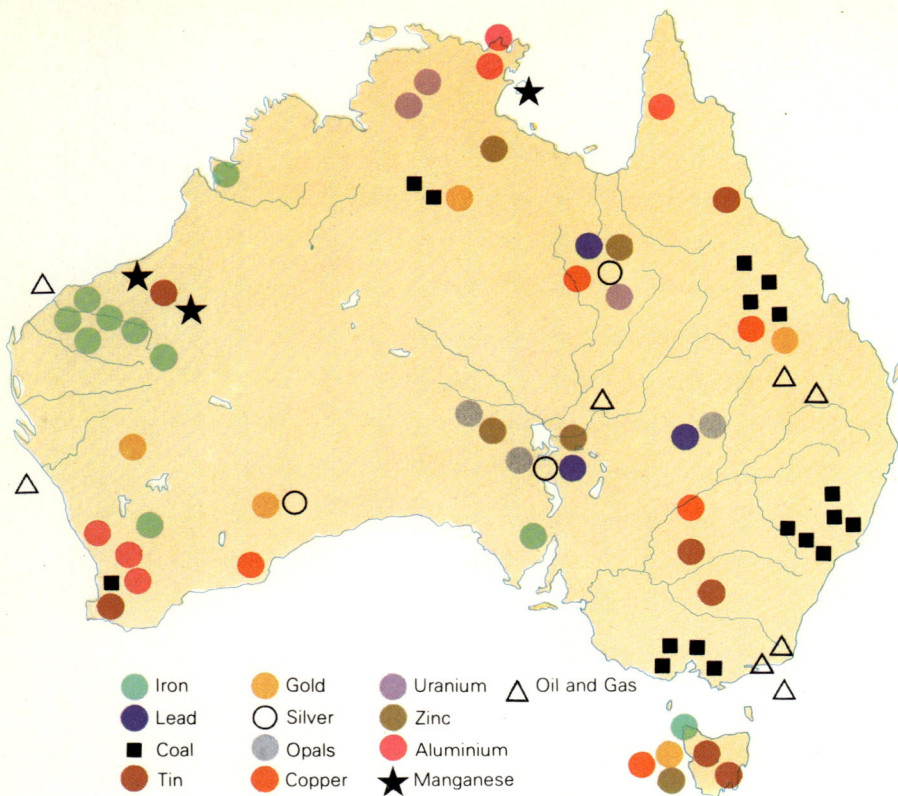

have also made their way to this beautiful part of the world – along with naturalists and anthropologists who have studied the unique social and family structures of the islands. Today, only a few tribes in Papua New Guinea keep to a life untouched by Western influences.

Above: The continent of Australia is a huge store of natural treasures.
Below: Living on the job, opal miners in hot Coober Pedy, Australia, have underground homes, often air conditioned. At their 'back door' may lie a fortune for the taking.

Economy

Skilled technology has greatly aided Australian agriculture, including the scattering of minerals from the air to render soils fertile. Bore holes have tapped the waters of the GREAT ARTESIAN BASIN and huge irrigation and hydro-electric schemes, as in the SNOWY MOUNTAINS, have made dry lands fruitful.

Alongside its agricultural wealth, a treasure-store of minerals has helped give Australia the nickname of the 'Lucky Continent'. In the 1800s the lure of gold and diamonds brought rough, tough fortune hunters here from as far away as China and the United States. Such sites as the KIMBERLEYS and BROKEN HILL have yielded untold wealth and fortunes are still made. In 1952, a miner, whose light aeroplane was forced

its capital, SYDNEY. The state has four main zones, running north to south. Sydney and many other major towns are sited on the fertile coastal strip. Inland, the tablelands include the BLUE MOUNTAINS and SNOWY MOUNTAINS. The first settlers found prosperity when a route across this barrier was made, opening up the western slopes and western plains beyond. In these regions some 50% of Australia's sheep are raised. In the far west is BROKEN HILL, for long Australia's major mineral source. New towns,

such as Albury, twin town with Wodonga, across the Victoria border, have been built to decentralize the state's economy. Covering 792,148 sq km, most of New South Wales has a temperate climate. The population is 4,955,000.
New Zealand consists of NORTH ISLAND, SOUTH ISLAND, Stewart Island, Chatham Islands and several minor islands. The capital is WELLINGTON. Over 60% of New Zealand's population is urban, but the economy is mostly dependent on farming. The main industries are those

processing farm products, but rapidly expanding industries include engineering, textiles, chemical manufacture and cars. The area is 268,665 sq km and the population is 3,142,800.
North Island, New Zealand, has broad, fertile coastal

Pohutu Geyser, Rotorua

plains and an eastern mountain range. Two in three New Zealanders dwell in North Island. WELLINGTON, the nation's capital and AUCKLAND, its largest city are sited here. So is its largest lake, Lake Taupo. Active volcanoes include Ruapehu (2,797 metres). Famous geysers around Rotorua shoot jets of steam and gas high in the air. Its area is 114,725 sq km.
Northern Territory is a huge but empty Australian state. Its capital, DARWIN, is in the monsoon zone of the far north. But, in the flat and hot interior, droughts of ten

years long are known. Some 25,000 Aboriginals live in reserves, mainly in ARNHEM LAND. Mining, cattle raising and tourism equally support the state economy. Bauxite and manganese are mined. Cattle are raised on huge stations in the outback. Tourism centres on ALICE SPRINGS. The first European settlement was in 1824, but the region was slow to develop. World War II brought many servicemen to Darwin, which was bombed by Japan. After the war many soldiers returned to live in Darwin. The population of

Over 60 per cent of the land in New Zealand can be farmed. Nine million cattle and some 57 million sheep are the main source of the country's wealth, but forestry is increasing in importance and New Zealand plans to be self-sufficient, using timber as a renewable energy source. Major hydro-electric schemes based on the high waters of South Island are also an important energy source.

It is unlikely that the Pacific islands will ever develop, as a whole, towards a thoroughly 'Western' lifestyle as they are too scattered to form large political units. Most are too small to attract the sellers of many consumer goods, and much of their produce is too perishable or too remote to export. But NEW CALEDONIA has

Below: One of the world's greatest-ever engineering projects is the Snowy Mountains HEP Scheme. Rivers running east to the sea were switched so that they would water plains to the west. Red arrows on the map show how tunnels turn the water back.

Above left: Pineapples grow well in hot Queensland, Australia. Bananas are also raised in a continent that spans a tropical far north to a cool south in Tasmania, where apples have been the traditional main crop. Today's transport costs have hurt the fruit trade.

Above: Australia grew rich 'off the sheep's back' and the plump Merinos on sale here in New South Wales still yield much of the nation's wealth. But farming is now highly mechanized, and few people live the traditional life of the outback sheep station.

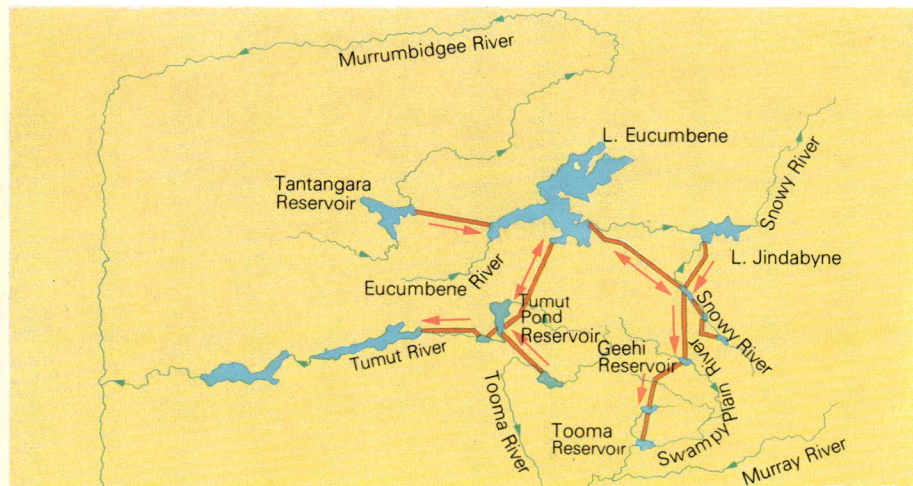

mineral reserves and exports nickel. The NEW HEBRIDES exports some manganese. And copper is the main export of PAPUA NEW GUINEA.

History and culture: Australia

For some 30,000 years, ABORIGINAL peoples had Australia to themselves. Far from the Western world, Australia was the last continent Europe colonized. In the AD 300s geographers guessed that a great southern continent might exist. They called it *Terra Australis Incognita*, the unknown southern continent.

Dutch explorers, among them Abel Tasman (1603-59), who discovered TASMANIA in 1642, led the way south. But hostile coasts and Aboriginals discouraged them. Then on 29 April 1770, the

the Northern Territory is 100,700.
Nullarbor Plain is a desert extending through Western Australia into South Australia and covers some 200,000 sq km. It is the world's largest limestone slab. Its name means 'no tree', but after rare rains the desert blooms dramatically.

O Ord River Dam in Western Australia created the country's largest artificial lake.

P Papua New Guinea is a tropical island country bordering West Irian in Indonesia to the west. Papua New Guinea reached full independence on 16 September 1975. But dense rain forests, high mountains and a rainfall averaging 2,000 millimetres annually make progress to a unified nation difficult. For example, hundreds of distinct languages are spoken, so the official language is now a form of 'Pidgin' English. Some tribes have only been sighted from the air. Headhunting and cannibalism survived until recently. Timber, copra, cocoa, coffee and rubber are

staple products. A new crop is palm oil. The Bougainville copper project is the main export money winner. Papua New Guinea covers 461,691 sq km and its coastal capital is Port Moresby. The population is 2,611,000.

West New Guineans

Paramatta is west of Sydney in New South Wales. It includes engineering, motor car assembly and textile works among many industries. Elizabeth Farm House, built in 1793, is Australia's oldest surviving building.
Perth is the capital of Western Australia and lies 19 km from the mouth of the Swan River. Freemantle, the state's main port, is sited here and is one of the world's most modern shipping terminals. Perth is a lively city whose citizens are 75% Australian born. Fine

buildings include St George's (Anglican) and St Mary's (Roman Catholic) cathedrals. Spacious parks such as King's Park grace the town and night horse-trotting is a popular sport in Gloucester Park. A 3,938-km-long rail link to Sydney was completed in 1970.
Polynesians are inhabitants of Polynesia, meaning 'many islands'. Scattered in a triangle formed by New Zealand, Hawaii and EASTER ISLAND, Polynesia includes American SAMOA, the GILBERT ISLANDS and Tuvalu, and FRENCH POLYNESIA. Tall, brown-

English navigator, Captain James Cook (1728-79), landed near the site of modern SYDNEY, with orders to claim for Britain this land glimpsed by earlier explorers. He reported that it was fit for colonization.

So, on 20 January 1788 the First Fleet landed at BOTANY BAY, bringing 750 convicts to start a settlement near the world's finest natural harbour.

Above: Solomon islanders fish by night in calm seas.

Below left: Benmore Dam, New Zealand, turns the nation's high waters into a power source.

Below: Dairy herds near snow-capped Mount Egmont graze on some of the world's best pasture.

European diseases and bloodthirsty persecution by White settlers reduced the numbers of Aboriginals, who were some 700,000 strong when the first Whites arrived. The Aboriginals had never fought over land ownership, finding room for all. But the settlers squabbled – landowners versus 'squatters'. By the mid-1800s Britain gradually stopped sending convicts, partly because it was no punishment to go to a land where a man might pick up a 48-kilogram nugget of gold. Instead immigrants flooded in, increasing the population by over a million in 20 years from 1860. Many who came to seek gold went on to grow rich on Australia's true wealth, her sheep and wheatlands.

Britain agreed that the colonies should move towards self government. In 1863 the colonies began to meet to discuss whether they should join in a federation or if each should go its own way. By January 1901, federation was agreed and from that time the states have run their own internal affairs. A federal capital was transferred from Melbourne to CANBERRA in 1927 to run affairs such as defence and trade.

Australia entered the 1900s with expanding cities and prosperous farms. In World War I, Australia volunteered readily to 'stand behind the mother country' in a far distant struggle.

The war boosted Australian trade and strengthened her voice in the world. But world depression in the 1930s hit the nation hard: 500,000 were out of work. Politics were bitter. In 1931 Britain gave Australia the right to make her own foreign policy. But when war broke out

skinned peoples, the Polynesians are skilled navigators and reached New Zealand, where they are known as MAORIS.

Q **Queensland** is Australia's second largest state, covering 1,707,520 sq km. Its eastern coast, 5,178 km long has 14 major ports to speed produce overseas. Fine grasslands in the east and north-west of Queensland make this the leading cattle state in Australia. Sugar cane is the main crop, but manufacturing, especially from wood and paper

products, forms half the state production. The population is less concentrated on the capital (BRISBANE) than in other states. Known as the 'Sunshine State', tourism is an important activity. The population is 1,960,700.

S **Samoa** is the name for two countries. Eastern, or American Samoa covers 197 sq km and has Pago Pago as its capital. Western Samoa, capital Apia, became the first independent Polynesian state in 1962. Both are in the eastern Pacific. Samoan peoples are

Polynesian and tuna fishing and canning, in addition to tourism, are the main activities. The population of Eastern Samoa is 35,000, of Western Samoa 152,000.

Snowy Mountains in NEW SOUTH WALES and VICTORIA has Australia's largest snowfield and national park – and one of the world's largest engineering schemes in a huge hydro-electric and irrigation undertaking. The scheme diverts the waters of the Snowy River so that instead of wasting eastwards to the sea they now flow west, bringing 2,446 million cubic

metres to irrigate the western plains and generate 4 million Kw of electricity. Seventeen major dams and 160 km of tunnels are involved in a scheme first planned in the 1880s and completed in the mid 1970s.

South Australia is the nation's major agricultural and industrial producer-state and the fastest growing in population. Half the population works in manufacturing industries, mainly centred on ADELAIDE, the state capital. The fertile Murray River basin has vineyards and other orchards. The semi-

arid Western Plateau includes a major Aboriginal reserve and the rocket range at Woomera. In the highland chain of mountains is the dramatic landscape of the Flinders Ranges. For South Australians, shark and fresh-

Vineyards, S. Australia

expression in their homeland, for example through Australia's own fine ballet, opera and theatre companies. In the past, too, many Australian writers and artists struggled self-consciously to break away from European traditions and create arts that would be specially Australian. Now, increasingly, they feel more free to choose personal subjects and styles.

One symbol of the new spirit is the world famous Sydney Opera House. The bold design of a young Danish architect, the Opera House was opened in 1973 after twenty years of problems and delay. At one stage it seemed that its soaring sail-like roofs could never be built. Now it is host to international stars of opera, ballet and drama.

Among Australia's opera stars are Dame Joan Sutherland (1926-) and Harold Blair (1924-). The dancer, choreographer and actor Sir Robert Helpmann (1909-) directed the Australian Ballet Company until 1975, while other leading ballet companies in Australia include the Australian Dance Theatre of South Australia, and the Queensland Ballet. Famous actors have included Judith Anderson (1893-1962) and Peter Finch

Above: Bora Bora island epitomizes an image of the world's southern oceans—the cone of an extinct volcano, its coral-crowned rim, and a blue lagoon. For centuries, adventurers, castaways, artists and traders have made this region one of the most mixed and exotic of earthly paradises.

Right: Coral reefs are formed from the stony skeletons of millions of tiny coral polyps (*far right*) continuously budding. Atolls are formed by coral reefs growing around an active volcano. Eruptions cause the volcano to sink below the level of the reef, leaving it exposed as islands.

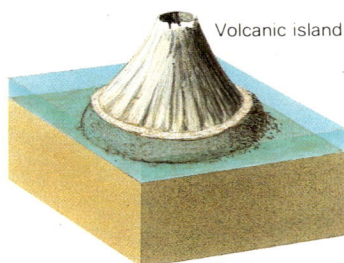

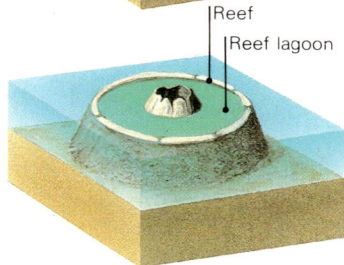

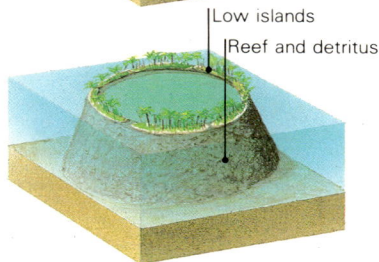

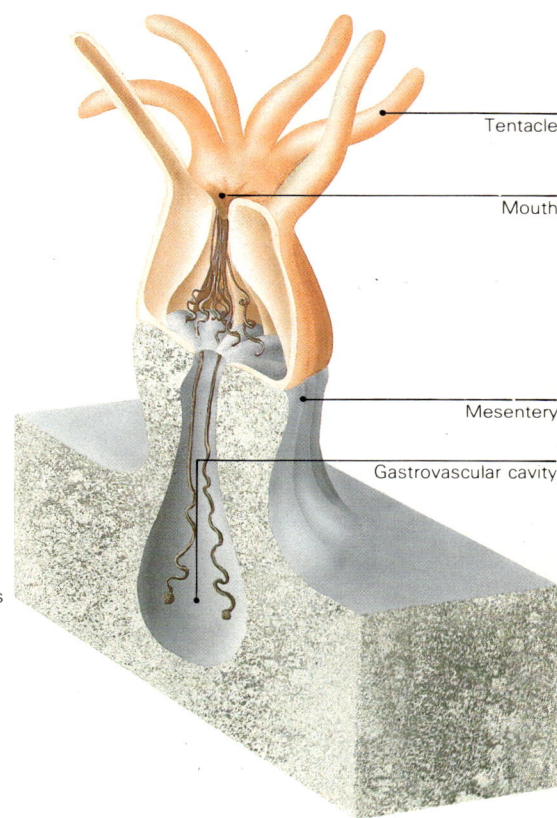

Volcanic island

Reef
Reef lagoon

Low islands
Reef and detritus

Tentacle

Mouth

Mesentery

Gastrovascular cavity

again in 1939 Australia once more sent men. They fought bravely in the Western Desert, but this time there was an enemy closer at hand. Fifteen thousand Australians went into harsh Japanese captivity at Singapore. And Japan, by raiding DARWIN on 19 February 1942, brought war to the doorstep.

After World War II, Australia opened her doors to many nations and foreign investors. The country boomed. It has become the world's fifth most prosperous nation. Trade with Britain declined and increased in turn with the United States and Japan. The arts in Australia have reflected the history of a fast-developing nation. In the past, many creative people left Australia to make their careers abroad. Now they can find

water fishing are popular sports. SA, first colonized in the 1830s, got its own constitution in 1856. Many migrants arrived in the 1960s and 1970s. The population is 1,217,600.

South Island, New Zealand, is dominated by the Southern Alps, where 17 peaks top 3,000 metres. Fast flowing rivers from the Alps generate electricity through hydro-electric schemes. In the lowlands the Canterbury Plains are among many fertile eastern areas on which sheep are raised. Its area is 153,940 sq km.

Sydney, capital of New South Wales, is Australia's largest and oldest city. A bridge, built in 1932 and 1,149 metres long, is a world famed landmark, as are the white concrete 'sails' of Sydney Opera House – home to the Sydney Symphony Orchestra and the Australian Ballet. Sydney and its vast suburbs, home to 59% of the state's peoples, is a thriving place with 25,000 factories, a major business and banking centre, and a port that handles some 4,000 vessels a year in the world's finest natural harbour. Ferries bring commuters to work in the inner city, dominated by high buildings and fine parklands. Nearby are 34 beaches, including Bondi and Manley which are famed for surfing. Inner suburbs have a lively, international air, with Greek and Italian communities and the well restored historical areas such as Paddington's terraced houses. Among many academic centres is the University of Sydney, Australia's first, founded in 1850. Captain Cook landed nearby at BOTANY BAY in 1770.

The town became a city in 1840. Its population is 2,717,000.

Tahiti, largest island of the Windward Group in French Polynesia, lies in the central south Pacific. The

Convict barracks, Hobart

artist Paul Gauguin made it his home. The mountains and coral fringes of its fertile coast, from which cocoa, sugar, copra and coffee are exported, make it an important tourist centre.

Tasmania is Australia's smallest state – an island about the size of Ireland. Long known as the 'Apple State', and supplier of 75% of Australia's apples, this crop has declined rapidly in the 1970s owing to the costs of packing and shipping overseas. But the mild climate favours other crops, such as hops. Tasmania is

Above: Kiri Te Kanawa, a Maori New Zealander, gained world fame as one of the foremost opera singers of the 1970s. Her success highlighted the problem for artists in small countries like New Zealand: those with great talent must take it abroad in order to win fame

(1916-1978), best known for his film roles.

Australia's film industry has recently been given much financial support from the Australian Film Development Corporation, and a 'new wave' of Australian films began to win prizes worldwide in the 1970s. They include *Picnic at Hanging Rock, Caddie, Newsfront* and *The Chant of Jimmy Blacksmith*. Many films were based on the novels of Australian writers. Patrick White (1912-) is the major Australian writer of the century, and won a Nobel Prize in 1973 for his novel, *The Solid Mandala*. The novelist Morris West (1916-) wrote the best-selling *The Shoes of the Fisherman*. Alan Moorehead (1910-) is the author of many novels, and was a distinguished war correspondent. Australia's dramatists include David Williamson (1942-), author of *Don's Party*. Major poets include Judith Wright (1915-) and Alec Hope (1907-).

Above: White sails of the Sydney Opera House match those of the yachts in the world's best harbour. But, for a time, it seemed that nobody could build this dream planned by a young Danish architect. Perseverance by the city fathers finally saw this national home of opera, ballet and drama through to completion.

In the visual arts Sidney Nolan (1917-) is the best known painter, particularly for his pictures of Leda and the swan, and the outlaw Ned Kelly. Sir Russell Drysdale (1912-) has painted the harsh landscape of the Australian interior.

The work of individual creative workers and of national artistic companies is aided by the Australia Council of the Arts, and the Australian Broadcasting Commission is the major patron of music in Australia. Arts festivals encourage the new vigour of Australian cultural life, most notably those at Adelaide and Perth.

History and culture: New Zealand

The native Maoris of New Zealand occupied the country for about 400 years before its discovery by Europeans in 1642. Later, sealers, whalers and Kauri seekers established settlements along the coast. These people had a devastating effect

also one of the world's most mountainous islands – and as a result is rich in hydro-electric power potential for industry. Though only 3% of Australia's population lives here, the state produces 8% of all Australia's electricity. Forests of pine, eucalyptus and myrtle cover half the state's area (67,540 sq km). Tasmanians are of 97% British stock. Keen yachtsmen, they held the first Hobart Regatta in 1838. Today, the capital, HOBART is still the destination of one of the world's great races, from Sydney to Hobart. The fact

that this island separated from the mainland some 11,000 years ago has preserved unique animals and plants such as the Tasmanian Tiger and Tasmanian Devil. A Dutch explorer, Abel Tasman, first sighted Tasmania on 24 November 1642 and named it Van Diemen's Land. It was claimed for England in 1802 and won its own local government in 1856. The population is 400,700.

Tonga, a Pacific island kingdom also known as the Friendly Islands, has been independent from Britain

since 1970. More than 150 islands make up the group, whose capital is Nuku 'alofa. Polynesian peoples live in Tonga, respecting since the AD 900s a line of sacred monarchs called the Tu'i Tonga. Queen Salote Tupous III, who reigned from

Queen Salote, Tonga

1918 to 1965, was a popular visitor in Britain. Tongatapu, extending to 260 sq km, is the largest island in the group which, in all, covers 699 sq km. Coconuts, copra and bananas are exported. The population is 96,000.

V Victoria is Australia's second smallest state but second highest in population. 70% of the land is farmed, but in so mechanized a way that only 7% of the population works on the land. Thirty per cent of the workforce is engaged in manufacturing industries,

mostly based in the region of Melbourne. Manufacturing earns twice as much revenue for the state as agriculture. Victoria, in Australia's far south-east, is temperate in climate and has four main regions. Gippsland lies behind the Ninety Mile Beach coastline and is a prosperous dairy farm region. Its northern parts are mountainous. Westward lies the central district where Melbourne stands on the Yarra River, with orchards, forests and plains nearby. Next in the western district cattle raising and dairy farm

Zealand began to trade with other nations, notably those of the Pacific Basin.

New Zealand's remoteness and small population has meant that organized cultural life cannot be on a large scale. The cost of bringing orchestras or stage productions from abroad is too high, for example. Many New Zealanders have had to make their artistic careers abroad, among them the world famous Maori singer, Kiri Te Kanawa.

There is, however, a national orchestra, three professional theatre companies, and in the 1970s a 'new wave' of New Zealand film-making began paralleling that in Australia. Important authors of this century have included the short-story writer Katherine Mansfield (1888-1923). The short story is a commonly practised medium among New Zealand writers.

A new development in New Zealand's cultural life is the fact that the Maoris are now creating a written tradition, recording stories and folklore previously passed down by word of mouth.

Left: A 'new wave' of fine Australian films was one of the nation's most important contributions to world culture in the 1970s. *Picnic at Hanging Rock* was based on a novel that told of mysterious disappearances from a girls' school early in the century.

Below: Tuvalu celebrates independence day in colourful dance. One of several South Sea communities to reach independence recently, Tuvalu faces a future with the problems confronted by all small nations.

on the Maori population by bringing European diseases into the country. They also provoked inter-tribal wars with the sale of muskets in the 1820s. New Zealand was annexed to Britain in 1840 and the Treaty of Waitangi was signed, guaranteeing the Maoris undisturbed possession of their lands. Land titles were, however, disputed and hostile Maori chiefs crushed before order was established in the 1800s. The Maoris now have four representatives in government, are four times as numerous as in 1900 and take an increasing part in their country's affairs.

New Zealand became an independent dominion in 1907, but its economy still entirely depended on Britain. It was greatly affected by the depression of the 1920s and 30s. Since World War II, an increased demand for food exports has boosted New Zealand's economy. When Britain joined the Common Market in 1973, New

ng are the major activities. The north region includes mountains, but also plains watered by tributaries of the Murray River. Most of the state's wheat is raised in this region. Irrigation projects in the north-west, based on the township of Mildura, have created a world-known dried fruit industry. European settlements began with a convict colony in 1803, which was quickly abandoned. Three expeditions, organized by Tasmanians, staked claims here in the early 1830s. By 1850 much of the state was occupied. Victoria's constitution dates from 1855. Its population is 3,647,500.

Wellington is the capital city of NEW ZEALAND. Sited at the far south of NORTH ISLAND on a fine natural harbour, it is the country's major port and commercial centre. Road and rail links make it the hub of the nation's communication network. The population is 140,000.

Western Australia is the nation's largest state, covering 2,498,355 sq km. Because much of Western Australia is dry, it has been the nation's slowest state to develop, but has prospered since World War II. Half the state's population live in the conurbation of the state capital, PERTH and its port at Fremantle. And 75% of the

Goldminers of Kalgoorlie

state's workforce dwell in these or other towns. But huge sheep stations prosper in the central and southern part of Western Australia. Gold, coal, oil, iron ore and nickel (found in huge deposits at Kambalda in 1966) enrich the state. The 'Golden Mile' of KALGOORLIE has been in production since the 1880s – and in 1979 world wide interest was raised among speculators at news of new mineral treasures in the KIMBERLEYS. The first settlement in Western Australia was in 1826. The population is 1,095,300.

Whyalla is the third largest city of South Australia and base of the Whyalla Shipbuilding and Engineering Works. From here in May 1972 the largest ship built in Australia to date, the *Clutha Capricorn* (a 78,000 tonne carrier) was launched.

Woomera in central South Australia has since 1947 been a base for testing guided missiles for the UK and Australia. Australia's first satellite was launched here in 1967. Woomera derives from an Aboriginal word meaning 'spear thrower'.

The polar regions offer hostile environments for people. But the Arctic and, possibly, the ice-covered continent of Antarctica contain resources which may assume great importance in the future.

Polar regions

Below: Although Antarctica is the world's most barren continent, it has huge riches not yet explored. The seas around it teem with life, in a complex chain that runs from minute organisms up to mighty whales. Many kinds of penguin flourish on the coast and its icebergs, which break continually from the huge ice cap.

Below right: For centuries Lapplanders followed the reindeer on their travels and found in them a source of meat, clothing, tools and—from their hide—shelter. The reindeer are still important in the life of this remote Arctic region, and their meat is still exported southwards. But few Lapplanders now lead the traditional hard life of the true nomad.

Both polar regions are the planet's radiators, drawing heat from warmer zones and reflecting it skywards. Both are regions of ice and snow, scenes of epic journeys of discovery. But in fact the poles differ greatly.

The Arctic is a small sea surrounded by continents. Nuclear submarines regularly pass 'below' the thin ice of the North Pole. Passenger aeroplanes fly 'above' it daily. The Antarctic is a huge continent surrounded by oceans. Though ancient Greeks guessed it was there, and Maori legend told of it, no one is known to have set foot on Antarctica until the 1800s. Today, some 800 scientists who brave its savage and sunless winter have many secrets still to find.

Antarctica

It is the world's most remote, highest and only treeless continent. Forming a rough circle around the Pole, the size of the United States plus Mexico, it lies buried beneath 90 per cent of all the world's snow and ice – to an average depth of 2,134 metres. If it melted, the world's sea level would rise 60 metres, drowning London, New York and Sydney. Yet Antarctica's climate is as dry as the Sahara's – fire is the hazard most feared by its explorers. Huge winds race clockwise round the continent, topping 160 kilometres per hour. The coldest temperature known on Earth, −88·3°C, was recorded in the Antarctic.

Huge mineral wealth must lie beneath the ice cap of Antarctica, but no technology yet known can reach it. Partly for this reason Antarctica is known as the 'peaceful continent' where no man has ever been killed in anger. The Antarctic Treaty, signed in 1959 by 14 nations, scrapped older maps that show the region sliced like a cake.

Reference

A **Antarctic Peninsula** is a mountainous region jutting 1,280 km from Antarctica towards South America. Its fiords and peaks resemble the landscape of Norway. Several nations claim part or all of it. Argentina calls it Tierra San Martin; Chile, Tierra O'Higgins; Britain, Graham Land and the US, Palmer Peninsula.

B **Beardmore Glacier** is a torrent of ice at the southern end of the Transantarctic Mountains. Robert Scott and Ernest Shackleton used it as a route to the pole. Cape Farewell is the southernmost tip of Greenland.

E **Ellsworth Mountains** are in the south of the Antarctic Peninsula and include the continent's highest peaks, Mount Tyree (4,965 metres) and Vinson Massif (5,139 metres). Ellsworth Mountains are named after Lincoln Ellsworth, the US aviator, who discovered their northern sector, the Senrinel Range, in 1935.

Eskimos have dwelt in the lands and ice cap of the Arctic for thousands of

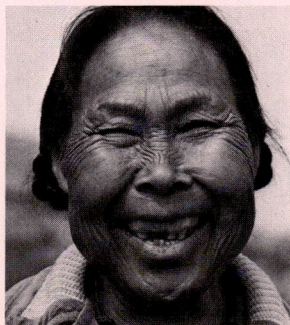

Eskimo, Greenland

years. Skilled hunters and trappers of caribou, fishes, seals, walrus and whales, they adapted to life in one of the world's toughest regions. Physically well suited to the climate, they are short and compact in body and have the flat faces, straight black hair and brown eyes of Mongoloid races. Traditionally, most Eskimos lived in tents in summer and stone or wooden houses in winter. The igloo, a circular snow block house, was more often a temporary shelter for hunters than a long-term dwelling. Great hospitality to all visitors has long been an Eskimo custom. Now few Eskimos remain untouched by European customs and technology. Many Eskimos have become skilled mechanics. But the change from old ways to a new lifestyle has not been easy for many.

G **Godthaab** is the capital of Greenland. It is a seaport, near the mouth of a fiord in a fishing and sheep raising region of south-west Greenland. Gondwanaland is the name given to the prehistoric super-continent

BERING SEA

EAST SIBERIAN SEA

CANADA

BEAUFORT SEA

U.S.S.R.

ARCTIC OCEAN

NORTH POLE

Queen Elizabeth Islands

Baffin Is.

BAFFIN BAY

Svalbard

Novaya Zemlya

BARENTS SEA

GREENLAND

Godthaab

Limit of pack ice

NORWEGIAN SEA

better planned expedition had won its way, without loss of life, to the heart of the last continent to be explored.

Its exploration continues and today, tourist cruises from New Zealand ply to a land through seas so dangerous that any sailor, in the days of sailing ships, could claim the right of putting both feet on the table after dinner if he had been to the Antarctic.

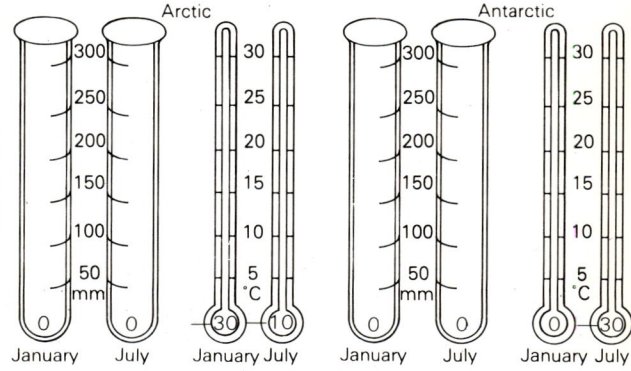

Arctic

300 250 200 150 100 50 mm

30 25 20 15 10 5 °C

January July January July

Antarctic

300 250 200 150 100 50 mm

30 25 20 15 10 5 °C

January July January July

Above: The Arctic and Antarctic have light snow instead of rain and their temperatures never rise above 0°C.

(with the pole as centre) between various claimant nations.

Since 1957 (the International Geophysical Year) it has been a 'continent for science' where all may move freely and military activity is banned. The Treaty runs out in 1989; then earlier claims, particularly on the ANTARCTIC PENINSULA, may be revived. Meanwhile, important research on the world's climate and magnetic field has been done. Air conditioning and nuclear power plants make life comfortable for scientists on Antarctica's bases today. But near the modern McMURDO STATION is the wooden hut raised by Captain Scott, whose doomed expedition to the pole began here in 1911. The bodies of his dogs and hay for his ponies will lie here for ever in Antarctica's great refrigerator. Scott reached the Pole, via the BEARDMORE GLACIER, to find a Norwegian flag, raised by Roald Amundsen (1872–1928) on 14 December 1911 – a month earlier. Amundsen's

WEDDELL SEA

QUEEN MAUD LAND

FILCHNER ICE SHELF

ANTARCTIC PENINSULA

ANTARCTICA

SOUTH POLE

Vostok

WILKES LAND

ROSS ICE SHELF

Mt Erebus

ROSS SEA

OATES LAND

of which Australia and Antarctica were once part.

Greenland is the world's largest island. Its 2,175,600 sq km lie mostly in the Arctic circle and only some 5% of the surface is ice free. On the southern coast, summers are cool but pleasant and some sheep are raised. But the sea's wealth of seals and whales has been Greenland's main source of livelihood, though mineral resources may be exploited in future. Greenland was an integral part of Denmark from 1953 to 1979. Then its own parliament, the *Landst-*

ing, was established. Greenland was a remote and little developed society until

Packing reindeer meat, Greenland

World War II, when its strategic position between the US and Russia brought

radar and weather stations there. Now air travel and an ultra modern telephone network of 90 stations has opened up the country.

Greenlanders are by race a mix of European and Eskimo peoples. There are few pure Eskimos.

Gunnbjorn's Mountain on the east coast is the tallest in Greenland, rising to 3,700 metres.

Icebergs, the chunks of ice that break off from ice shelves in polar regions, may drift far; regular patrols chart their course in north-

ern shipping waters. One iceberg 145 km long was sighted in Antarctica. But most are about 1.6 km long and rectangular.

Ice shelves occur where polar ice spreads from the land over the sea. Ross ice shelf in Antarctica is larger than France.

Lapps dwell on the arctic edges of Scandinavia. Some 30,000 strong, they are the last survivors of the people who lived in Europe in the Ice Age and went north with the ice as it retreated. The reindeer has

The Arctic

Northern Russia, Scandinavia, Alaska and the world's largest island, GREENLAND, border the North Pole located in the frozen Arctic Ocean. The Indians who settled in America came this way from east to west. Some stayed in the far north and are known as ESKIMOS. Later, when reindeer herds retreated north with the snows of the Ice Age, LAPPS followed them to the Arctic.

It is now one of the world's fastest developing regions. Modern technology can tap its oil and gas resources. Greenland, for long an undevelopable country, is now prospecting its mineral wealth. Russia even raises strawberries under glass within the Arctic Circle. US military bases have brought some prosperity, but also such problems as alcoholism to many Eskimos.

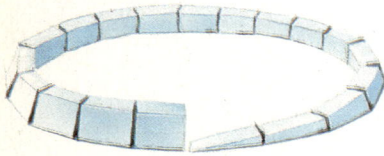

Below: The kayak is still used by Eskimos for fishing and hunting.

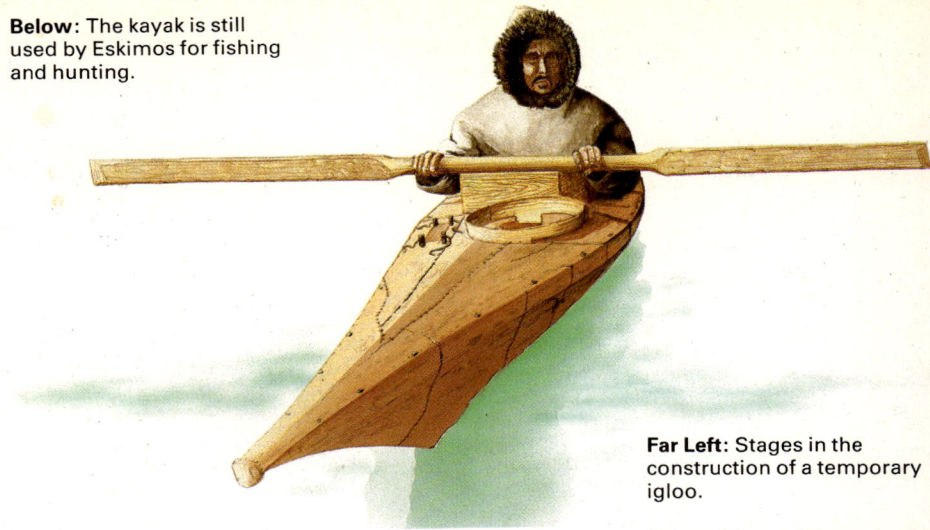

Snow blocks are placed in a ring with their top surfaces sloped.

More rows are added, inclined slightly inwards.

The dome so formed has an entrance hole cut in it.

The entrance to the igloo is protected by blocks.

Modern exploration began with a search for a North West Passage – a trade route from east to west. Explorers like William Baffin (1584–1622), Henry Hudson (c.1600s) and Martin Frobisher (c.1535–94) left their names on the map, but failed to find a viable route. There are now plans to build a massive icebreaker to open one up. Less severe in climate than Antarctica, the north polar region is rich in wild life: seals, walrus and polar bears can approach the neighbourhood of the pole itself across the pack ice. No lives were lost on the two great polar expeditions; in the first, Fridtjof Nansen (1861–1930) a Norwegian, attempted to reach the pole by allowing his ship to freeze into the ice and drifting with it. The successful assault on the pole was by Americans, Robert Peary (1856–1920) and Matthew Henson, on 6 April 1909.

Far Left: Stages in the construction of a temporary igloo.

Below: The umiak, made of walrus skin stretched over a frame, is still used, often with an outboard motor.

Below: Stages in the construction of a kayak. The open design of the framework (1–3) makes the craft light and manoeuvrable. Sealskin is stretched tightly across the frame and hunting tools are attached (4).

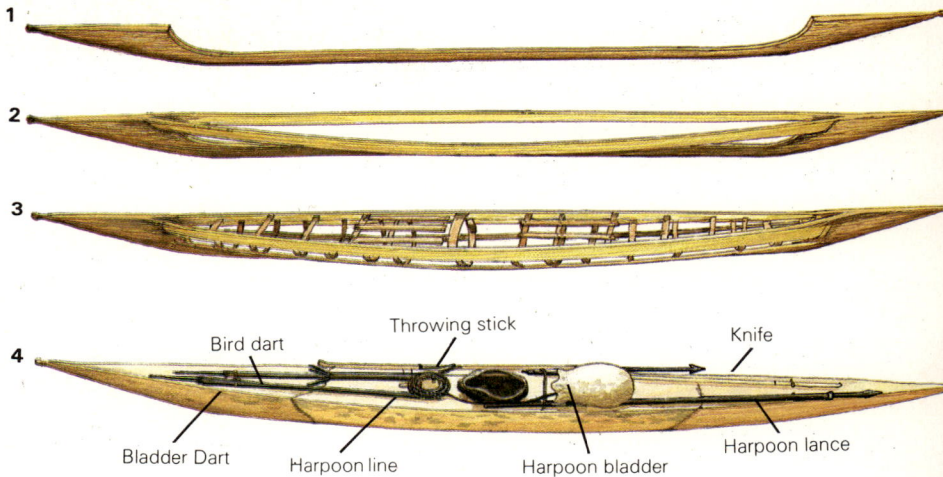

1

2

3

4

Bird dart   Throwing stick   Knife

Bladder Dart   Harpoon line   Harpoon bladder   Harpoon lance

---

always been their source of food, clothing, and shelter. Few now follow the herds, but instead trade reindeer products to southern lands. **Little America** was the name of five bases established in Antarctica by the US.

M **McMurdo Station** is now the main US base on Antarctica, and is sited on the southern end of Ross Island. It is a sprawling, 100 hut village powered by a nuclear reactor and obtains fresh water from the sea through a desalination plant.

Nearby, Robert Scott's first hut is maintained by New Zealand as an historical monument.
Mount Erebus is the only recently active volcano in Antarctica. Always topped by a white plume of gases, it is 1,140 metres high.
Mount Terror, extinct neighbour of Mount Erebus in Ross Island, Antarctica, is 994 metres high.

N **North Pole** was first reached by Robert Peary (1856-1920), the American explorer, on 6 April 1909.

S **South Pole** was first reached by Roald

North Pole – 13 base

Amundsen the Norwegian polar explorer (1872-1928) on 14 December 1911. There is now a US base here. A striped pole, topped by a globe and surrounded by the flags of the nations that signed the Antarctic Treaty, marks the pole. Also in Antarctica is the Pole of Relative Inaccessibility, marking the region least accessible from the coast. A Russian base, Sovetskaya, was built here.

T **Thule** is a major US air base on Cape Athol in north-west Greenland. Origi-

nally a World War II base, developed in 1952 as a stop on the transpolar route from the US to Europe. There is a 365-metre-high radio and radar tower and a ballistic early warning station.
Transantarctic Mountains form one of the world's greatest mountain chains, stretching 4,800 km from Oates Land to the Filchner ice shelf.

V **Vostock** is a Russian base established at the Geomagnetic Pole in 1958.

Index

Page numbers in **bold** type refer to the reference sections. Page numbers in *italics* refer to illustrations.

A
Abadan, 6
Abidjan, 33
Aboriginal, 49, *49*, *52*, 57
  decline, 58
Accra, 33
Adam's Bridge, **10**, 11
Aden, **3**
  economy of, 8
Addis Ababa, 33
Adelaide, **49**
Aegean Sea, 4
Afghanistan, **10**
  agriculture, 11, 14
  climate, 11–12
Africa,
  agriculture, 42, *42*, 43
  art, *39*
  birthrate, 36
  civil wars, 46–47
  climate, 34–35
  communications, 45, *45*, 46
  economy, 40–42
  exports, 42–43
  European influences, 40, 43
  fishing, 43, *43*
  forestry, 42
  hyrdro-electric power, 44–45
  independence movements, 46–48, *48*
  instruments, **38**
  languages, 37–38, *37*
  manufacturing, 45
  map, *35*
  mining, 43–44, *44*
  non-indigenous peoples, 39–40
  peoples, 37–38
  physical features, 33
  population, 33, 36–37
  problems, 33
  religions, 40
  size, *33*
  vegetation, 36
  wildlife, 36
Ahmedabad, **10**
Ainu people, *17*
Ajanta, **10**, 16
Aleppo, **3**
Alexandria, 33
Algeria, **33**
  life expectation, 37
  oil, 43
Algiers, 33
Alice Springs, **49**, 53
  climate, *50*
All Blacks, *54*, 55
Amman, **3**
Amritsar, 10
Amundsen, Roald, 63
Anatolia, **3**, 4
Andaman and Nicobar Islands, **10**
Anderson, Judith, 59
Angkor, **26**
Angola, **33**
  independence, 47
  oil, 43
Ankara, **3**, 6
  climate, *3*
Antananarivo, **33**
Antarctic
  climate, 62, *63*
  differences with Arctic, **62**
  minerals, 62
Antarctic Peninsular, **62**, 63
Antarctic Treaty, 62
Arabian peninsular, 5
  climate, 5
  life styles, 6–7
  physical features, 5
  population, 6
  vegetation, 5
Arab–Israeli wars, 9, *9*
Arnhem Land, **49**
Arctic,
  differences with Antarctic, 62
  extent, 64
  resources, 64
Ashanti, 37
Aswan High Dam, **34**, 44
Auckland, **49**, 55
Australia,
  agriculture, 52
  arts, 59–60
  climate, 52–53
  communications, 54
  European influences, 53
  history, 57–58
  immigration, 50, 53, 58
  manufacturing, 56
  mining, 56, *56*
  peoples, 53–54
  Second World War, 59
Australian Alps, **49**
Australian Capital Territory, **49**
Ayres Rock, **49**

B
Baffin, William, 64

Baghdad, **3**
Bahrain, **3**, 5
Bali, **26**
  Hinduism, *29*, 30
  peoples, 30
Ballarat, **50**
Bamako, **34**
Bandaranaike, Mrs Sirimawo, 16, *16*
Bandung, **26**, 30
Bangalore, **10**
  climate, 12
  population growth, 15
Bangladesh, **10**
  agriculture, 11, **14**
  climate, 12
  vegetation, **10**
Bangui, **34**
Banjul, **34**
Bangkok, **26**, 29, *30*
Bantustans, **34**, 48
Barossa Valley, **50**
  agriculture, 52
Basra, **3**
Beardmore Glacier, **62**, 63
Beirut, **3**
Belgian Congo, 46
Benares, see Varanasi
Benin, **98**
Bhutan, **11**
  independence, 16
  vegetation, 11
Bissau, **34**
Black Sea, 4
Blair, Harold, 59
Bombay, **11**
Bona Island, *59*
Bophuthatswana, see Bantustans
Borneo, **26**
  vegetation, 27
Borobudor, **26**
Bosphorus, 4
Botany Bay, **50**, 58
Botswana, **34**
Brahmins, 13
Brazzaville, **34**
Brisbane, **50**
British Anglo-Persian Oil Company, 8
British Solomon Islands, **50**
Broken Hill, **50**, 56
Brunei, **26**
  peoples, 30
Buddhism, 20, *25*, 28, 31
Buddhist-Hindu-Jain civilization, 16
Bujumburg, **34**
Burma, **26**
  climate, 27
  minerals, 31
  peoples, 28
  physical features, 27
  political unrest, 32
Burundi, **34**
  economy, 41
  farming, 41

C
Cabora Bassa Dam, 44
Cairo, **35**
Calcutta, **11**
  steel, 14
Cameroon, **35**
  peoples, 39
Canaan, 5
Canary Islands, **35**
Canberra, **51**, 58
Canton, see Kwang-chow
Cape Town, **35**
Cape Verde Islands, **35**
Casablanca, **35**
Caspian Sea,
  climate, 4
Caucasoids, 37
  Somalis, 37
  Sudan, 37
Cebu, **27**
Central African Empire, **35**
Chad, **35**
  economy, 41
Cheetahs, *36*
Chiang Mai, **27**, 29
China, 17
  agriculture, 20, 22
  climate, 19
  economy, 22–23
  history, 24–25
  industry, 23
  Kuomintang, 25
  physical features, 18
  religions, 20
  vegetation, 19
Chittagong, **11**
Chopsticks, *20*, 22
Christchurch, **51**
Chungking, **18**
Climate,
  Africa, 35–36
  Antarctica, 62
  Eastern Asia, 19–20
  Oceania, 52
  South Asia, 11–12
Cocos Island, **51**
Colombo, **12**
Communes, 20, *20*, 21
Comoro Islands, **36**
Conakry, **36**

Confucianism, 20
Congo, **36**
  oil, 43
Cooper, Pedy, **51**
Cook, Captain, James, 58
Cyprus, **3**, 9
  climate, 4
  economy, 8
  life styles, 5
  physical features, 4
  population, 5

D
Dacca, **12**
Dakar, **36**
Damascus, **3**
Dardenelles, 4
Darjeeling, **12**
Darwin, 51
Dasht-I-Kavir, 4
Dasht-I-Lut, 4
Date palm, 41
Dead Sea, **4**
Deccan, **12**
  climate, 11
  physical features, 11
  vegetation, 11
Delhi, **12**
Desai, Morarji, 16
Djebel Toubkal, **36**
Djibouti, **36**
Dodoma, **36**
Drakensberg, 33, *34*, **36**
Drysdale, Sir Russell, 60
Dunedin, **52**
Durban, **36**
  climate, *35*

E
East African rift valley, 33–34
Easter Island, **52**
Eastern Asia,
  climate, 19–20
  peoples, 20
  physical features, 18
  size, 18
  vegetation, 19
Eastern Ghats, see Deccan
East Timor, **27**
Egypt, 9, **36**
  agriculture, 43
  economy, 41
  manufacturing, 45
  oil, 43
Ellora, **12**, 16
Equatorial Guinea, **37**
Eritrea, **37**
Eskimos, 64
  igloos, *64*
  kayak, *64*
  umiak, *64*
Ethiopia, **37**
  agriculture, *40*
  Christianity, 40

F
Fiji, **52**
Finch, Peter, **60**
Freetown, **37**
French Polynesia, **52**, 55
Frobisher, Martin, 64
Fula, 37

G
Gabon, **37**
  vegetation, 36
Gabarone, **37**, *47*
Gambia, **38**
Gaza, **38**
Geelong, **52**
Ghana, **38**
  food exports, 43
  population, *37*
Ghandi, Mrs, 16
Gibson Desert, **52**
Gilbert Islands (Kiribati), **52**
Gobi, 18, **18**
Godthaab, **62**
Golan Heights, **4**
Great Artesian Basin, **52**
Great Barrier Reef, **53**
Great Leap Forward, 23, 25
Greenland, **63**
Greenlanders, **63**, 64
Guinea, **38**
  bauxite, 44
Guinea-Bissau, **38**
  vegetation, 36
Gunnbjorn's Mountain, **63**

H
Hanoi, **27**, 29
Harbin, **18**
Hausa, 38
Hawaii, **53**
  climate, 53
  US influence, 55
Heliopolis,
  climate, *3*
Helpmann, Robert, 59
Hemitic Berbers, 37
Henson, Matthew, 64
Himalayas, 10, **12**
  agriculture, 11
Hinduism, *29*

Hindu Kush, **18**
Hiroshima, **18**, 25
Hittites, 6
Hobart, **53**
Ho Chi Minh, 32
Ho Chi Minh City, **27**, 29
Hokkaido, **19**
Hong Kong, **18**, **22**
  climate, *17*
  colonial development, 25
  economy, 24
  industry, 23
Honshu, **19**
Hope, Alec, 60
Hua Kuo-feng, 25
Hudson, Henry, 64
Hyderabad, 13

I
Ibadan, **38**
Ibn Saud, 9
Icebergs, **63**
Ice shelves, **63**
India, **13**
  agriculture, 14, 16
  caste system, *12*, 13
  dress, 12
  industry, 14
  life styles, 12–13, *13–14*
  Pakistan and, 16
  politics, 16
  population, 12
  religion, 12–13
  resources, 15–16
  vegetation, 10
Indonesia, **27**
  agriculture, 31
  climate, 27
  fishing, 31
  independence, 32
  life styles, 30
  Malaysian war, 32
  minerals, 31
  peoples, 28, 30
  physical features, 27
  vegetation, 27
Inner Mongolia, **19**
International Geophysical Year, 63
Iran, **4**
  climate, 4
  life styles, 6
  oil and, 7–8
  physical features, 4
  population, 6
  social change, *4*, 6, 8
Iraq, **4**
  British rule, 9
  vegetation, 5
Isfahan, 5, 6
Islamabad, **14**
Ismir, 6
Israel, **5**
  Arab-Israeli war, 9
  economy, 8
  languages, 7
  population, 7
  vegetation, 5, *5*
Istanbul, **5**, 6
Ivory Coast, **38**

J
Jakarta, **28**, 30
Japan, 19
  climate, 19–20
  economy, 23–24
  feudalism, 24
  history, 24
  life styles, 22, *23*
  military history, 25
  Oceania and, 50
  physical features, 19
  religions, 20, 22, *25*
  Second World War, and 50
  vegetation, 19
Java, **28**
Jerusalem, **5**
  Wailing Wall, *8*
Jidda, **5**
Jogjakarta, **28**, 30
Johannesburg, **38**
Jordan, **5**
  British rule, 9
  economy, 8
  vegetation, 5

K
Kabul, **14**
Kalahari, **39**
  climate, 35
  San, 37
Kalgoorlie, **53**
Kalimantan, **28**
Kampala, **39**
Kampuchea, **28**
  civil war, 32
  physical features, 27
  Vietnam war, 32
Kanawa, Kiri te, *60*
Kanpur, **14**
Karachi, **14**
Kariba Dam, 44, *44*
Kashmir, **14**
  war of 1947, 16
Katanga, 46
Katmandu, **14**

Kenya, **39**
  rift valley, 34
Khartoum, **39**
Khmer Rouge, 32
Khoi-San, 39
Khyber Pass, **14**, 16, *16*
Kigali, **39**
Kimberleys, **53**, 56
Kimono, 22
Kinshasa, **39**
Kitakyushu, **20**
Kobe, **20**
Kuala Lumpur, **28**
Kuching, **28**
Kun Lun, **20**
Kurdish tribes, *4*, 6
Kurdistan, **6**
Kuwait, 5, **6**
Kwang-chow, **20**
Kyoto, **20**
Kyushu, **20**

L
Labuan, **28**
Laccadive Islands, **14**
Lagos, 39
Lahore, **14**
Lake,
  Chad, **36**
  Eyre, **54**
  Nyasa, 34, **43**
  Tanganyika, 34, **46**
  Toba, **29**
  Victoria, 34, **47**
Languages,
  Africa and, 37
  Arabic, 37
  Bantu, 38
  Swahili, 37
  West African, 37–38
Laos, **29**
  physical features, 27
  Vietnam war, 32
Lapps, **63**, 64
Lebanon, **6**
  British rule, 9
  economy, 8
  vegetation, 5
Lesotho, **39**
Lhasa, **20**
Liberia, **39**
Libreville, **39**
  oil, 43
Lilongwe, **40**
Little America, **64**
Lome, **40**
Longyi, 28
Luanda, **40**
Lusaka, **40**
Lu-ta, **20**
Luzon, *27*, **29**

M
Macao, **20**
  'boat-people', *18*
  colonial development, 25
  physical features, 18
Madagascar, **40**
  languages, 39
  peoples, 39
  vegetation, 36
Madeira Islands, **40**
Madras, **15**
Malabo, **40**
Malacca, **29**
Malawi, **40**
  farming, 41
Malaya, **29**
  independence, 32
Malaysia, **29**
  customs, *28*
  independence, 32
  life styles, 29
  oil, 31
  peoples, 28–29
Maldives, 11, **15**
  climate, 12
  independence, 16
Mali, **40**
  life expectation, 37
  Muslims, *40*
Manila, **30**
Manufacturing industry,
  South Africa, 45
  South-east Asia, 31
Maoris, 49, **54**
  cultural influences of, 61
  history, 60–61
  meeting house, *54*
Mao Tsetung, 21, 25
Maputo, **41**
Marble Bar, **54**
Marcos, President, 32
Mariana, **54**
Maseru, **41**
Mau Mau, 46
Mauritania, **41**
Mauritius, **41**
Mbabane, **41**
McMurdo Stadium, 63, **64**
Mecca, **7**
Medina, **7**
Melanesians, **54**
  life styles, 55
Melbourne, **54**
Merino sheep, 52, **57**

Mesopotamia, 5
Micronesians, **55**
  life styles, 55
Mindanao, **30**
Mining
  South Africa, 43–44
  South-east Asia, 31
Mogadishu, **41**
Mohammed Reza
  Pahlavi, *8*
Moluccas, **30**
Mombasa, **41**
Mongolia, **21**
  agriculture, *18*, 21–22
  climate, 19–20
  economy, 21–22
  life styles, 21
  physical features, 18
  vegetation, 19
Monrovia, **41**
Moorhead, Alan, 60
Morocco, **41**
Moroni, **42**
Mountains
  Atlas, 34, **34**
  Blue, **50**
  Cameroon,
   climate of, 35
  Elburz, 4
  Ellsworth, **62**
  Erebus, **64**
  Fuji, 19, *19*
  Isa, **55**
  Kenya, 33, **42**
  Kilimanjaro, 33, *36*, **42**
  Kosciusko, **55**
  Terror, **64**
Mozambique, **42**
  climate, 36
  physical features, 34

N
Naga Hills, **15**
Nagasaki, **21**, 25
Nagoya, **21**
Nairobi, **42**
Namibia, **42**
  Hottentots, 39
Nanking, **21**
Nara, **21**
Narbad, **15**
Nasser, Colonel
  Gamel Abdel, 46
N'Djamena, **42**
Negroids, 37
Nehru, Kawahrlal, 16
Nepal, **15**
  climate, 12
  life styles, 13
  vegetation, 11
New Caledonia, **55**
  French influence, 55
Newcastle, **55**
New Hebrides, **55**
New South Wales, **55**
New Zealand, **56**
  arts, 61
  climate, 52
  economy, 57, 61
  history, 55, 60–61
  hydro-electric
   power, 57
  immigration, 55
  independence, 55, 61
  influence of
   Britain, 50
  life styles, 55
  physical features, 52
  vegetation, 52
Niamey, **42**
Nicosia, **7**
Niger, **42**
  farming, 41
Nigeria, **42**
  civil war, 47
  dress, *39*
  economy, 41
  oil, 43
  tin, 44
Nilotes, 38–39
Nolan, Sidney, 60
North Island, New
  Zealand, **56**
  physical features, 52
  population, 55
North Korea, **21**
  agriculture, 24
  climate, 20
  economy, 24
  influences, 22
  life styles, 22
  physical features, 18
  religions, 20
  vegetation, 19
  war, 25
North Pole, **64**
North Territory, **56**
  uranium, 56
North-West Passage, 64
North Yemen, 5, **7**
  economy, 8
Nouakchott, **43**
Nullabor Plain, **57**

O
Oceania, 49
  economy, 56

European exploration,
  49
  map, *50*
  peoples, 49
  size, 49
Oil, 7
  importance of, 7
Oman, 5, 7
OPEC, 7
Ord River Dam, **57**
Organization of Petroleum
  Exporting Countries
  (OPEC), 7
Osaka, **22**
Ouagadougou, **43**

P
Pacific Islands,
  climate, 53
  economy, 57
  peoples, 55
  vegetation, 53
Pakistan, **15**
  agriculture, 11, 14
  civil war, 16
  climate, 12
  dress, 12–13
  history, 16
  India and, 16
  population growth, 15
Palestine, **7**
  British rule, 9
  'Palestinian
   problem', 9
  vegetation, 5
Pamir Knot, **22**
Papua New Guinea, **57**
  climate, 53
  peoples, 49
  size, 53
Paramatta, **57**
Peary, Robert, 64
Peking, **22**
Penang, **30**
Persia
  history, 8
  population, 6
Perth, **57**
Philippines, **30**
  agriculture, 27, *27*, 30
  climate, 27
  fishing, 31
  history, 32
  independence, 32
  manufacturing, 31
  minerals, 31
  peoples, 28, 30
  religions, 30
  Spanish influence, 32
  vegetation, 27
Phnom Penh, **28**
Polar regions, *63*
Polynesia, **57**
  life styles, 55
Poona, **16**
Population
  South-east Asia, 90
Port Louis, **43**
Porto Novo, **43**
Praia, **43**
Pretoria, **43**
Pusan, **22**
Pygmies, 39
Pyongyang, **22**

Q
Qatar, 5, **8**
Quathlamba, *see*
  Drakensberg
Queensland, **58**
  agriculture, 52
  climate, 52
Quezon City, **31**

R
Rabat, **43**
Rangoon, 29, *31*
Reunion, **43**
Reza Khan, 8
Rhodesia, *see*
  Zimbabwe Rhodesia
River
  Brahmaputra, **11**
  Darling, **51**
  Euphrates, **4**
  Ganges, **12**
  Godavi, **12**
  Hwang Ho, 18, **19**
  Indus, 12, **14**
  Irrawaddy, 27, **28**
  Jordan, 5, **5**, *5*
  Keno, *34*
  Limpopo, **40**
  Mekong, 27, **30**
  Murray, **55**
  Niger, **42**
  Nile, **43**
  Orange, **43**
  Salween, 27, **31**
  Tigris, **73**
  Yalu, **25**
  Zaire, **48**
  Zambesi, **48**
Riyadh, *5*
Rub Al Khali, 5, **8**
Rwanda, **44**
  economy, 41

farming, 41
Ryukyu Islands, **22**
  physical features, 19

S
Sabah, **31**
  peoples, 29
Sahara, 35, **44**
  climate, *34*
  farming, 42
Saigon, *see* Ho Chi
  Minh City
Saint Helena, **44**
Salisbury, 44
Samoa, **58**
San'a, **8**
Sao Tomé & Principe, **44**
Sapporo, **22**
Sarawak, **31**
  peoples, 29
Sarong, 28
Saudi Arabia, 5, **8**
  importance of, 7–8
  oil, 7
Scott, Captain, 63
Sea of Marmara, 4
Senegal, **44**
  groundnuts, 43
Seoul, **23**
Seychelles, **44**
Shah Abbas, 8
Shanghai, **23**
Shenyang, **23**
Shikoku, **23**
Sian, **23**
Sierra Leone, **44**
Singapore, **31**
  climate, *26*, 27
  economy, *31*
  life styles, 29
  manufacturing, 31
  peoples, 29–30
Sinkiang-Uighur, **23**
Snowy mountains, **58**
  hydro electric
   schemes, 56
Somalia, **45**
  economy, 41
  independence
   movements, 47, *48*
South Africa, **45**
  climate, 36
  economy, 41
  farming, 42–3
  gold, *43*, 44
  life expectation, 37
  manufacturing, 45
  physical features, 34
  racial situation, 40, 48
South Australia, **58**
South-east Asia,
  agriculture, 30
  climate, 27
  dress, 28–9
  economy, 30
  history, 31–2
  life styles, 28–9
  manufacturing, 31
  map, *26*
  minerals, 31
  physical features, 27
  population
   density, 26
  religions, 27
  size, 26
Southern Asia,
  caste system, 13–14
  climate, 11–12
  industry, 14–15
  life styles, 12–13
  map, *10*
  physical features, 10
  population, 12–13
  population
   growth, 15–16
  size, 10
  vegetation, 10–11
South Island,
  New Zealand, **59**
  physical features, 52
South Korea, **23**
  climate, 20
  economy, 24
  influences, 26
  Korean War, 25
  life styles, 26
  physical features, 18
  religions, 20
South Pacific
  Commission, 55
South Pole, **64**
South Vietnam, 32
South-West Africa, **45**
South-west Asia
  economy, 7–8
  extent of, 4
  history, 8
  map, *3*
  non-oil states, 8
  population, 5
South Yemen, 5, **8**
  economy, 8
Sri Lanka, **16**
  agriculture, 14
  climate, 11
  dress, 12
  physical features, 11

politics, 16
population growth, 15
vegetation, 11
Sudan, **46**
  agriculture, 43
Suez Canal, **46**
Sulawesi, **31**
Suleiman, 8
Sumatra, **31**
Surabaja, 30, **32**
Sutherland, Joan, 59
Swahili, 37
Swaziland, **46**
Sydney, **59**
  climate, *50*
  history, 58
Syria, **8**
  British rule, 9
  economy, 8
  vegetation, 5

T
Tahiti, **59**
Taipeh, **23**
Taiwan, **24**
  agriculture, 24
  climate, 19–20
  economy, 23–4
  influences on, 22
  physical features, 19
Tanzam railway, *45*
Tanzania, **46**
  farming, 41
  languages, 37
  rift valley, 34
Taoism, 20
Tartars, 6
Tasman, Abel, 57
Tasmania, **59**
  agriculture, 52
Taurus mountains, 4, **9**
Tehran, 6, **9**
Tel Aviv, **9**
Thailand, **32**
  Buddhist monks, 29
  dress, 29
  minerals, 31
  physical features, 27
Thar desert, 11, **16**
Thimpu, **16**
Thompson, J., *53*
Thule, **64**
Tibet, **24**
  climate, 19
  vegetation, 19
Tien Shan, **24**
Tientsin, **24**
Togo, **46**
Tokyo, **24**
Tonga, **60**
Tonle Sap, **32**
Transantarctic, **64**
Transkei, *see*
  Bantustans
Tripoli, **46**
Tsingtao, **25**
Tungabhadra Dam, *14*
Tunis, **47**
Tunisia, **47**
  oil, 43
Turkestan, 25
Turkey, **9**
  agriculture, *6*
  climate, 4
  economy, 8
  history, 8–9
  life styles, 6
  physical features, 4
  population, 5–6
  westernization, 6

U
Uganda, **47**
  rift valley, 34
Ulan Bator, **25**
United Arab
  Emirates, 5, **9**
United States
  influence in
   Hawaii, 55
  oil, 8
  Vietnam War, 32
Upper Volta, **47**
  economy, 41

V
Varanasi, **16**
Vegetation
  Africa, 36
  deserts, 36
  Eastern Asia, 19
  Oceania, 52–3
  savanna, 36
  South Asia, 10–11
  uplands, 36
Victoria (Australia), **60**
Victoria Falls, **47**
Victoria (Hong Kong), **25**
Victoria (Seychelles), **47**
Vientiane, 29, **32**
Vietnam, **32**
  dress, 29
  fishing, 31
  minerals, 31
  physical
   features, 27
  War, 32

Volta Dam, 44
Vostock, **64**

W
Waitangi, Treaty of, 61
Walvis Bay, **47**
Water buffalo, 94–5
Wellington, 119, **61**
West Bank, Jordan, 9
West Bengal, climate, 12
Western Australia, **61**
Western Ghats, *see* Deccan
Western Sahara, **47**
West Irian, **32**
  climate, 27
West, Morris, 60
White, Patrick, 60
Whyalla, **61**
Williamson, David, 60
Windhoek, **48**
Wolof, 38
Woomera, **61**
Wright, Judith, 60
Wuhan, **25**

Y
Yangtze Kiang, **25**
  agriculture in, 18
Yangtze Plain, 18
Yaounde, **48**
Yokohama, *23*
Yoruba, 38

Z
Zagros Mountains, 4, **9**
Zaire, **48**
  copper, 44
  independence, 46
  oil, 43
  peoples, 39
  rain forests, 36
Zambia, **48**
  copper, 44
Zamboanga, **32**
Zanzibar, **48**
Zimbabwe Rhodesia, **48**
  independence
   attempts, 47–8
  life expectation in, 37

Acknowledgements

Contributing artists
Creative Cartography, Nick Cudworth, Howard Dyke, Sue and Dave Holmes, Cathy James, Dave Mallett, Ralph Stobbart, Tony Yates.

The publishers also wish to thank the following:
Adespoton Film Servies 47T
Bryan & Cherry Alexander 62TR
Associated Press 45TR
Australian News and Information 49B, 51B, 52B, 53TR. B, 55B
Bo Bojesen 25T
Anne Bolt 41B
Camera Press 16C
Camera Press/J. Carnemolla/P. Prenzel 56T
Camera Press/M. Kaplan 43C
Camera Press/David Moore 49TR, 58T, 59T
J. Allan Cash 7T, 16T
Colorpix 13C, 45TL
Colorsport 53TL, 54T
C. T. O. Films/Denis Davidson Associates 61T
Daily Telegraph Colour Library 9T, 60TL
Daily Telegraph Colour Library/Nicholas Guppy 62TL
Douglas Dickins 8T, 12B, 13B, 14C, B, 16B, 17B, 18B, 19T, 20B, 22B, 24B, 25B, 27T, 28B, 30T B, 31T B, 46C
Mary Evans Picture Library 59B
Peter Frankel 33T, 34TL, 36T, 37T, 40C, 41T, 47T
Sonia Halliday 6C
Robert Harding Associates 12T, 14T, 15T, 18TR, 24C, 25T, 29T, 31C, 53C
Robert Harding Associates/Sybil Sassoon 34C
Anwar Hussein 61C
Alan Hutchison Library 6T B, 11T C, 21B, 32C, 33B, 36B, 37B, 38B, 39T, 42B, 43T, 44B, 46B, 48T
Alan Hutchison Library/Sarah Errington 45B
Alan Hutchison Library/C. Nairn/Granada Disappearing World 55C
Louis-Yves-Loirat/C. D. Tetrel 8C
Macdonald Educational 47B
Macquitty Collection 4B
Tony & Marion Morrison 4T
High Commissioner for New Zealand 54B, 56B
Novosti 64B
Popperfoto 9B, 32C, 40B, 50B, 55T, 58B, 61B
G. R. Roberts 49TL, 54C, 57TL TR, 58CL CR
John Topham Picture Library 3B, 5B, 7B, 8B, 10B, 11B, 13T, 15B, 19B, 23B, 26B, 27B, 29B, 32B, 35B, 39B, 43B, 57B, 60B, 62B, 63B
John Topham Picture Library/Bente Fasmer 52T
Mireille Vautier 5C, 22T, 23T, 28T
D. C. Williamson 18TL
Jerry Young 5T
Zefa/Baglin 52C
Zefa/Franscnia 34TR